FASCIST SCOTLAND

Gavin Bowd teaches French at St Andrews University. He has published widely on Scottish, French and Romanian culture and politics. He is also a poet, fiction writer, journalist and translator.

FASCIST SCOTLAND

CALEDONIA AND THE FAR RIGHT

GAVIN BOWD

BIRLINN

First published in 2013 by
Birlinn Limited
West Newington House
10 Newington Road
Edinburgh
EH9 1QS

www.birlinn.co.uk

ISBN: 978 1 78027 052 4

British Library Cataloguing-in-Publication Data
A catalogue record for this book is available from the British Library

Typeset by Iolaire Typesetting, Newtonmore
Printed and bound by Grafica Veneta
www.graficaveneta.com

'It is a terrible thing', said Miss Carmichael, 'to see the best of our lads marched off, generation after generation, to fight the battles of the English for them. But the end is upon them. When the Germans land in Scotland, the glens will be full of marching men come to greet them, and the professors themselves at the universities will seize the towns. Mark my words, don't be caught on Scottish soil on that day.'

Evelyn Waugh, *Officers and Gentlemen*

Contents

List of Illustrations

Rudolf Hess. The Deputy Führer's 'peace mission' to Scotland in May 1941 still provokes speculation.

The Duke of Hamilton denied all acquaintance with Hess, but had been a prominent friend of Nazi Germany.

North of the Cheviots, Mosley's Blackshirts came up against religious sectarianism and the Scottish national question.

Thomas Carlyle was an inspiration to Fascists and the bunker bedtime reading of Adolf Hitler in the twilight of the Third Reich.

Nazi turned SNP supporter, the warrior-writer Graham Seton Hutchison enjoys some Alpine air with nordic youth.

Already in 1923, the Scottish Renaissance poet Hugh MacDiarmid was calling for a native 'species of Fascism'.

As early as May 1931, the Glasgow *Evening Times* drew parallels between Scottish nationalism and the Nazi Party on the rise in Germany.

The Scottish Protestant League's hatred of all things 'Papist' led it to support Spanish anticlericalism before rallying to a latter-day Martin Luther, Adolf Hitler.

Charles Saroléa, Edinburgh University's first Professor of French, was an outspoken supporter of Fascism.

The Duchess of Atholl paid heavily for her support of the Spanish Republic and opposition to the politics of appeasement.

In 1938, the affair of Mrs Jessie Jordan, Dundee hairdresser and German spy, became a sensation in the Scottish press.

After a hapless career as a spy, Norman Baillie-Stewart served the Nazi cause on radio.

The rabidly anti-semitic Captain Archibald Maule Ramsay was the only MP to be interned during the Second World War.

Propaganda for the Wood Elves (Ian Hamilton Finlay, in collaboration with Harvey Dwight).

Acknowledgements

I would like to thank the following for their help and inspiration while writing this book: Dani Bruns, Stephen M. Cullen, Mairi Cunningham, Nigel Dennis, Alec Finlay, Ray Furness, Stuart Kelly, John Manson, Annie Tindley, Agnès Villette, Ian S. Wood, Matt Worsley and Annette Zimmermann.

Prologue

At dusk on 10 May 1941, an enemy aircraft was plotted off the coast of Northumberland and made landfall close to the Farne Islands. Wing Commander the Duke of Hamilton, then on duty at RAF Turnhouse near Edinburgh, received a report from the Royal Observer Corps that the enemy aircraft was an Me110 fighter-bomber. The duke thought this to be a mistaken identification as this type of plane had only once before been seen as far north as Northumberland, and, without extra fuel tanks, could not make a return flight to Germany.

The audacious pilot of this intruding aircraft was Rudolf Hess, Deputy Führer of the Third Reich. He had begun his journey in Augsburg, Bavaria, navigating northwards with the help of transmitting stations in Denmark – Jackal, Jasmine and Hyena – before turning westwards. On two Ordnance Survey maps covering the south of Scotland and the north of England, Hess had marked railways and prominent landmarks. With a red arrow he had indicated his planned destination: Dungavel House, near Glasgow, home of the Duke of Hamilton.

On approaching the coast, Hess spotted the peak of the Cheviot. In a letter to his five-year-old son 'Buz', he would describe a 'heavenly, polar-like view'.[1] Hess's manoeuvres, and the arrival of a bank of mist on the coast-line, confused the Spitfires scrambled to intercept him. Instead, the Deputy Führer climbed up the side of the Cheviot Hills and slid down into Scotland. He then headed for St Mary's Loch. On this late spring evening, there were still people working in the fields, and Hess waved cheerfully to them from treetop level. His aircraft sped on at 300 mph, burning up its fuel. At about 22.45 he passed very close to Dungavel House.

The Observer Corps in Galashiels reported the enemy aircraft's entry into the Ayr Sector of No. 13 (Fighter) Group. Normal action was taken to intercept, and a Defiant fighter took off in hot pursuit. Meanwhile, Hess passed over the Renfrewshire constituency that the Duke of Hamilton (then Marquis of Clydesdale) had represented in parliament for ten years, before arriving over the west coast, where he saw what he described to Buz as a 'fairy-like view', with 'steep mountainous islands visible in the moonlight and fading twilight'. After the Cumbrae Islands, he turned inland and tried to use the railway line to Kilmarnock to lead him towards Dungavel. But fuel was getting very low and it was now necessary to bale out. He climbed to 6,000 feet, feathered the propellers and opened the cockpit roof. Pushing with his legs, he fell backwards into the air. His parachute opened while the Me110 crashed and burst into flames at 23.09 hours. The RAF report read: 'It was with disappointment that the Wing Commander learnt that [the Defiant's] guns had not been fired. Later it was reported that the enemy aircraft had crashed two miles from Eaglesham close to Mearns Road and that it was definitely an Me110. A German having baled out had been captured.'[2]

On landing, Hess had lost consciousness. He told Buz:

> I woke in a German-looking meadow, not realising where I was and what was happening to me. When I first saw my parachute lying behind me, it became clear to me that I had arrived in Scotland, the first landing place of my 'Plan'. I was lying some ten metres from the front door of the house of a Scottish goatherd. People came running towards me, alarmed by the burning aircraft. They looked at me in a compassionate way.

He had landed at Floors Farm, 12 miles to the west of Dungavel House. He was lying ten metres from the cottage of a ploughman, Donald McLean, who had been preparing to go to bed when he heard the noise of the aircraft, and had gone to investigate when he saw a parachute floating down. On helping the man to his feet, he noticed he was wearing a foreign uniform underneath his flying clothes. McLean asked him if he was German, to which Hess replied in English, 'Yes, I am Hauptmann Alfred Horn. I have an important message for the Duke of Hamilton.'

While an elderly neighbour went off to report the incident and get help, McLean helped Hess into the cottage he shared with his mother. The Deputy Führer was offered a cup of tea but said he preferred a glass of water. His hosts were impressed by Hess's air of authority, uniform of fine soft cloth, expensive gold wristwatch and magnificent flying boots lined with fur. Two Home Guard officers turned up at the cottage, one of them the worse for wear, and the captive was eventually transferred to Maryhill Barracks in Glasgow.

In conversation with the Scottish Area Commander of the Observer Corps, Major Graham Donald, 'Alfred Horn' declared that he was on a 'special mission' to see the Duke of Hamilton. Donald was sure that he was in fact Rudolf Hess and reported: 'he is, if one may apply the term to a Nazi, quite a gentleman ... I found him to be a very interesting, and quite pleasant fellow, not in the least of the tough young Nazi type, but definitely an officer who might be a very important man in higher Nazi circles'.[3]

On 11 May, at 10.00 hours, the Duke of Hamilton arrived at Maryhill Barracks with an intelligence officer. They first examined the prisoner's effects: a Leica camera, photographs of himself and a small boy, and some medicines, as well as visiting cards of Professor Karl Haushofer and his son, Dr Albrecht Haushofer. The duke then entered the room of the prisoner. The prisoner, whom he had no recollection of ever having seen before, at once requested to speak with him alone. The duke asked the other officers to withdraw. There followed a conversation in English:

The German opened by saying that he had seen me in Berlin at the Olympic Games in 1936, and that I had lunched in his house, he said, 'I do not know if you recognise me but I am Rudolf Hess.' He went on to say that the Führer did not want to defeat England and wished to stop fighting. His friend Albrecht Haushofer had told him that I was an Englishman who, he thought, would understand [Hess's] point of view. He had consequently tried to arrange a meeting with me in Lisbon. He went on to say that he had tried to fly to Dungavel and this was the fourth time he had set out, the first time being in December. On the three previous occasions he had turned back owing to bad weather. He had not attempted to make the journey during the time when Britain was gaining victories in Libya, as he had thought this might be interpreted as a weakness, but now that Germany had gained successes in North Africa and Greece, he was glad to come.

The very fact that the Reich minister had come to Scotland in person, Hess explained to the duke, showed his sincerity and Germany's willingness to make peace:

> [The Führer] was convinced that Germany would win the war, possibly soon but certainly in one, two or three years. He wanted to stop the unnecessary slaughter that would otherwise inevitably take place. He asked me if could get together leading members of my party to talk over things with a view to making peace proposals. I replied that there was now only one party in this country. He then said he could tell me what Hitler's peace terms would be. First, he would insist on an arrangement whereby our two countries would never go to war again. I questioned him as to how that arrangement would be brought about, and he replied that one of the conditions, of course, is that Britain would give up her traditional policy of always opposing the strongest power in Europe. I then told him that if we made peace now, we would be at war again certainly within two years. He asked why, to which I replied that if a peace agreement was possible, the arrangement could have been made before the war started, but since, however, Germany chose war in preference to peace at a time when we were most anxious to preserve peace, I could put forward no hope of a peace agreement.

Hess then requested that the duke ask King George VI to give him 'parole', as he had come unarmed and of his own free will. He further asked him to inform his family that he was safe. He also asked that his identity not be disclosed to the press. The wing commander concluded: 'From previous photographs and Albrecht Haushofer's description of Hess, I believed that this prisoner was indeed Hess himself. Until this interview I had not the slightest idea that the invitation in Haushofer's letter to meet him in Lisbon had any connection at all with Hess.'[4]

The Haushofer connection helps us understand Hess's motives. Albrecht Haushofer's father was a key figure in the German school of geopolitics, and was notably the theorist behind the policy of *Lebensraum* or 'living space', Germany's need to collect the resources and land of neighbouring countries. After the Great War, Rudolf Hess, an army veteran embittered by the humiliation of Germany at Versailles, keenly followed Professor Haushofer's lectures at the

University of Munich and became his personal assistant. Hess then became óne of the founder members of the Nazi Party. After the failure of the 1923 *Bierkeller Putsch*, Hess and Hitler found themselves in Landsberg Prison. It was there that Hess transcribed and edited Hitler's autobiography and manifesto, *Mein Kampf.* Personal contact with Karl Haushofer and the work of the school of geopolitics influenced the Führer's *Weltanschauung.* Hess had earlier become acquainted with the professor's son, himself a brilliant geopolitician and poet, though not a Nazi. In the 1930s, Hess would turn to him as an adviser on foreign affairs.

James Douglas-Hamilton, grandson of the duke, explains further the Hamilton–Haushofer–Hess 'nexus':

> Albrecht Haushofer spoke English like an Englishman, had a great admiration for the British Empire, and wanted Germany to have peaceful relations with Britain. In August 1936 Albrecht Haushofer met a group of British MPs at the Berlin Olympic Games, one of whom was the Marquis of Clydesdale, who became Duke of Hamilton in 1940. Clydesdale was of interest to the Germans, because he had been the first man in the world to fly over Mount Everest. Aviators in those days were regarded in much the same way as the early astronauts, and aviation was looked upon as a top priority by the leaders of the Third Reich. Clydesdale kept in contact with Albrecht Haushofer and, after a skiing holiday in Austria, visited him and his father at Hartschimmelhof in January 1937. Clydesdale later sent his book *The Pilot's Book of Everest* to Karl Haushofer, who replied saying he would review it in the *Zeitschrift für Geopolitik.* What Clydesdale did not know was that four days after his visit to the Hartschimmelhof, Hess would arrive. He would be told about Clydesdale's visit, and be shown *The Pilot's Book of Everest*, which interested him greatly.[5]

It was this mutual acquaintance, increasingly alarmed by the expansionist policies of Hitler, who put the idea in Rudolf Hess's head that the Duke of Hamilton was a man open to a peace agreement. Although profoundly sceptical about the possibility of peace, given Hitler's track record of breaking treaties, on 8 September 1940 Albrecht Haushofer suggested to Hess 'a personal meeting on neutral soil with the closest of my English friends, the young Duke of Hamilton, who has access at all times to all important persons in London, even to Churchill and the King'.[6] On 23 September, Haushofer wrote to 'my dear Douglo', asking whether he 'could find time to have a talk with [him] somewhere on the outskirts of Europe, perhaps in Portugal'.[7] This letter was intercepted by MI5 and not seen by its addressee until March the following year, and no reply was sent.

Despite the silence, Hess did not give up on his mission, which he prepared in secret with the complicity of his adjutant, Karlheinz Pintsch. The flight to Scotland apparently caused consternation in the Nazi leadership. On hearing the news at Berchtesgaden, Hitler burst into tears. In a Nazi Party statement, Hess was described as having undergone severe physical suffering for some years, which had led him increasingly to seek relief in the various methods practised by mesmerists and astrologers. He was an 'idealist' who had fallen prey to 'tragic hallucinations'. A letter left behind 'showed traces of mental disturbances'.[8] Josef Goebbels commented privately that 'there are situations which even the best propagandist in the world cannot cope with'. He noted in his diary: 'What a spectacle for the world: a mentally deranged second man after the Führer.'[9] The BBC may have crowed about the unmasking of the 'moth-eaten myth of Nazi might',[10] but Hess's unwilling hosts were either bewildered or flippant. After a good dinner, Winston Churchill is said to have declared: 'Well, Hess or no Hess, I am going to see the Marx Brothers.'[11] Nevertheless, Hess was soon placed under special guard and considered a potential war criminal.

Like Dungavel House, the geopolitical objective had not been reached. A preliminary report by the Foreign Office noted that 'when he contemplates the failure of his "Mission", [Hess] becomes emotionally dejected and fears he has made a fool of himself'. The Deputy Führer had flown from Augsburg under the impression that his prospects of success were much greater than he now realised:

> He imagined that there was a strong Peace party in this country, and that he would have the opportunity of getting in touch with leading politicians who wanted the war to end now. At first, he asked constantly to see leaders of the Opposition, and even imagined himself as likely to negotiate with a new government. He is profoundly ignorant of our constitutional system, and the unity of this country. He has constantly asked to have a future meeting with the Duke of

Hamilton, under the delusion that '*der Herzog*' – perhaps because of his rank! – would be the means of getting him contact with people of a different view from the 'clique' who are holding Hess prisoner i.e. the Churchill government. His confusion of mind on all this is extreme.[12]

On 15 June 1941, Hess wrote to his son:

Buz, take notice, there are higher fate-forming forces – if we wished to give them a name, we would call them divine forces – which intervene, at least when it is necessary in a great event. I had to come to England and speak hope of understanding and peace. Often, we do not understand the decisions which are sometimes hard; at a later date, their importance will always be recognised.

Hess's motives and his state of mental health were, and still remain, objects of speculation. After a brief sojourn in the Tower of London, he became the only prisoner at 'Camp Z' in Surrey. There, every conversation he had, with members of the Scots Guards and Coldstream Guards as well as Lords Beaverbrook and Simon, intelligence officers and psychiatrists, was recorded in order to glean intelligence and delve the depths of the German's psyche. They did not get far with 'Jonathan', who was increasingly despondent, hypochondriac, paranoid and suicidal. 'Fate-forming forces' meant the war had taken another course: with Hitler's invasion of the Soviet Union, Britain now no longer stood alone – though the compulsively suspicious Stalin could not help seeing in Hess a conduit for Churchillian treachery. The 'great event' had turned out to be a tragi-comic incident. The now former Deputy Führer, whose letters to the Duke of Hamilton and the king were never delivered, withdrew into dreams of a return to Scotland, and sketched a Highland country house from which, after the war, he would indulge his passion for walking and cycling.

Historians Ron Conyers Nesbit and Georges van Acker have convincingly challenged the sometimes outlandish myths surrounding the flight of Rudolf Hess: that British military intelligence induced Hess to make his flight; that Hess was in fact acting with Hitler's knowledge and as his emissary; that he could not have flown over German territory without authorisation; that he was escorted for part of his flight by the architect of the Final Solution, Reinhard

Heydrich; or even that the man who flew to Scotland was an imposter. Nesbit and van Acker also dismantle the thesis that, at Dungavel House, the Nazi peace envoy was awaited by the dukes of Kent and Buccleuch.[13] As for the Duke of Hamilton, he successfully sued the Communist Party of Great Britain, in February 1942, for a pamphlet asserting that Hamilton and Hess were friends and that the duke approved of the Nazi regime.

But how far had Rudolf Hess flown from reality? After all, such distinguished Scottish peers as the dukes of Hamilton and Buccleuch and the earls of Erroll and Glasgow, along with much of the British ruling class, had not been averse to 'peaceful arrangements' with Hitler before 1939: the peoples of Austria, Czechoslovakia and Spain could vouch for that. As late as October 1939, the Duke of Hamilton had written to *The Times*: 'The moment the menace of aggression and bad faith has been removed, war against Germany becomes wrong and meaningless (. . .) We do not grudge Germany Lebensraum, provided that Lebensraum is not made the grave of other nations. We should be ready to search for and find a just colonial settlement'.[14] Organisations such as the Anglo-German Fellowship and the Link looked favourably on the Hitlerite energy resurrecting Germany, and sought both to avoid a repeat of the carnage of the Great War and to support a rampart against the evils of Bolshevism. Such sympathies were not restricted to the 'Cliveden set'. The world of aviation had been particularly favourable to the Third Reich: the editor of *The Aeroplane*, C.G. Grey, wrote in 1936 that Germany was now ruled by 'sensible middle-class men of real intelligence', who had 'freed Germany from Communism and disruption by Oriental square-heads'.[15] More broadly, opinion polls in the late thirties showed the popularity of Germany in a considerable minority of the British public, with it coming third in a list of people's favourite countries after the United States and France.

This Germanophilia was expressed by some non-aristocratic Scots. In March 1939, one Samuel Strachan of Pollokshaws, Glasgow, wrote to the *Anglo-German Review*:

> I would place the majority of Germany's critics in this country in the following categories: first, the ignorant, who know nothing whatever about their subject; secondly, political journalists who obey the instructions of their bosses; and thirdly, the evilly disposed critic whose

intention is to harm Germany in every possible way (...) Having
visited most of the big towns in Germany, I can truthfully say that I
have seen more poverty and misery in one district here in Glasgow
than I saw anywhere in the Reich.[16]

On 28 April 1939, the Glasgow and West of Scotland branch of the
Link held an evening of Schubert, 'Mr Kayser's trio and the singing
of Miss Constance Vanstone and Miss Betty Doherty being greatly
appreciated'.[17] As late as June 1939, three months after the Nazi
invasion of what remained of Czechoslovakia shattered residual illusions, the Link could boast that its Glasgow branch had successfully
held a musical evening, a 'mystery' bus tour and numerous rambles
in the surrounding countryside. In August 1939, Reichsmarschal
Göring had discussed with Hitler the idea of his flying to Britain to
offer peace. It was therefore not as a victim of 'tragic hallucinations'
that Hess made his ill-fated flight to Eaglesham.

Although Fascism in Britain is normally associated with England,
and especially the East End of London – and even then dismissed
as a marginal political phenomenon – Fascism did find support in
Scottish society. Scotland has provided its own cohort of traitors,
idealists and fanatics for extreme racist, nationalist and authoritarian
politics. From Dumfries to Alness, one of the main ideologies of the
first half of the twentieth century found its standard-bearers. But
when Fascism crossed the Cheviots, it found itself in a restless part of
a multi-nation state, riven by sectarian hatreds. Rudolf Hess felt the
natives looked at him in a compassionate way, but Scottish Fascism
had to carve out a niche in a crowded market for bigotry.

1

Mosley's Lost Legion

In the early twentieth century, Scotland could be fertile ground for the politics of xenophobia. On 15 May 1915, after a German U-boat sank the *Lusitania* with the loss of more than 1,000 lives, a crowd wrecked a butcher's shop in Annan belonging to one C. Feyerband. There had already been strident demands from the Scottish labour movement for strong immigration controls in the run-up to the 1905 Aliens Act. Politicians, both Independent Labour Party and Conservative, as well as trade unionists, joined these calls and in 1919, the year of the 40-hour strikes and mass agitation in Glasgow, there were violent anti-black riots. These riots, which occurred in nine British port towns, involved thousands of whites and dozens of black men. Behind these figures lay a background of economic competition in the merchant shipping industry as it began to contract in peacetime. In the case of Glasgow, sailors from Sierra Leone were made the scapegoats for the social and economic pressures felt by white sailors and the wider white community. Three sailors, one black and two white, received serious injuries. On 18 June 1919, in the aftermath of the race riots, one 'Hal O' the Wynd' adopted a bitter tone in the *Evening Times*: 'In this country Sambo has been usually regarded with general toler-ance. We have looked upon him as an "amoosin' cuss", who would never create anything approaching a problem.' Racial tension on the waterfront was not limited to this incident. One of the grievances of Emmanuel Shinwell and the Seafarers' Union was the use of cheap Chinese labour. Red Clydeside could also be brown.[1]

The First Fascisti

Nevertheless, the first 'Fascists' did not emanate from the radical Left, nor from the Scottish Nationalists, despite Hugh MacDiarmid's call for a 'Scottish fascism' as early as 1923, after Mussolini's march on Rome. Instead, the Right, terrified at the imminence of Bolshevik insurrection, and inspired by the robust actions of Il Duce, founded the British Fascisti (BF). As Richard Griffiths points out, Fascist Italy 'presented, to many, the picture of a country that had turned from chaos to order, from widespread poverty to comparative affluence'.[2] The BF were founded in 1923 by Rotha Lintorn-Orman, a young woman from a military family, who had served during the Great War in an ambulance unit in the Balkans. Basically a Conservative movement, obsessed by the threat of civil emergency, the BF fought the shadow of the Russian Revolution. It seemed that Fascism had come to save Italy from Bolshevism. Lintorn-Orman's movement would be based upon this new, virile regime. On the enrolment form of the BF, entrants undertook 'to uphold His Most Gracious Majesty King George V, his heirs and successors, the established constitution of Great Britain, and the British Empire', and to 'render every service . . . to the British Fascists in their struggle against all treacherous and revolutionary movements now working for the destruction of the Throne and Empire'. The BF's activities included stewarding Conservative Party meetings, waving Union Jacks, and shouting 'for King and Country'. Despite their admiration for Mussolini, there was, in their literature, an absence of corporatism or revolutionary doctrine. The membership was predominantly from the military and the gentry.

Scotland played its role in this burgeoning movement, notably in the case of the eighth Earl of Glasgow, born in 1874. As Commander Lord Kelburn, he had landed at Vladivostock in 1917 to succour British subjects who were stranded by the events. His *Times* obituary in 1963 remarked that 'what he saw of Bolshevik brutality appalled him, and his horror of Communism was to colour the next twenty years of his life, and to lead him into some indiscretions'.[3] The BF had a Glasgow branch and city centre headquarters, and marched in Glasgow on Armistice Day 1924. Their HQ in Pitt Street would become that of the British Union of Fascists in Glasgow some ten years later.

Scotland therefore contributed to the fight against 'Communist poison and Godless Soviets'. In June 1925, the *British Fascist Bulletin* carried a report by Miss Blake, Area Commander for Edinburgh, on 'Women's Units and Fascist Sunday Schools'. While in Scotland, she 'was greatly struck by the predominance of the very poorest kind of women, who were among the very keenest members. This, in my mind, is due to two things: the wearing of uniform by all members who can afford to do so, thus doing away with class distinction, and the fact that kitchen meetings are held everywhere, especially in the poorest parts of the cities . . . A further point of interest very noticeable in the Scottish units is the fact that the slack member has been almost entirely "eliminated"'.

At a meeting in Edinburgh, General Blakely had denounced a 'Gang of internationalists seek[ing] control of the world'. The Earl of Glasgow described the fascist movement as 'a lifebuoy for a drowning man', while Mrs Hamilton More-Nisbett, vice-president of the Women's Units in Scotland, spoke of the menace to Christianity posed by communist and socialist Sunday schools. At the Berkeley Hall in Glasgow, the general traced the Bolshevik conspiracy to its source: 'we found a gang of internationalist Jews, having their headquarters in Berlin, whose secret aim was the absolute control of a chaotic and defenceless world.'[4]

Later that month, the *Bulletin* reported on the Women's HQ at 34 Shandwick Place, Edinburgh. Three kitchen meetings had taken place in poor parts of the town, while a 'Helping Hand Fund' had been set up 'for our poorer Fascist sisters', who had been interviewed by the *Evening News*. In Glasgow, recruiting progressed favourably. In Ayr, the Countess of Eglinton and Winton accepted office as Country Commander for Ayrshire and Wigtownshire, while 'Miss Thorneycroft, of Plean House, has promised to give a drawing-room meeting at Plean next month with a view to starting Fascists in Stirlingshire, a very "Red" district'.[5]

In July 1925, the *Bulletin* announced that in Glasgow, Fascists had inspired the spirit of patriotism. There had been clashes with Communists at Central Station. The Fascists had boarded the train taken by Harry Pollitt, Communist leader: down the aisle, they had sung 'Rule, Britannia' and the national anthem, drowning out 'The Red Flag'.[6]

A fortnight later, Lord Ernest Hamilton, in his editorial 'What is Fascism?', called for 'a more robust, egoistic patriotism'.[7] His prayers seemed answered on 16 August, with a Fascist demonstration at the evening service at the Ross Street Unitarian Church, Glasgow. The Blackshirts 'sang the National Anthem with the Church at the conclusion of the service as a protest against the persistent preaching of revolution by the Minister, Mr R. Lee'.[8] There were actions against the Red Councils of Action in Glasgow, Edinburgh and Methil. Scottish Fascists set up children's clubs, and sold Fascist cigarettes, ties and pennants. That said, the *Bulletin* gave much more news from Tunbridge Wells and Tooting, as well as of the exploits of the London Cycling Club.

The year 1926 would pose a decisive challenge to the BF, and the Scottish section in particular. Certainly, there was a promising start. In February 1926, the *Bulletin* wrote of the success, in Glasgow, of speakers' and ju-jitsu classes. There was a fund-raising bazaar, and, what's more, the vice-president the Earl of Glasgow had returned from Ceylon. In March 1926, it was reported that, at the bazaar and carnival in the McLellan Galleries, 'the numerous side shows and attractions were managed by assistants in fancy dress, which added to the gaiety of the proceedings. The Newton Players, an excellent concert party, gave three performances, while a "Palais de danse" was run in two sessions'. There were promising developments in the Tradeston branch, 'the Troop Leader in charge allowing the use of push cycles in his shop to Fascists to help in the distribution of literature. In fact, he has the nucleus of a "mobile column" which may yet prove very useful'.[9]

But the General Strike of May 1926, which seemed to justify anti-Bolshevik fears, tore apart the organisation. BF offered their help to the government's strike-breaking Organisation for the Maintenance of Supplies. This help was refused, unless they gave up calling themselves Fascists, and dismantled their paramilitary organisation. This was rejected by the Fascist Grand Council, which precipitated the departure of Earl of Glasgow to form the Loyalists. The rapid collapse of the General Strike, with its dire consequences for the British labour movement, made apocalyptic fears of revolution appear unjustified. The BF's decline followed, with remaining strength concentrated in the London area. On 6 June 1926, the *Bulletin*, renamed the *British Lion,* affirmed Fascist principles: the king, promotion of class friendship, improvement of social conditions, preferential treatment for ex-servicemen, inter-Empire trade, and purification of the British race. Notable by their absence were Scottish 'Command Notices', in comparison with those of Ulster, Dublin, Birmingham, and the Northern, Western and Southern Commands.

However, in August 1927, the *British Lion* could announce that Glasgow Fascists were at work again. Members of the Glasgow branch of the BF had rallied again, and on 1 July 'went over the top', the enemy being the Glasgow Occult and Psychic Investigation Society. The psychics had said:

> These are Pyramids and they prophesy a World War in May, 1928, or 1929. The extremists of both classes will fight it out to the bitter end. The oppressed will rise. Seven years later [that being 1936], our coasts will not be visited. The steamers will but steam around, refusing to enter our ports because of the unsanitary after-effect of the Revolution.

The *Lion* reported that 'a brief speech by the Troop Leader of the British Fascists bluntly told those on the platform that they were nothing but Bolshies and their doctrines nothing but unadulterated, polluting Bolshevism'.[10]

In 1928, the Fascist John Colquhoun of Glasgow addressed 'This Nationalism' that would harass the movement throughout its history: 'During the last few months we who are carrying the Fascist banner into the enemy camp in Scotland have heard quite a lot about Scottish nationalism. This is, to our mind, nothing but Socialism disguised under the cloak of Nationalism.' What was really wanted in Scotland was 'more British Fascism, which is the only thing that will bind us closer to the Empire and the throne'. The Socialists who preached '"universal brotherhood"while making us antagonistic to each other by their so-called nationalistic doctrines, should be shunned by all who believe in the Empire Brotherhood'.[11]

The struggle for hegemony did not cease. In June 1929, the Fascists announced a Patrol wedding: 'The wedding took place at Ballimore Otter Ferry, Argyll on Wednesday June 12, of Miss Barbara Macrae, daughter of Lieutenant-Colonel and Mrs Macrae-Gilstrap, of Eileen Donan, to Captain Henry Laharde Mayne, formerly of the KOSB.' The London Special Patrol, of which she was OC, 'were mostly Scotch and were devoted to her although most rigidly disciplined and relentlessly kept up to the mark'. The London Special Patrol therefore felt 'the loss of such an officer and are only consoled by the fact that she remains an honorary member and has promised to visit the Patrol whenever she comes south'.[12] The new Mrs Mayne settled down at Barguillean Farm, Taynult, Argyll, but did not abandon her convictions. In the same issue that described the Patrol wedding, she announced the creation of a Fascist Dogs' Club.

But the pioneers of British Fascism did not benefit from the dramatic upheavals exacerbated by the Wall Street Crash. While Britain's overall unemployment rose from 11% in 1929 to around 22.5% in 1932, it rose to disproportionate heights in Scotland, from 12.1% to around 27%. Symptomatic of internal strife on the far right was the *British Lion* article of 1 March 1932, asking 'Who began Fascism in Great Britain?'. In its final years, the BF cast around for a coherent identity, from No Surrender in Ulster to out-and-out Nazism. The autumn issue of 1933 contained a double page spread on 'the death camps of the Soviets' and 'why we are anti-semitics'. In March 1934, the BF was denouncing the Austrian Fascist but anti-Nazi Engelbert Dollfuss, and reprinting the 'Horst Wessel' song. In April 1934, the BF had adopted as emblem the 'spiral', for its 'cosmic significance' as 'creative force'. It also denounced the 'Messiah' Arnold Leese, founder of the Imperial Fascist League. But the energies of the cosmos no longer served them, and the *British Lion*'s last issue appeared in autumn 1934. A year later Lintorn-Orman, ravaged by drink and drugs and dogged by lurid rumours of orgies and other 'indecent practices', died at the age of 40.

Against the Old Gang

On Hogmanay 1929, John Buchan, Perth-born author of *The Thirty-nine Steps*, wrote in the *Morning Post*: 'but for the bold experiment of Fascism the decade has not been fruitful in constructive statesmanship'.[13] However, up until the 1930s, there was no major organisation in Britain which could emulate Mussolini's example. This appeared to change with the emergence of the New Party, originally conceived by ex-Labour minister Sir Oswald Mosley as an organisation independent of the mainstream political parties, and which would be committed to Keynesian economic strategies. Mosley had serious connections with Scotland: he was close to several Clydeside MPs, and his initial programme was similar to the ideas of James Maxton.

The New Party campaign in Scotland was launched with a rally in the City Halls of Glasgow in March 1931. *The Glasgow Herald* reported that the interruptions were of a humorous nature. The appeal of the New Party was shown by the size of the meeting (a full hall and at least 2,000 people who could not obtain admission) and the range of speakers, which included Oswald Mosley, Cynthia Mosley, Robert Forgan (MP for West Renfrewshire), John Strachey MP for Birmingham Aston and Rosslyn Mitchell (former MP for Paisley).

Robert Forgan had been MP for West Renfrew since 1929. On 24 February 1931, he had sent a private letter of resignation to Ramsay Macdonald. For him, the strategy and policy pursued by the National Government were 'far removed from what was advocated at the General Election in 1929'. Promised investment in public works and public health had not materialised. He concluded:

> The electorate was asked to believe, with the sanction of the Labour Party, that the Liberal leader was not to be trusted: now an alliance has been entered into with a partner who less than two years ago was held up to ridicule and dishonour. It is such a contradiction and subterfuge (of a kind practised by all Parties) that has brought politics into disrepute with a large section of the community. It may be all in accordance with the character of the old game: but a more serious conception of the function of Government is necessary if the needs of the nation are to be met. Holding this opinion, I can do no other than resign from a Party that is content to tolerate indefinitely the futility of present parliamentary methods and the trend of present Government policy.[14]

Thus, in Forgan's eyes, the action proposed by Mosley was the only real way of addressing the slump.

Significant disturbances took place at the next New Party mass meeting, in the Flesher's Haugh, Glasgow Green. According to the police, it attracted 8,000 people, but the press amplified its importance, and that of the incidents following the arrival of 200 members of the Communist-controlled National Unemployed Workers Movement (NUWM). *The Glasgow Herald* reported 'New Party Rally Uproar'. According to *The Scotsman*, 'a loud burst of cheering, mingled with boos and jeers, greeted Sir Oswald as he made his way from a gaily decorated motor car to the platform'. He was assailed by cries of 'traitor'. Introduced by Robert Forgan, Mosley denounced the 'noisy futility' which reduced the House of Commons to 'the conduct of a girls' school in hysterics'. The youth of the nation were 'discarding the old ways and demanding a new movement. If you are prepared to make a new start in Britain to get rid of the old men and the old measures, join with us, fight with us, and on the ashes of the past, its failures and its betrayals, we will build a new Britain and a model State of which we can be proud'. Mosley went on to denounce the threat of sweated labour from poorer countries: 'They could not make the working classes of Britain fight for their salvation until every Hottentot in Africa had joined the ILP. They should take action to protect the home market, and to protect the workers from the chaos of world conditions.' The New Party held that 'the worker and employer should both be protected by a scientific system which served efficiency in industry, good wages to the worker, and low prices to the consumer'. At the end of the speech, some of the crowd – estimated at 15,000 by *The Glasgow Herald* and 40,000 by *The Times* – had stampeded towards the platform. *The Daily Express* reported:

> After replying to numerous questions which had been put to him, Sir Oswald stepped forward to the front of the platform, looked resolutely in the face of the crowd which surged towards him, and with a cry of 'Now boys', leaped to the ground. His supporters quietly followed, and the crowd, taken by surprise, scattered, completely nonplussed. It was only a moment, however, before they rushed back to the rear of the Mosley party, making a concentrated attack with razors, stones, life preservers, walking-sticks, and other missiles. The mob stampeded, and for a few seconds there was complete confusion, women and children jumping into the shrubbery as the crowd surged past them.

Sticks and stones were thrown, and the England rugby internationalist Peter Howard and others in the civil 'bodyguard' 'had their clothes cut, evidently with knives or razors'. An effort to strike Sir Oswald Mosley with a life-preserver was also frustrated. Apparently unperturbed, the Leader 'waved a nonchalant au revoir to the noisy assembly as the car moved off'.

Seen in the Central Hotel by a *Scotsman* representative after the meeting, Mosley said the gathering was 'one of the best he had ever addressed'. He confirmed to the *Daily Express* journalist that he himself 'saw razors flourished'. Peter Howard added: 'Two or three men came up and kicked me on the shins. They persisted, and I stood it as long as I could. I did not want to go for the wrong man, so I just watched and singled out the best kicker. I let him have it when he kicked me again. That stopped the kicking.' Another famous tough associated with the New Party, the boxing champion Ted 'Kid' Lewis, declared: 'I was continually kicked, but I did not retaliate. I know how to hit,' he added significantly, 'and that is why I never use my fists outside of the ring.'

Nevertheless, on 23 September 1931, Glasgow's Assistant Chief Constable played down the incidents in a report to the Under-Secretary of State at the Scottish Office: 'An ambulance squad and a large body of police were in attendance during the meeting. No complaints of any kind were received by the police, and no person was injured. The reports in the daily newspapers regarding this meeting were greatly exaggerated.'[15] Nevertheless, the robust reaction to the New Party, which involved the substantial Jewish working-class presence in the west of Scotland, would mark out Glasgow as a relatively 'no-go' area for Mosley: in the course of the thirties, he would look rather to Edinburgh and other parts of Scotland.

The New Party may have made the headlines, but it failed to make an electoral impact in Scotland. In the October 1931 rectorial election at Glasgow University, Compton Mackenzie made a major breakthrough for the Scottish Nationalists, while Mosley polled an embarrassingly low 21 votes out of 2,323. At the general election, even Robert Forgan and Major C. Randolph Dudgeon, sitting MPs who had come over to Mosley from the Labour and Liberal Parties respectively, polled poorly, with 4% for Forgan in Renfrewshire and 3% for Dudgeon in Galloway. This electoral disaster contrasted sharply with the performance of the Nationalists and the Communists: the Nationalists received 11% of the vote in West Renfrew. Mosley's illness, the electoral failure of the New Party candidates under the first-past-the-post system, the consequent disillusionment of Mosley's initial support, and the growing strength of Fascism in Europe all served to suggest to Mosley that what was needed was an out-and-out Fascist party with a clearly defined programme.

It was not that there was no sympathy for Fascism among the Scottish elites. In April 1933, the Union Debating Society of St Andrews University invited a German government language tutor, Otto Wagner, to propose the motion: 'This House approves of the

Nazi Party, and congratulates it on its splendid work in the reformation of Germany.' According to the Society's Annual Report, 'Herr Wagner overcame the language difficulties with such skill'. The minutes of the debate recorded that 'the 75 members on the floor with a further 50 in the gallery' passed the motion with a clear majority. Wagner reported to his masters in London that the debate was widely reported in the Scottish press, and that the success of the motion contrasted with 'anti-German' ones proposed elsewhere in Great Britain, notably at the London School of Economics.[16]

One of the speakers, and the university's future convenor of debates, was George K. Young, whose right-wing radicalism had led him to try to thwart the National Government candidate in the East Fife by-election of 1933 and even to help Labour. In November 1933, to a packed chamber, Young spoke in opposition to the Student Representative Council's motion 'This House deplores the rise of Fascism'. Although the motion was carried, most of the floor speakers argued from a pro-Fascist standpoint. St Andrews students would confirm their right-wing reputation in February 1934 with the defeat of the motion 'That socialism is the only solution for man's problems'. In November 1935, 'That National Socialism spells the damnation of Germany' was carried by 'a fairly small majority'. At this event, it was minuted that 'Mr Thompson, moving the counter-motion, gave a good imitation of General Goering, in boisterous mood, and indeed was so funny that he broke down several times himself'.[17]

Nevertheless, despite such pro-Fascist sympathies among Scotland's gilded youth, after the British Union of Fascists (BUF) was finally launched in October 1932 a second Scottish launch had to be held a year later. It was not until late in 1933 that the movement established a branch in Edinburgh, under the leadership of a Major Sleigh. However, on 12 January 1934, *Blackshirt* announced:

Fascism in Scotland is making great headway, and it is expected that at least three new branches will be opened in Edinburgh during the present month. An interesting innovation in uniform, peculiar to Scotland, is being introduced. This is the kilt, to be worn with the blackshirt. The colour will be a neutral grey, tartan being impossible, as the Fascist policy is to embrace all clans and classes. This does not mean any attempt to interfere with the wearing of Clan tartan, for only when the member is in uniform will the BUF kilt be worn.

A Fascist dance would be held that weekend, and it was 'expected that there will be an excellent performance'.[18] In March, it was announced that in Motherwell 'the re-organisation of this branch has eliminated certain disturbing factors, and the branch will grow all the stronger for this pruning'.[19] Motherwell would became a pocket of strong BUF activity, following the recruitment of some very active members, in particular a Mr and Mrs Nixon. The branch held rallies, maintained a Fascist Hall and were granted leasehold of the tennis courts at Calder Park. Lady Mosley (Sir Oswald's mother), visiting the Motherwell branch in June 1934, would speak at the tennis courts and the Fascist hall. She was reported as saying that she 'didn't know of any branch of the movement that had started on such strong lines as the one in Motherwell'. The neighbouring town of Wishaw also witnessed big levels of BUF activity, involving meetings, social events and rallies.

In this first spring of Scottish Fascism, Edinburgh was rapidly consolidated, with the creation of a blood transfusion corps, made up of 30 members including four women, and a defence force. That March, according to *Blackshirt*, Dundee 'received a shock': 'an "advance guard" of Blackshirts penetrated still further north and held a successful surprise meeting on the spacious city square'. Greenock was now assured of 'a fine Defence Force. Several young men, some of them well-known boxers, are already training in Defence Force work'.[20] In April, at the Gardners Hall in Edinburgh, a debate between Willie Gallacher and Captain Vincent Collier attracted more than 700 people, 'nearly all socialists'.[21]

Scotland's first UF rally was at the Drill Hall, Dumfries on 6 April 1934. According to *The Scotsman*, it was attended by around 3,000 people and, despite an overnight attempt at sabotage, the audience was mainly well-behaved: 'The Communist element was in evidence, but their singing was drowned by broadcast music before Sir Oswald went on to the platform. Sir Oswald spoke from a table draped with the Union Jack.' After rebuking the Communists, Mosley argued against the weakening of the link between Scotland and England on the grounds that both would suffer. He maintained, however, that it was thoroughly understandable why the Scots had grievances with Westminster: under Fascism, Scottish questions would be settled by Scotsmen 'on the spot'. They would be assisted in their work by the 'corporate system'. As regards agriculture, 'Fascism alone, through the corporate system, had the policy to provide the market which agriculture lacked through an increase in the purchasing power of the great towns, by raising wages and salaries as science increased the power of industry to produce.' Mosley argued that tariffs and quotas were ineffective. There should be total exclusion of foreign foodstuffs, except from the Dominions. Ominously, however, 'during Sir Oswald's speech there was an interruption lasting two minutes, during which two men had to be ejected from the hall. Following the disturbance two Blackshirts received blows to the head, and had to be assisted to an ante-room to receive attention'.[22]

A Special Branch summary of April 1934 gave a sober assessment of the beginnings of Fascism north of the Cheviots. At a time when the BUF had 120 branches in England and Wales, with nine regional and area headquarters, Scotland still only had a temporary headquarters, under Richard Adolph Plathen, who was at that time seconded to Scotland. Membership in Aberdeenshire, Aberdeen, Argyll and Ayrshire was nil. It was reported that the Earl of Glasgow 'was at one time connected with the movement but has since left it'. Dumfriesshire counted about 100 members: 'The membership is reported to be growing especially since the visit of Sir Oswald Mosley on the 6 April. No great importance is to be attached to the movement, which is not sympathetically received by the local press, Liberal or Conservative.' Fife, Inverness and Glasgow still counted nil, while Edinburgh had about 50 Blackshirts. This branch had already proved schismatic:

> A branch of the BUF was formed in Edinburgh in November 1933 under Major Sleigh and Mr Geddes. After the arrival of a Captain Collier from the National HQ in London friction occurred, and the original Edinburgh leaders broke away and formed a Scottish Union of Fascists with National HQ at 44 Hanover St, Edinburgh. This party wears the usual Fascist badge with the addition of a St Andrew's Cross. They appear to be in sympathy with the SDSA [Scottish Democratic Self-government Association], of which the leader is Miss Wendy Wood. The BUF and the SUF both continue to display activity, but no great importance is to be attached to them.

The strength of Fascism in Renfrewshire was unknown: 'Some indications of the Fascist movement are reported. They are attributed to

Dr Robert Forgan's previous association with the West Renfrewhire constituency'.[23]

The first success story was the Dalbeattie branch, led by James Little. At that time, Little was the most successful BUF leader across the border. By summer of 1934, he was promoted to Officer-in-Charge, Scotland. He was a bank manager, town hall clerk and a well-known and respected figure in the social life of the town. At the end of the month, *Blackshirt* praised Dalbeattie: 'this branch has been dubbed by the local press "the cradle of Fascism" which is regarded as a great compliment by the members'.[24]

In September 1934, Special Branch reported that the Dumfries branch had about 400 members, although their real activity was questioned:

> A fairly large percentage of the numbers are described as 'passive' members, who do not attend the meetings held in the HQ of the local branch, nor wear the Blackshirt uniform. A large number of that class consists of business men, mostly in a small way. It is said that it is intended to make Dumfries the HQ for Scotland. This branch is regarded as one of the most flourishing in Scotland.[25]

The deep south therefore seemed particularly propitious terrain. In May a very successful dance was held in Gatehouse of Fleet and a badminton court furnished with the proceeds. The 'Reds' had 'miserably fizzled out in their threat to drive the Blackshirts out of Dalbeattie'.[26] In Dumfries, the Women's Branch had begun to hold highly popular physical culture classes.

However, the high-point of BUF activity in Scotland in 1934 was the visit at the beginning of June by the Leader himself. At the Usher Hall, wrote *Blackshirt*, 'the Leader was heard by people representative of all classes and all political beliefs. There were in the audience: ministers of religion, prominent lawyers, city councillors, farmers, clerks, shop assistants and artisans'. He presented to this august audience a policy that was 'British first, the Dominions next, and the foreigners nowhere'. In 'Scotland re-visited', 'Anglo-Scot' wrote at length on the Scottish situation and the Leader's visit. He was not insensitive to the rise of separatist sentiment:

> It is interesting indeed to go north after an interval of many years, to Scotland once more, to hear Mosley speak on Fascism for the

first time in the ancient Scottish capital. Edinburgh outwardly seems
to change very little with the years; there are the same grey stone
houses, the same beautiful Princes St facing the Castle Rock, the
same dour Scots accent heard on every hand that warms the heart of
the returning traveller. But one thing struck me at first sight – on the
flagstaffs of the city flies an unwanted flag, the St Andrew's Cross of
Scotland. During my whole stay in Edinburgh I have seen only one
Union Jack and that was draped on the table of the Fascist platform.
The many trials which have beset the Scottish people within recent
years have made them bitter and inclined to blame the Southerner
for their present plight. The trend of industry southwards has its
serious effects in England, but here it is interpreted as a deliberate
attempt of the Sassenach to save himself at the expense of Scotland.[27]

It was in such a spirit that the people of Edinburgh thronged to
hear Mosley at the Usher Hall, the greatest one in the city. There
were some demonstrations by Scottish Nationalists outside the hall,
but these were 'soon drowned by Communist rowdyism, showing
clearly that it is with the Hammer and Sickle of Moscow, not with
the St Andrew's Cross, that Fascism has ultimately to contend in
the North'. Inside the crowded hall, Mosley began with a strong
challenge to the separatists:

> He points out that it is all very well to say that the English have no
> right to speak in Scotland (ironic applause), but the English might
> retaliate by insisting that no Scot has a right to speak in England;
> they might even carry out the dire threat of returning Ramsay Mac-
> donald to his native land (groans and laughter). He then proceeds
> to show that it is possible to solve our economic problems only by
> planning the joint resources of Britain and that it is the very lack of
> planning which has caused the serious trend of industry southwards,
> which has intensified the sufferings of Scotland.

For 'Anglo-Scot', the reactions of the listeners were entirely different
from those of an English audience:

> Where sentiment avails but little, Mosley's reasoned economic argu-
> ments win intelligent response; especially his analysis of the ship-
> ping problem, with irrefutable statistics to support his clear-cut logic.

Again, in the questions at the end – which come thicker and faster than at any Fascist meeting which I have attended in England – intelligent criticism is everywhere made manifest.

Needless to say, *The Scotsman* gave much more coverage to the less 'reasoned' street fighting that followed the meeting in the Usher Hall:

Between 300 and 400 uniformed Blackshirts attended the meeting and acted as stewards, and it was on the departure of these that the trouble developed. Contingents had come from Manchester, Newcastle, Glasgow and Edinburgh, and their appearance outside the hall apparently raised the ire of the large crowd which had gathered in the vicinity. Later there were fights between groups of Blackshirts and their opponents, principally near Tollcross, and a bus was stoned. Six or eight Blackshirts, and several civilians, including a bus driver, had to receive attention at the Royal Infirmary, and one was detained.

During the meeting, about 100 Communists marched repeatedly around the hall, where at one time a crowd of between 2000 and 3000 people collected. After half an hour mounted police were called. The Dumfries bus was made the object of a special attack. An ugly situation developed in Melville Road, when a bus of Manchester Blackshirts was attacked.

Nevertheless, *The Scotsman* remarked on the charismatic presence of the Fascist orator: 'The Black Shirt leader entered the hall to the tape of a Fascist hymn, and spoke behind a table draped with the Union Jack. Gigantic loud speakers on the platform, where he was a solitary figure, amplified his powerful voice.' Mosley's speech 'was accompanied by characteristic gestures. At one moment he spoke with his left hand on his hip and his right arm and fingers extended. At other times both his hands grasped the buckle of his belt, with its emblem of the fasces; at rare intervals, while driving home some particular point of his policy, his fist was clenched. It was a fluent oration expressed with logical arrangement'.[28]

For 'Anglo-Scot', the success of this meeting was 'indicated by the enthusiastic recruiting that has followed the Leader's stirring message'. It was therefore unnecessary to attach any great importance to the riotous incidents which happened when his men left the hall:

They were deliberately engineered by a small Communist minority. Indeed, I myself travelled in the same train with three Communists from London to Edinburgh who arrived shortly before the meeting. The worst elements gathered from Canongate and Tollcross, and because of the prohibition of a march by the city authorities, our men had to leave the hall in motor coaches. Finding our men at a disadvantage, Red hooligans surrounded the coaches and rained stones and bricks, smashing the windows and seriously injuring several of our men. One of them is still in the Edinburgh Infirmary with glass splinters in his eyes.

'Anglo-Scot' therefore reached this satisfied and optimistic conclusion:

On my return from the North, I feel that one thing alone can restore the loyalty of Scotland to the Union, and that is the early formation of a planned Corporate State in Britain, with which Scotland may be assured her rightful place; in which her local industries would be governed by Scotsmen, and her local cultural traditions preserved and strengthened as a precious part of the great communal heritage of the British people . . . It is the disintegrating influences of a corrupt and effete clan which are at present driving the two countries apart. Fascism, here as elsewhere, will restore co-operation and understanding for the mutual benefit of all.

Yet the incidents at the Usher Hall had made the uniformed troops of Mosley's legion look, if not effete, then at least curiously effeminate. A week later, *The Scotsman* reported on the trial of Allan Stewart, a young labourer, who was found guilty of 'having conducted himself in a disorderly manner in Castle Terrace on 1 June and assaulted William Mill of Dumfries by tripping him and kicking him'. The constable told the trial: 'The Blackshirts were not offensive. They appeared to be a very cowed party, and were trying their hardest to get away from the situation.'

The events in Edinburgh anticipated the debacle, six days later, of Mosley's meeting at the Olympia in London. This gathering in the largest hall in the land, disrupted by anti-Fascists who were in turn brutally dealt with by Blackshirt stewards, tarnished the image of Mosley's movement and led to the discontinuation of support by

Lord Rothermere and the *Daily Mail*. The BUF creed would not die, but it would drift even further from the mainstream of British politics.

Later in the fateful month of June, it was the turn of the Leader's mother to tour the Scottish branches, starting in Edinburgh, as reported by *Blackshirt*:

> She had consented to be photographed by Press cameramen among the group of Blackshirts on the pavement at the door of the premises. As the picture was about to take place, she smilingly remarked: 'It would not do for the Leader's mother to appear as though she were trying to hide the black shirt', and removed her costume coat, which almost completely hid her uniform, before posing with the Blackshirts.

Lady Mosley then visited Edinburgh Royal Infirmary to visit Joseph Wood, of Manchester, who had lost an eye on 1 June. In Dumfries, she presented a black flag with the BUF emblem in yellow and a Union Jack, then 'exhorted the members of the branch to defend the colours with their lives, and to follow them to victory. The members saluted the colours with the Fascist salute, and two Blackshirts played bagpipe music'.[29]

Attempts were made at developing activists and creating a Fascist culture. Thus, in July 1934, *Blackshirt* reported on the success of speakers' classes, as well as sporting activities:

> Scottish Blackshirts are well to the fore in sports, and inter-branch tug-of-war contests are being arranged. It is hoped also that there will be a contest between an English and a Scottish team. Next winter there will be at least six Blackshirt football teams in South Scotland, and negotiations for a Blackshirt Football League are being made. The Dumfries Life-Saving Team have been greatly augmented, and now patrols a 30-mile stretch along the Solway Coast.[30]

Indeed, that summer, the south of Scotland was a hive of wholesome activity:

> A new development for Blackshirts in Scotland is the commencement of a Health Dancing Class by WAO Mitford Hone and women Fascists now keep themselves fit by eurythmic exercises. Women

members are also attending the Speakers' Classes which are being run by BO Hatton Duff. So great was the attendance at a Whist Drive and Dance held in the Queensberry Hotel, Dumfries, that a larger hall is being taken for the next one. Blackshirt Life-Saving Patrols upon the shores of the Solway Firth are much appreciated and their ambulance men have already handled twelve minor cases.

The activities of Fascists in the South of Scotland had led to the establishment of two more sub-branches, one at Lockerbie and the other at Thornhill. Upwards of 300 gathered at Lockerbie to hear DBO Hone.[31]

Blackshirts sought to emulate this in the west of Scotland. Certainly, the BUF seems to have failed to absorb a large number of BF members – estimated to be around 400 in Glasgow in May 1934. This may be explained by Lintorn-Orman's hostility to the 'Communist' Mosley, as well as the inactivity of the Glasgow membership. Nevertheless, in August 1934, under the title 'Fascist Enterprise', *Blackshirt* reported that two Glasgow Fascists had shown in a very practical way their enthusiasm for the movement:

Fascist Salmond, of the Propaganda Dept, and Fascist Corrin, have given several days of their holiday to the work of spreading Blackshirt agricultural policy in the farming district of South Lanarkshire. They made no attempt to hold meetings, realising that in such a scattered district personal contact would bring better results. They visited the majority of the farms and cottages in the vicinity of Lamington, Culter, Symington, Coulter, Winston, and Roberton. Their tour was successful. They were met with courtesy and were given every chance to explain Blackshirt policy. The people were interested and decidedly sympathetic. One farmer said, 'Thank heaven somebody is at last taking an interest in workers on the land. I have read all Sir Oswald Mosley's speeches and am sure he has got hold of the right policy.' These two enthusiastic Fascists are paying a return visit shortly, when the farmers and farm workers will have had time to read the literature left with them.[32]

However, back in the large urban centres, the wild scenes at the Usher Hall had inaugurated a campaign of anti-Fascist violence which would continue into the late 1930s. In August 1934, 700 people gathered at an open-air meeting in Albert Crescent, Queen's Park, Glasgow. *Blackshirt* noted:

> Within a short space of time some 600 people were present, their number being largely composed of Communists. Mr Oliver was allowed to speak with little interruption for some 30 minutes. Communists made desperate efforts to sell anti-Fascist literature, having decided, as Mr Oliver said, that they could not do so at their own meeting.[33]

The following month, at an open-air meeting in Dennistoun, 'one of the Reds, with the usual Communist "bravery", kicked Fascist Salmond in the back and then ran hurriedly away'.[34] Also in Glasgow, six Blackshirts on a sales drive 'were attacked by large numbers of Communists led by a Jew, and armed with lead-piping and knuckle-dusters. Owing to the overwhelming noise of their attackers, they were compelled to return to their HQ'. Later in the evening APO Baxter, accompanied by five Fascists, three in uniform and the others in plain clothes, walked away from the HQ and up Bath Street. At the junction of West Campbell Street and Bath Street they 'were attacked by a mob of some 600 Reds, again led by a Jew. The Communists, having concluded their own meeting, had obviously been lying in wait for the Blackshirts. The Blackshirts retreated towards their HQ. A few months later a cobblestone was flung which struck APO Baxter behind the ear. He fell to the ground, half-stunned. Regaining his feet he was immediately attacked by a Communist, wielding a piece of lead-piping'.[35]

In the same month, such Judeo-Communist viciousness was contrasted with the encouraging developments down south:

> Six months ago a few people assembled in a small hall in Dumfries. They had been asked to listen to a lecture on British Fascism, and it is very probable that curiosity was the main reason for their presence there. This was the first time anyone in Dumfries had seen a Blackshirt or heard anything of the Fascist policy, but as the speaker proceeded with his address it was evident that the interest of the small audience had been aroused. This was the beginning of the Dumfries branch, and the three Blackshirts present were the advance guard of Fascism in the Border county of Dumfries. On Monday, last week, the new

HQ of the Dumfries Branch and South West Scotland were opened. Anyone who had an opportunity of inspecting the new premises, decorated in grey, black and gold, would find it hard to realise how short a time has passed since the beginning. As the officers inspected the Defence Force, to the accompaniment of the wild music of the pipes, I thought of the trials, successes, disappointments and minor triumphs since that small first meeting on a wet March evening. Fascism has come to stay in Dumfriesshire. The Lowland Scot is slow to move, but underneath his dour exterior glows the ancient Border courage, which the Leader, with his stirring message of hope and patriotism, has rekindled once again.[36]

October brought more 'amazing examples of Red hooliganism' on the mean streets of Glasgow:

Hundreds of Communists demonstrated on Tuesday outside the Blackshirt HQ in Bath St. Headed by a flute band they marched up and down outside the HQ, screaming and shouting. Nearby streets became blocked with people and police were called to restore order. Three Blackshirts were set upon by a gang of rowdies as they were walking along Gordon St on Thursday. Fierce hand-to-hand fighting took place in the presence of a large crowd attracted by sounds of the struggle. The Blackshirts quickly got the upper hand and chased the rowdies away. One of the Blackshirts then addressed the crowd, explaining that the incident they had just witnessed was a nightly occurrence and was typical of Communist attempts to terrorise the Fascists.[37]

At the beginning of November, Glasgow Fascists fought back with the opening of a winter campaign at St Andrew's Halls:

Valuable publicity was given to the meeting by the Reds who had chalked the streets throughout the city, urging all 'Class conscious workers' to demonstrate outside the building. DBO Tiffin opened the meeting with a vigorous attack on the misrepresentation of the alien controlled press and further exposed the sham of so-called liberty. At the conclusion of Mr Tiffin's speech, an anti-fascist rose to his feet and began to shout, but within a few seconds the Blackshirt stewards had removed him and the meeting proceeded undisturbed.

Mr Bryham Oliver followed with a clear and lucid explanation of the Blackshirt economic policy. Outside, during the meeting, wild scenes were witnessed and the police were forced to draw their batons and charge the mob. Owing to the presence of the hostile mob, nearly two hundred ticket holders decided not to enter the building in case they were involved in a fight.

After the meeting it was claimed there had been a strong stream of enquiries at the branch HQ, seeking further info on the fascist movement.[38] Not to be outdone, that very week 'Blackshirt uniforms were much in evidence at a Blackshirt dance held in Edinburgh'.[39]

If Mosley's Scottish legion had begun to march north of the Cheviots, it was already torn by peculiarly Scottish contradictions. Religious sectarianism and the question of the union coalesced to divide and weaken Scottish Fascism. Firstly, the Mosley brand had to compete with an established Scottish tradition of bigotry that went back to the Reformation. More recently, as Colin Kidd has shown, in the late eighteenth and nineteenth centuries, 'Anglo-Britishness was recast as a shared Teutonic racialism', promoting an idea of the Scottish people that excluded the inferior Celts and Irish.[40] Indeed, Scots 'played an important role from the beginning in the incubation of racial thought'.[41] The pioneering work of the Gothicist John Pinkerton was added to in the nineteenth century by George Combe, who saw the racialist potential in phrenology, and above all by Robert Knox, who asserted in *The Races of Men*: 'To me the Caledonian Celt appears a race as distinct from the Lowland Saxon of the same country, as any two races can be: as negro from American; Hottentot from Cafre; Esqiumaux from Saxon'.[42] This Lowland Teutonist perspective was enthusiastically shared by the prophet of Ecclefechan, Thomas Carlyle, whose fear and loathing of the Celt compromised even his sympathy for the Irish during the 1840s.

Between the two world wars, a section of the Church of Scotland associated with reverends Duncan Cameron and John White was in the forefront of campaigns against the 'threat' posed by Irish Catholic immigration and the 'Red' politicians it naturally supported. In May 1923, the General Assembly of the Church of Scotland had received with appreciation a lurid report on 'The Menace of the Irish Race to our Scottish Nationality'. Thus began an official Presbyterian campaign against Scoto-Irish Catholics that would continue up to the outbreak of the Second World War. The Presbyterians seemed to be endeavouring to revive the Great War spirit of unity by, in the words of Stewart J. Brown, 'directing hostility toward a group that could be labelled as outside the covenant, as an impure element polluting Scotland's race and culture'.[43] In 1928, John White, the architect of Church Union the following year, asserted in a speech: 'when race and soil conspire to evoke both loyalty and patriotism in a people, the moral qualities of a great and permanent nation are secured'.[44]

Fatefully, however, the BUF considered Protestants and Catholics to be equally capable of being good Britons. The BUF's decision to delete anti-Catholic articles from its charter in 1933, and Mosley's well-known personal stance and history of support for Irish separation from Britain – most notably in his denunciation of atrocities by the Black and Tans – convinced the Scottish Protestant League (SPL), led by Alexander Ratcliffe in Glasgow, and Protestant Action (PA), led by John Cormack in Edinburgh, that they should oppose the BUF. They were formidable opponents: 1931 had seen the crushing of the New Party in Scotland, but also the election of Ratcliffe as councillor for Dennistoun with more votes than all of his opponents combined.

Ratcliffe was not, however, averse to Fascism: in the summer of 1933, he had been close to the short-lived Scottish Fascist Democratic Party (SFDP), founded by William Weir Gilmour. Weir Gilmour was, in the words of Tony Milligan, 'a man steeped in the ethos and politics of urban Scotland'.[45] From working as a miner he had gone on to become a surveyor, and had become active in the ILP, working for the weekly *Forward* as well as lecturing for the Scottish Labour Colleges. He was also a delegate to the Glasgow Trades Council and shared the Scottish far-left's admiration for Daniel De Leon's ideas of industrial democracy. What attracted them in De Leon's thought was his critical stand-point in relation to existing trade-union organisation, and his support for the dismemberment and reorganisation of unions on an industry-by-industry basis. This was to form the basis for an industrially organised socialist democracy. Weir Gilmour identified Mussolini's corporate state as the embodiment of this ideal. Quickly recognised as an important young convert, Weir Gilmour had been adopted as the New Party candidate for Coatbridge in 1931 and polled 2.1%, a result which was moderately better than the other two non-MPs who stood for the New Party in Scotland.

Weir Gilmour saw the success of the Nationalists and of the SPL and PA as a blueprint for Fascist work in Scotland. At its inception, the Charter of the SFDP read:

> Clause 4: Expulsion from Scotland of all members of Roman Catholic Religious Orders. Repeal of Section 18 of the 1918 Education (Scotland) Act, whereby non-Romanists in Scotland are compelled to pay for the upkeep of Roman Catholic schools.

> Clause 5: Prohibition of Irish immigration into Scotland.

For Weir Gilmour, the Mosley movement was 'run by Roman Catholics, organised by Roman Catholics, in the interests of Roman Catholics'. On the launch of his paper *The Commonweale*, Weir Gilmour wrote to Ratcliffe: 'I know that so far as Scotland is concerned there are important Fascist political moves in the offing. I am not at liberty to speak further than this. But if this paper were started it would give Scottish Fascism a definitely anti-Romanist line, and indirectly would influence and educate the English party to adopt the same line'.[46] At first, the BUF adopted a relatively conciliatory position. On 16 June 1933, in *Blackshirt*, the following disclaimer was made on 'Fascism in Scotland': 'The new movement in Scotland embraces the Corporate State policy and indeed has embodied much of the policy of the BUF in its programme . . . We disagree, however, entirely with their attitude towards Roman Catholics. Further, we think they go too far in their ideas of Scottish self-government. We agree that purely Scottish matters should be settled on the spot in Scotland under Fascist organisation. We think, however, that some of the more extreme proposals of the Scottish Movement would tend to break up national unity.'[47] The sectarian issue alienated Ratcliffe. The SFDP announced that they were reconsidering their robust position on Catholic schools and Irish immigration. By December 1933, Ratcliffe was adamant that Protestants should leave both the SFDP and BUF.

In the *Vanguard* of 27 December 1933, Ratcliffe headlined with 'Why I resigned from Scottish Fascists'. The minister recalled the initial enthusiasm Weir Gilmour's party had engendered:

The people began to ask themselves the question, 'Is this a movement in Scotland, at least a political movement to enable us to do something practical with the co-operation of Protestant organisations to put Rome off the rates, to sweep the convents and monasteries from the country and to sweep Rome from the country altogether?'

The first issue of *The Commonweale* had been sold out within a week. Thousands more copies were asked for and could not be procured. The SFDP's anti-Catholic, anti-Irish charter had 'stirred up the hearts of the people of Scotland'. Ratcliffe told his followers: 'I am not a Fascist at all in so far as political matters are concerned, and never was. I was a member of the SFDP ... because that constitution was consistent with clean political administration and with my own principles as a Protestant Protagonist in Scotland.' Then he received a fateful letter from Weir Gilmour: 'the attitude of the SFDP towards religious matters is being completely reviewed just now, and I think that the result will be drastic alterations in the Constitution of the party'. While Weir Gilmour was hauling down the flag, Ratcliffe did not believe in 'hanging fire':

Organisations may come, and organisations may go, but the Scottish Protestant League goes on forever. (Loud applause) ... Oh let us beware of these shilly-shally, namby-pamby, milk and water sort of Protestants who grow hot and cold. That is not what we want in Scotland. My friends, Christ has no use for that sort of thing. [48]

Weir Gilmour and his brief adventure were consigned to hell along with other pro-Catholic Fascists. Already in November 1933, Ratcliffe had thundered: 'Von Papen, Mussolini and Oswald Mosley have received the Papal blessing and the Concordat has made Germany practically a Catholic state ... the Papacy is behind Hitler in his devilish work.'[49] The electoral advances of the SPL – five council seats won in November, with a vote dwarfing that of the Communists – allowed Ratcliffe to fill the anti-Catholic niche in Glasgow, while the growth of the BUF put paid to the SFDP. If anything, the SFDP's initial sectarianism put Catholics off joining the BUF's ranks and further weakened Fascist organisation in the west of Scotland.

Ratcliffe's autocratic personality eventually led to division and defeat for the SPL, with the leader losing his seat to an anti-Ratcliffe alliance in October 1934. But he continued to be a noisy presence.

Throughout the late thirties, Ratcliffe and his *Vanguard* gave full vent to their sectarianism. Pamphlets came thick and fast: *The Horrible Lives of the Popes of Rome*; *The Abominable Confessional*; *Convent Life Unveiled*; *A Great Exposure*; *Roman Catholics and Crime* and *Liguori the Filthy*. Papist fascism was also singled out for attack. On 25 April 1934, Walter Allen analysed 'Fascism and Vaticanism':

> The sinister influences at work behind Fascism and Dictatorship would appear to be of Jesuit origin and design, for the Jesuits are aiming at a World dictatorship ... Popular sovereignty is disappearing in Europe. These great continental powers have passed under irresponsible dictatorships. Two others face the prospect of restoring the Bourbon and Hapsburg dynasties. These are the most dangerous and reactionary ruling families of modern times.

This movement to restore the Hapsburgs in Austria included a Fascist dictator as head of government. What's more, efforts were 'definitely under way to extend Fascism to Ireland and Spain. The Barbarian pretender awaits in Belgium the opportune moment to fly to Paris and assume the reins of power'. Allen concluded:

> As the alliance of Fascism and Vaticanism sweeps away democracy in Europe, Austria now appears the next victim. A few weeks ago it looked as though Ireland would be the first to follow Italy and Germany. But that Rome-cursed island has permitted Roman Catholic Austria to rush in front of it in the mad scramble for Fascist dictators.[50]

In February 1935, Walter Allen claimed that *The Protocols of the Learned Elders of Zion* had been authored by Jesuits.[51] On 1 May 1935, the *Vanguard* spelled out its position: 'The Pope is the cause of all the trouble in the world. Being the direct descendant of the Devil, the Prince of Darkness, he is used by Satan to delude millions of men and women who have souls to be saved.'[52] On 8 January 1936, *Blackshirt*'s approval of Section 18 of the Education Act attracted Protestant ire:

> These Mosleyists and Joyceites of the BUF become a menace to the Protestants of the British Empire when they openly seek to bolster up the furtherance of Popery at the public expense throughout the

British Empire. And let us make it perfectly clear to these people, that so far as Scotland is concerned, they will never make headway even with their organisation, never mind with their politics, until they recant on the Papist school question.[53]

In what was characterised as 'an amazing article', 'Fascism and Rome's Jesuits', David Wilkie wrote: 'Fascism is not an instrument of capitalism; it is an instrument of Rome. Its aim is not to "reinstate" capitalism, but to take advantage of the political and economic situation in its entirety to re-establish the political supremacy of the Vatican.'[54] What's more, Catholicism was the 'spawning-ground of both Communism and Fascism'. As for the 'Dollfuss Massacre', the massacre in Vienna was 'St Bartholemew's Day over again, with Austrian Social Democrats taking the place of French Huguenots'. A week later, it was asserted that Hitler was made chancellor 'by papal intrigue'. 'What is to be noted,' declared the *Vanguard*, 'is that von Papen, like Hitler, is a Roman Catholic.'[55] As late as January 1939, Ratcliffe's mouthpiece declared: 'Hitler is a Papist, and he learned the art of persecution as a Roman Catholic. He is also an Austrian, and this makes him a very superstitious Roman Catholic'.[56]

The sectarian issue also affected Fascist activity in the east. On 11 May 1934, *Blackshirt* reported:

The practice of certain parties in Scotland to mix religion with politics has caused some local opponents to try to draw Fascists into the controversy. Their refusal to accept the challenge of a hot-headed and ignorant tub-thumper to discuss the matter on the Mound last Sunday led to attempts to involve them in a fight. The Defence Force held its ground and with the assistance of a large and sympathetic section of the audience succeeded in avoiding trouble.[57]

By 1935 the BUF had three branches in Edinburgh and Leith, a central branch, a west of Edinburgh branch, and a Leith branch. But by then radical politics in Leith and Edinburgh were dominated by John Cormack's Protestant Action. Leith was PA's stronghold, with the movement capturing six seats in the 1936 municipal elections, but PA also made its presence felt across Edinburgh, in violent attacks on Catholics and with massive street demonstrations: on 25 June 1935, no fewer than 10,000 Protestants had been mobilised to disrupt an open-air procession of the Blessed Sacrament. Like his arch-rival in Glasgow, Alexander Ratcliffe, John Cormack tarred the Blackshirts with the 'Papist' brush. The PA leader would tell the *Edinburgh Evening Dispatch* in November 1936: 'all out energies will be directed against the Fascists. When I get control I will put a ban on Fascists on the streets'.[58]

With its leader's bodyguard, Kormack's Kaledonian Klan – whose very name says something about Cormack's racist credentials – divided into Kommissionaires and Kustodians, Protestant Action applied 'physical Christianity' to the streets of Edinburgh and Leith, not hesitating to beat up Catholic priests in broad daylight. To the tune of 'The Old Rugged Cross' they sang:

> Over dear old Scotia,
> The Fiery Cross we display,
> The Emblem of Klansmen's domain.
> We will for ever be true,
> To the Red, White and Blue
> And British will always remain.

They seemed to be playing the tune of many. In 1935, PA obtained 23.6% of the vote in local elections, and this rose to 32.1% in 1936.

Protestant Action was essentially a religious party, taking the Reformation, rather than the Nation, as its main point of reference. But it was the closest Scotland got in this period to a mass fascistic movement. Tom Gallagher remarks: 'Cormack dominated his own movement as completely as Hitler and Mussolini exercised power in their own respective parties. Protestant Action's very existence as a popular movement hinged on the presence of its leader, who derived his authority from his magnetism and from the power of the oratory rather than from any office he might hold within the organisation or on the council'.[59] On Cormack's Klan, Stephen M. Cullen rightly remarks that 'the squadrist tactics of PA in Edinburgh look far more "fascist" than anything the BUF did in Scotland'.[60] Indeed, the PA's running battles through the impoverished Catholic areas of Cowgate, Grassmarket and Canongate strongly resembled the BUF's contemporaneous anti-Jewish campaigns in the East End of London. Scottish 'anti-Fascism' was therefore not necessarily the left-wing internationalism of popular myth. Cullen concludes: 'the complexities of religious politics, especially religious street politics, was a primary cause of the failure of the BUF in Scotland, and it appears that older traditions of intolerance, in a sense, an older authoritarian tradition, helped defeat the new authoritarianism of the BUF'.[61]

It seemed that, in Scotland, the BUF could only lose. If Glaswegian Fascists had gained notoriety for flirting with Protestant extremism, in Edinburgh the BUF was attacked for being under Papist influence. In October 1934, on Princes Street, a heckler told the BUF's Director of Policy, Raven Thomson: 'a lot of your Blackshirts are Italians and you're under the Pope of Rome'.[62] During the local elections of October 1937, Fred Douglas, Communist leader in the capital, declared: 'The Protestants are noisily appealing to religious prejudices to disrupt Labour; the Fascists are trying on the same game with the Catholics.'

The BUF's line on the Scottish question also produced confusion and splinters. It might have been expected that the BUF would be sensitive to the Scottish dimension, given that Raven Thomson was a Scot. In *My Life*, Mosley remembered:

This exceptional thinker emerged from the study at the age of nearly forty to become a man of action and one of the finest fighters for our cause we ever knew. Intellectually Raven Thomson towered above the men I had known in the Labour Cabinet of 1929, and in firmness of character he seemed in an altogether different category to most of the contemporary politics.[63]

Thomson was born into a prosperous Edinburgh family in 1899: his maternal grandfather was the renowned architect, Alexander Thomson. At Merchiston Academy, he specialised in sciences, to which he later attributed his interest in theories. In July 1918, he left Merchiston and enlisted in the Royal Engineers. On his return to Edinburgh he met and married Lisbeth Röntgen, descendant of the discoverer of the X-ray. On receiving an inheritance from his grandfather, Thomson left for the USA with his wife and her daughter Helga. There Thomson engaged in private study, concentrating on engineering, and developed 'strong feelings against capitalism in general'. He briefly studied at the University of Heidelberg before becoming, in 1926, a partner in a London engineering firm, while his wife set up a domestic service agency importing young women from Germany. Thomson was marked by his

reading of Oswald Spengler's *Decline of the West*. At first attracted to
Communism as a possible solution to the enveloping crisis, Thomson
then saw in Fascism the embodiment of his ideal civilisation. In *Civilization as Divine Superman. A Superorganic Philosophy of History* (1932),
Thomson took inspiration from 'the hives, ant-heaps, and termite-hills
[that] form new living entities as individual and distinct, as active and
intelligent, as any higher animal'.[64] Civilisation, claimed Thomson, 'is
not the servant of man. It is his master and tyrant; the superman that
directs and enforces his actions to the greater glorification of himself,
and grants him the immense advantages of co-operation and speciali-
zation only as a reward for abandoning his freedom of action to the
higher aims of the communal spirit'.[65]

In *The Coming Corporate State*, the BUF's Director of Policy gave
specifics on the 'superorganic' structuring of a Fascist Britain:

Political – Central government welding the nation together by the
exercise of authority.

Economic – the science of organisational planning upon functional
lines for the production and distribution of wealth.

Cultural – the release of individual enterprise for more energy of
invention and design.

Scotland would find her place in a Britain-wide corporate system:
the seat of the Shipbuilding Corporation would be in Glasgow, while
the 'category council' for jute would be in Dundee (Sheffield would
look after cutlery). The House of Lords would contain presidents
and leading members of learned societies but also 'the leaders of local
cultural bodies in Wales, Scotland and elsewhere, who are striving to
maintain invaluable local traditions'.[66] But if Raven Thomson found
inspiration in the past, it was not a Scottish one:

The Tudor Period, the high point of our own national life, found its
expression, not only in the seafaring and Empire building of Walter
Raleigh and Francis Drake, but in the philosophy and science of Francis
Bacon and the poetry and drama of William Shakespeare. It will be in
recovering the 'age of faith' of Christendom and the vital energy of Tudor
England that we may realise in part the great future of our nation.[67]

Against this Anglocentric vision, T.W. Denholm-Hay had, in the middle of 1934, formed the Scottish Union of Fascists, with an initial membership of 70, and added the saltire to its emblem. The SUF established links with Wendy Wood and the Democratic Scottish Self-Government Organisation. However, the SUF could not compete with the better-organised, better-funded and infinitely more visible BUF, especially around the time of the Usher Hall rally; and after a very short life, its members quickly joined the Duke of Montrose's Scottish Party, then eventually the SNP.

By the end of 1934, the BUF had probably around 1,000 members in Scotland. The two Edinburgh branches appear to have had approximately 160 members between them, and there may have been close to 120 in Glasgow, with 400 in Dalbeattie and 120 in Dumfries. Its Scottish membership figure was therefore around double that of the Scottish Party's, but, significantly, a good deal less than the approximately 5,000 members of the National Party of Scotland. Mosley's legion was therefore failing to profit from either the religious or the national divide.

The national BUF leadership, based in London, seems to have been indifferent and even hostile to the cause of Fascism in Scotland. The BUF spent little time explaining the place of Scotland within their proposed Fascist Britain. Only one relevant policy pamphlet was produced, entitled *Fascism and Scotland* (1934), and articles in the Fascist press about Scotland tended to concentrate on particular issues such as the fishing industry, agriculture or the need for a Forth road bridge. *Mosley's Fascism: 100 questions asked and answered* (1936) put the question of Scottish and Welsh home rule in eighty-second place. For the BUF, Scotland shared many of the same economic problems as England, and such problems could only be solved within the context of Britain and the Empire.

The BUF branches in Scotland also received less financial support than those south of the border, and only rarely had the benefit of meetings addressed by well-known national Fascist figures, such as Mosley or William Joyce, who was later infamous as 'Lord Haw-Haw'. Robert Forgan had initially played a leading role in the movement and, through the secretive January Club, succeeded in bringing establishment figures into the Fascist orbit, notably Lord William Scott, brother of the eighth Duke of Buccleuch and future Unionist MP for Roxburgh and Selkirkshire, and Sir Adrian

Baillie, Unionist MP for Linlithgow. But personality issues had led to Forgan being exiled to the Scottish organisation in early 1934, and then, in the midst of a financial scandal, resigning from the party itself. The *Blackshirt* of 12 October 1934 read: 'It is with great regret that we announce Dr Forgan's resignation from the position of second in command of the BUF, rendered necessary by the state of his health.'[68] According to Weir Gilmour and anti-BUF Protestant extremists in Edinburgh, Forgan had left the movement because he found out it was run by Catholics. Another, more plausible, explanation for Forgan's break with Mosley was that he was by then a spy for the Board of Jewish Deputies.

On 19 March 1935, Special Branch reported:

> All the members of the administrative staff of the movement in Scotland have been discharged. They received a grant of £500 per annum from HQ, but considered this insufficient and demanded £3,000 a year as the absolute minimum. Sir Oswald Mosley decided, therefore, to dispense with their services, as he considers that the Scottish Branches will be able to build up a healthy movement without such assistance.

At the end of February, it was estimated that in Glasgow there were 50 to 60 members, and *Blackshirt* sales of about 52: the movement was 'on the downward grade and the membership has dropped about 50% since October last'. Edinburgh had about 80 members, but here too 'the movement has never been popular and now appears to be on the downward grade'. This was at a time when BUF membership reached its high point of 50,000. Special Branch noted with reason and caution: 'Fascism represents a phase in the development of European thought, and it has roots in this country in real discontents.'[69]

In March 1935, all paid BUF staff in Scotland were dismissed, saving the movement £500 a year, but, perhaps, fatally undermining any hope of further progress by the Fascists in Scotland. Special Branch remarked: 'There has been serious trouble in the Scotland area, where membership has greatly declined.'[70]

This neglect of Scotland would not cease and could try the patience of even the most loyal Mosleyite. Richard Plathen had been a prominent member of the New Party, in which he was assistant to the Director of Organisation of NP's youth club. After the demise of the NP, Plathen moved to the BUF, rising to become Inspector for Scotland in 1936, a position he held until September 1938, when he married Maire Inglis, the Edinburgh West leader. Within the BUF, Plathen was renowned for his loyalty to Mosley, and his dedication to the movement. However, shortly after his appointment as Inspector for Scotland, the Special Branch reported that Plathen was 'continually complaining of the lack of support from headquarters'.[71]

Even isolated successes could weaken the Scottish Blackshirts, as in the case of John Hone, an engineer who had first become interested in Fascism while working in South Africa. On his return to Scotland he joined the BUF in Dumfries, and quickly rose to the rank of Officer-in-Charge. But he was promoted to Northern Inspection Officer in 1935, thereby depriving the Dumfries branch of its main motor of success.

Nevertheless, the struggle continued. In February 1935, William Joyce, the BUF's Director of Propaganda, made a tour of the Scottish branches. On 22 February 1935, *Blackshirt* announced that Scotland was 'prepared for Fascism'.

> At Dumfries the audience was small but appreciative. Here Mr Joyce began his campaign with an exposition of the advantages which Scotland would derive from corporate organisation and representation. He showed that all the legitimate aspirations of Scottish Nationalists would be satisfied in a system which permitted the affairs of Scottish commerce to be discussed and organised by Scotsmen.[72]

Despite hecklers, a meeting in Dalbeattie was highly successful. On the following day, Joyce 'conversed with very many of the townspeople, who showed the greatest sympathy with fascism'. The Bathgate meeting was attended almost exclusively by industrial workers and the unemployed. The speaker was given 'a very courteous and attentive reception, and the interest of the audience was sustained for 3 hours'. The Edinburgh meeting gave the Edinburgh people 'an opportunity of seeing how the Communist hooligan offends against the Public Meeting Act with the connivance of the Conservative Press. Though the audience consisted, for the most part, of noisy and dirty anti-fascists, Mr Joyce succeeded in explaining the policy; and he answered questions with practically no interruption'. The meeting closed with the singing of the National

Anthem, 'which finally prevailed over the incoherent noises made by the Reds'. At Inverness, Mr Joyce spoke to 'an excellent audience and dealt mainly with the problems of the Highlands, and especially with their need of financial assistance and secure agricultural markets'. The *Blackshirt* article, no doubt penned by Joyce himself, concluded:

> Mr Joyce's campaign shows that Scotland is prepared to welcome Fascist propaganda, and that the work done by B.O. Little and his loyal Scottish Fascists has already made a marked and favourable impression on Scottish public opinion. The opposition offered by irresponsible Edinburgh Communists stands in the most emphatic contrast with the courteous, attentive, and sympathetic consideration granted to Fascist policy by the average Scottish audience.

At these meetings, Joyce had needed to give the Fascist answer to the demand for Scottish autonomy:

> Mr Joyce said that Scotland and England had been linked together in the past and must be together in the future for the good of both. There was no value in the proposal that Scotland should be separated from England; the remedy did not lie in the setting up in Scotland of a replica of Westminster, of which the English people were now so tired. But there was every justice in the statement that Scottish affairs did not receive at Westminster the consideration which they deserved.

There needed to be financial assistance for Scottish agriculture and the construction of a Forth road bridge. To develop industry, Scotland would become a land of corporate activity. Foreign foodstuffs would be banned, while the successful experiment of producing oil from coal indicated a radiant future for the country.

In April 1935, successful activity was even reported in the stronghold of Cormack's PA:

> Leith is an ancient Scottish burgh now amalgamated with the more modern city of Edinburgh. It is actually one of the most 'depressed' areas in the UK. The first Blackshirt activities in the town met with fierce opposition, but a little perseverance has met with considerable

success, and a new branch, under the supervision of J.A. Pringle, is making rapid progress. An open-air meeting at the 'Foot of the Walk', on Monday evening attracted a considerable audience, which listened to Mr Bryham Oliver without a trace of hostility.[73]

That month, the Edinburgh Blackshirts carried out a motor-car 'raid' on a district of Midlothian hitherto untouched: 'A quick tour was made of several small villages and towns, including Loanhead, Lasswade, Dalkeith and Musselburgh. Several inquiries were made as to when meetings would be held in the district, the greatest interest in this respect being shown by residents of Dalkeith.'[74] In May, the Edinburgh Blackshirts extended their activities beyond the city boundaries 'with excellent results':

> Members of the Scottish HQ branch have been 'nursing' the Border town of Galashiels. Several members held a weekend camp there and 'showed the flag' and followed it up with an open-air meeting. There is now the prospect of a group being formed. Leith and Portobello Blackshirts encamped at Dalbeattie, in which until recently Scottish HQ were situated. The climax of this activity took place when a party of 20 Edinburgh Fascists made the journey to Newcastle for the Leader's meeting. The party travelled in motor-cars and arrived back in the capital in the 'wee sma' oors'. The Leader specially honoured the Edinburgh Fascists by addressing them in Newcastle branch premises, assuring them of his keen interest in the progress of the Movement in Scotland.[75]

There seemed to be no more no-go areas for the BUF in Scotland. In July 1935, Dundonian Fascists Cook and Walker 'commenced an intensive canvass of shopkeepers and others in the central districts of Dundee. Support for the *Blackshirt* sales has been promised, and thus begins the grim struggle for the "Red Stronghold of the North"'.[76] Dundee libraries were even agreeing to make the *Blackshirt* available.

The Abyssinian crisis, which started with Mussolini's invasion of Haile Selassie's Ethiopia and provoked sanctions by the League of Nations, became a focus for (Mussolini-funded) Blackshirt activity – and anti-Fascism. At the beginning of September, a crowd of 5,000 gathered at the Mound when Vincent Collier launched a National 'Peace Campaign'. Communists and socialists who were present in considerable numbers 'gave an angry roar when Collier said: "Our pacifists would drive us into war, but these same people are those who would not fight for King and country if Britain were threatened from without"'. According to *Blackshirt*, 'favourable comments were heard among the listeners, and on the Fascists leaving the Mound people shouted to the speaker: "Come back again"'.[77] Then Edinburgh began the Peace Campaign activities in earnest. On the following Saturday, 'thousands of green-coloured leaflets were distributed among supporters at the Hibernian Football Club match'.

At the end of the month, Raven Thomson returned to his homeland to explain Fascist policy. He started with a meeting in Berwick-upon-Tweed. To the 400-strong audience, he 'emphasised the need of leadership to solve modern difficulties. He concluded with the Fascist appeal for peace which was very well received; not a voice was raised for war, and general agreement was expressed for the Blackshirt policy. The speaker asked the audience to let the Government know that it did not back the policy of sanctions. Opposition was negligible.'

At a meeting in Leith, despite the frequent interruptions from Communists, he 'succeeded in delivering his message. He said that Fascists considered that Communism was the wrong way to change the position; it was dangerous and anti-Christian'. Fascists said to the working people: 'Do not waste your time fighting a class war with a lot of other people who are just as much caught up in this despotism of high finance as you are.'

Communists and other anti-Fascists crowded the ballroom of the Aberdeen Music Hall, where a Fascist meeting was to be held. When Thomson went on the stage, there was 'pandemonium' in the hall:

> A man stood on a seat, waved a red flag and conducted a mass choir in the singing of the Internationale. This was followed by catcalls and more choral work. The speaker's voice was never heard, and after the noise had reigned incessantly for some time Chief Constable McConnach walked up the centre aisle to inform the crowd that organisers had told him that the meeting would not be held. As the demonstrators left the hall there were calls for 'three cheers for the defeat of Fascism'.

Blackshirt reached a now familiar conclusion: 'once again the Reds have shown their fear of free speech'.[78]

In October, there were violent scenes in Edinburgh. The speakers' platform was smashed to pieces and Blackshirts had to defend themselves at a national peace campaign meeting at the Mound:

> Remarkable scenes were witnessed at the close of the meeting. A section of the crowd (the largest ever seen at the Mound for the past several years, and estimated at over 10,000) swept some of them to the tram lines in Princes Street. One Blackshirt was thrown to the ground and few escaped without at least bruising caused by the violence of the opposition. Rush after rush was stemmed by the Blackshirts and a handful of police. In the third rush the platform was smashed, but the speaker resumed almost immediately, standing on the wreckage.

After 40 minutes, police requested the closure of the meeting. The alarming scenes 'attracted many more thousands of people, who congregated on the pavements in Princes Street, and as the Blackshirts walked back to their HQ in Hope Street, they were followed by a huge crowd which completely held up traffic'.[79] Nevertheless, the West Edinburgh District could boast of holding 33 open-air peace meetings and distributing 40,000 peace pamphlets. Active opposition had 'promoted solidarity among members. The active strength has further increased by a number of new members'. Gauging the receptivity of the general public to the Fascist message was, however, rendered impossible by the BUF's decision not to present candidates at the general election of November 1935, opting instead for 'Fascism Next Time'.

As regards Edinburgh's rival city, Bryham Oliver promised that 'Fascism will save Glasgow'. That city, wrote Oliver, had indeed prospered, but 'upon the blood of the millions of negroes whom she transported to the American plantations; prospered upon the tobacco and the cotton which they produced; prospered upon the blood and sweat of unnumbered agricultural workers, Scots and Irish alike, who have been drawn into the mesh of her industrial machine and condemned to live in slums the like of which the world can hardly equal'. Modern Glasgow was gangster-ridden: 'It is true that they have not taken to the machine-gun of Chicago, but the knife and the razor are in daily use. The revolver and the sawed-off shotgun are by no means unknown.' The gangsters 'begin with collecting for a local football team and end with brutal murder for the maintenance of their vested interests in the districts'. The energy of such men had to be channelled into a Fascist future:

Give these men an ideal to live for; give them social and economic justice; teach them the virtues of discipline and obedience; and the Glasgow gangster will show an example to the world: loyal to the core when once his heart is gained; ready to fight maybe, but ready to postpone the fighting if there is a job of work to be done and he feels that it is up to him to do.

Glasgow gangsters were 'the men whose fathers fought in those days when men's endurance was tested to the breaking point; the "Jocks", who maintained not only the strength but the spirit of many a wavering line'. They were men 'who, given proper leadership, will yet rebuild a greater and a better Glasgow, founded, not upon the slave labour of American plantations but upon her essential services in the rebuilding of Britain herself'.[80]

Such sentiments were echoed in the January 1936 issue of *Fascist Quarterly*. Reviewing Alexander McArthur and H. Kingsley Lang's *No Mean City: a Story of the Glasgow Slums*, N.R. Temple wrote:

This in the literal sense is a terrific book – a book, that is, to strike terror into any reader but a Fascist, since it portrays the stark horrors of capitalistic democracy, for which Fascism alone can find a remedy. . . . Here is the 'Decline of the West', described not as by Spengler, in the light of the philosophy of History, but as seen at close quarters – human beings herded helpless in their reeking tenements, born to be hopeless, becoming more heartless than the beasts in their worse than bestial environment.

No Mean City showed how civilisation had 'turned back to conditions of the jungle'. Considering such frightening characters as the 'Razor King', it 'would be an error to call these young fellows Communists. Those who have votes vote Communist because the Communist candidate is noisiest, but they have no belief in that or any cause. Life is empty – barren of loyalty, equally of hope'. For Temple, this damning report on contemporary Glasgow was of great political use:

Read and spread abroad this first-hand information; spread it, above all, wherever there is contentment with the country's (or the 'City's') accumulated wealth, while men decay. The authors pose no remedy – in fact, until there shall descend upon us the vision without which the people perish, no remedy exists. The sickness of civilisation is a sickness of the soul and there is no cure but Fascism. [81]

Elsewhere in *Fascist Quarterly*, there were attempts to resuscitate historic Scottish figures. In his review of Hamilton Fyfe's *Keir Hardie*, John Beckett wrote:

Hardie believed in uncompromising fighting, and could not under-stand the Parliamentary method of fighting in public and negotiating in secret. He believed in Committees of one and getting things done. He had little economic knowledge but a burning desire to benefit his class and country ... What a Blackshirt Hardie could, and would, have made![82]

In July 1936, with a long essay-cum-anthology, 'Thomas Carlyle – National Socialist', William Joyce, himself a founder of the 'Carlyle Club', staked a claim on one of Scotland's finest and most controversial nineteenth-century intellectuals:

Thomas Carlyle ranks first amongst British heralds of the Fascist revolution. Other great thinkers who preceded him showed in their writings some of the main tendencies of Fascist philosophy, and of their number Shakespeare and Goldsmith contributed much; but in all the vast extent of Carlyle's writings there is nothing that could be recorded as other than the product of a National-Socialist mind. He himself had the spirit of National Socialism long before the name existed. His words are always the words of a patriot. His passionate love of country might, in his own day, have failed to satisfy the tests of patriotism, because it was no abstraction that he loved, it was the people; and herein precisely lies the fundamental difference between the old patriotism and the new. The old concerns itself with dead and outer lineaments. The new concerns itself with the very reality of the people, and is patriotism because it is socialism in the only honour-able sense that may be attached to the term.[83]

Thomas Carlyle's doctrine of leadership and authority demonstrated that without discipline freedom was impossible. Equally repulsive to him were snobbery and class war. He believed in the dignity of labour but rejected the socialist 'wage-slave'. Creative intellect and heroic action were his guiding lights: 'He can conceive of no people acting as a community save under the direction of a class of leaders'.[84] He also wanted to build a real British Empire.

For Joyce, Carlyle 'rightly stressed the connexion between the ownership of land and the power to influence the culture of a nation'. However, he did not fully foresee the effects of the Industrial Revolution. He could hardly visualize the day when everything should be ruined, and the agriculturalist, the farmer, the landowner, reduced to a position of miserable impotence, laiden with the chains of Jewish usury'.[85] A committed enemy of liberalism, Carlyle believed Parliament prevented things being done, and hated the sordid materialism of the Manchester School. Joyce concluded: '[his] hardness and purity of thought should set an example to those who hold the steel creed of an iron age, which, in the words of Mosley, "cuts through the verbiage of illusion to the achievement of a new reality"'.[86]

Scotland's Ernst Jünger: Graham Seton Hutchison

Despite *Fascist Quarterly*, the BUF does not seem to have attracted the support of Scottish intellectuals. Hugh MacDiarmid followed a distinctive path of Scottish national-communism, while John Buchan's early admiration for Mussolini did not detach him from mainstream conservatism. The only other significant Scottish writer to be attracted to the far right in this period was Lieutenant-Colonel Graham Seton Hutchison.

Seton Hutchison's father came from Inverness, and he claimed to have records of forebears on the battlefield of Culloden. However, his parents settled in London. He recalled: 'I was schooled mostly in England, with the sons of moderately wealthy middle-class people to whom their self-importance and money were the only real gods. And they were extremely class-conscious. From the beginning, I knew I was different, but could not tell then why I mostly preferred the company of country boys and workshops lads to that of the smoothed-down conventional, polite young gentry with whom I rubbed shoulders in the class-rooms and jolted more savagely on the playing fields'.[87] After passing through Sandhurst, Hutchison regained contact with his Scottish martial roots, being commissioned in the King's Own Scottish Borderers, then serving with a militia battalion of the Argyll and Sutherland Highlanders. He had a brilliant war career, receiving the MC and DSO and being mentioned in dispatches four times, finishing as a lieutenant-colonel in the Machine Gun Corps. He also gained a reputation for brutality towards shirkers and deserters. Seton Hutchison remembered thus an episode in the fighting at Meteren in early 1918: 'After an hour of the action, I made a very full reconnaissance with my adjutant. We discovered in the Belle Croix estaminet beside the mill a crowd of stragglers, fighting drunk. We routed them out, and, with a machine gun trained on them, sent them forward towards the enemy. They perished to a man'.[88] It was rumoured that Seton Hutchison had mown down 38 out of 40 retreating British soldiers. Such behaviour inspired Kenneth Alford to compose his tune 'The Mad Major'.

After the Great War, Seton Hutchison became active in the ex-serviceman movement, as first chairman of the Old Contemptibles Association, and founder member of the British Legion. His war experience was expressed in *The History and Memoir of the 33rd Battalion Machine-Gun Corps*, memoirs such as *Footslogger* and *Warrior*, and, under the name Graham Seton, best-selling thrillers such as *The W Plan*, the first of a series involving journalist and spy Colonel Duncan Grant. This literary debut received praise from critics as diverse as D.H. Lawrence, Sir Arthur Conan Doyle and Lord Baden-Powell.

Despite, or because of, his patriotism and taste for warfare, Seton Hutchison had deep sympathy for defeated Germany. A year spent in the Upper Silesian Commission, in 1920–21, convinced him that the Versailles peace settlement had wronged Germany, something which he expounded upon in *Silesia Revisited*: 'The Supreme Council in Paris, modifying the recommendations of the Plebiscite Commission, bargaining together, made a travesty of the principle of self-determination in the Treaty of Versailles. The Partition [of Silesia] was sprung upon the world, supported by special pleading and specious propaganda.'[89] He would become an apologist for German revanchism, frequently visiting that country and cultivating links with Hitler and the Nazis. It is also alleged by Richard Griffiths in *Fellow Travellers of the Right* that Seton Hutchison was paid by the Germans as a publicist.

To this growing attraction to German Nazism was added conversion to the social credit theory of Major C.H. Douglas. Douglas proposed to bring production and purchasing power into line thanks to a 'National Dividend' and a 'Just Price' mechanism. The major targeted the baleful influence of 'usury' as well as the 'abstraction' of parliamentary democracy. Inevitably, among many Douglasites, criticism of capitalism tended to coalesce with anti-Semitism.

The work of Seton Hutchison seemed to strike a chord with Hitler's favourite author, the warrior-writer Ernst Jünger. In *Footslogger*, Seton Hutchison recalled the German's appreciation of his history of the machine-gunners:

> Herr Jünger, great fighter, a German subaltern, author of *The Storm of Steel*, one which I consider to be the greatest story of sheer reporting emanating from Germany concerning the War, wrote to me: 'By sending me the wonderful war story you have given me a pleasure as undeserving as it is great. It delights me to know that during the War and even though on opposite sides we have been so near to each other'. He returned to me, 'with his sincere affection', another volume of his own, *Feuer und Blut*, and inscribed in it a dedication, which translated reads: 'To Colonel G.S. Hutchison, in memory of nights spent under the same sky'.[90]

Footslogger records Seton Hutchison's drift towards Nazism. Dismissing the theories of Karl Marx as 'dismal',[91] he also denounced the bankruptcy of the parliamentary system: 'Like many others I recognised that the democratic machine had already reached the zenith of its usefulness, and that to give expression to the ideals of the war generation and those who had followed after, some new form must be discovered.'[92] Although he remembered that Jewish classmates in Hampstead had turned out to be good sportsmen, there are hints of anti-Semitism in reminiscences of his time in Silesia:

> In no part of the world have I observed squalor so hopeless, so devastating as that of the considerable town of Bensin. More than 80% of its inhabitants are Jews, and in all the cities of Poland a percentage of this race almost as high dominates the population. But the Jews of Poland alone understand financial and commercial technique.[93]

In the 'filthy' Krakow ghetto, a crowd of Jews clamoured for the banknotes he waved from his car.

Indeed, this anti-Semitic tendency, which preceded that of Mosley and the Blackshirts, had already manifested itself in a novel, *The Governor of Kattowitz*:

The men are grotesque with jewellery and paste gems; sheathed in coloured cloths and garish silks, suitings cut to absurdity, with hands fat and stubby like an oakum picker's, and finger-nails like claws: their female attachments, with fleshy parts well displayed, are obscene in their fatness, decked with coloured finery, their faces and arms smooth as if with distemper.[94]

The ending of *Footslogger* is the first of a series of calls for regeneration and renewal. Great Britain, he asserts, 'is in a receding economic position'; the moral sense of the nation 'is doped'; some 'insidious, soul-destroying paralysis is creeping over the civilised world'.[95] To confront and defeat such decadence, 'We want Men!' A race of Supermen, 'efficient, experienced, courageous; untied by prejudice or party',[96] could replace the moribund old with the vitality and virility of youth. The great outdoors could cleanse the body politic, as an erstwhile foe now demonstrated:

Germany, efficient, progressive, emerging from the humiliation of the War, has refound its soul in the beauty of Nature. More than two million young people, members of the *Jugendherberge*, using more than two thousand well-established, magnificent hostels, last year, went forth from their cities to rediscover the god of the spirit in the smell of the loam, the tang of the myrtleberry, the music of the stream, and the sigh of the hills, mounting higher and higher, crag upon crag, boulder upon boulder, even as a ladder to Heaven. The country is not despoiled by those youthful spirits, nor would it be in Britain.[97]

Seton Hutchison's vision was elaborated the following year in *Warrior*: 'Warrior has proceeded without halt from the day of the Proclamation of War to the Armistice, fighting, training, marching, playing ... and fighting again. Here, on the highest peak of human history, yet unafraid, Warrior stands.'[98]

The anti-Semitic drift of Seton Hutchison also expressed itself in *Arya. The call of the future*, which offered a critical analysis of the British government in India and proposed a monarchical federal system. The author remarked that 'both the teaching of the New Testament and the Vedantas hold up to opprobrium the gross materialism of the Semite ideology and conduct of life'.[99] In the new India, governed by the 'Aryan principle', usury would be forbidden 'and usurers submitted to the most severe penalty. No measure can be calculated more swiftly to win the confidence of all India – its vast peasant population – to the new form of government'.[100]

Seton Hutchison was unimpressed by Mosley's imitation of Mussolini and, after Hitler's victory in 1933, attempted to carry out his messianic mission by founding a Nazi 'party' of his own: the National Workers' Movement, which then became the National Socialist Workers' Party, and finally, in 1936, the National Workers' Party. His avowed aim was to create a movement that was violently pro-Nazi, anti-Semitic, and in favour of ex-servicemen and a 'classless' society. His 1933 autobiography, *Meteor*, was a eulogy to Hitlerism. It began with a 'meeting with the enemy' in the aftermath of the Great War: exchanges with Bavarian peasants and the adjutant of the Alpine Corps aroused a sense of 'blood brotherhood' which was toasted with Highland colours. The author proceeded obsessively to attack usury and the nefarious influence of Jews in Britain and abroad. Countering anti-Nazi propaganda, he declared: 'The Jews, throughout the world, have a sufficient task in the cleansing of their own stables, and in the ordering of the lives of their own nationals, without entering into the institutions of these other peoples which gave them hospitality.'[101]

The 'Nazi Gospel', Seton Hutchison concluded, 'as a work of social construction … defies reasoned criticism, while it is provocative of honest reflection'.[102] *Meteor* ended with 'a call and a creed – the national workers' movement – programme and policy'. Identifying close affinities between the National Government's Political Economic Plan, 'whose Chairman is Israel Moses Sieff', and the *Protocols of the Elders of Zion*, he declared:

> Anyone can observe, if he will but think, that the real, the only prob-
> lem is to relate productive capacity with consumptive capacity. That
> implies only a change in financial technique. But it does imply the
> destruction of the Jewish financial system, which is enslaving the
> world. British people are not going to be such fools as to hand over
> the whole genius of their race to a gang of unscrupulous, greedy alien
> financiers, to whom are joined other unscrupulous careerists. No. Not
> on your life.[103]

To pursue a policy of 'national regeneration', the media, education and arts would be cleansed of subversive propaganda; aliens would be excluded from employment; British and Empire trade would be fostered and friendly relations established with like-minded nations; and the Treaty of Versailles revised 'in pursuance of the traditional British policy of "Fair play"'.[104] The Means Test would be abolished, and a National Industrial Insurance as well as a Fair-Wage standard introduced. All movements and associations, on both ends of the social scale, whose objectives were directed towards class warfare, would be destroyed. In a new Britain devoid of the vested interest of corporations and classes, the government would 'provide recreation and entertainment for the people designed to recapture the traditional spirit of "Merrie England", develop a policy of National Physical Training and bring up the nation in 'the spirit of true religion'.[105] The policy of the National Workers' Movement, he concluded, 'is one which appeals to the heart and to the intellect . . . The Mission of the British Race is not yet ended'.[106]

Seton Hutchison also used his literary talents to expound this vision. In *Blood Money* (1934), he offers, through the main character Colonel Malcolm Graham, a damning indictment of the post-war settlement:

> The curtain had been rung down upon the last act of the great conspiracy whereby politicians bartered national honour and swapped the blood of the battlefield for financial privilege and territorial concessions. Great Britain at Versailles had been represented by men who were neither statesmen nor gentlemen. The usurers, who whispered in their senile ears, extracted their blood money from the tomb. The Hall of Mirrors witnessed the triumph of wickedness, not the exaction of penalty for wrong, but the most monstrous display of greed, fraud, and hypocrisy which the world has ever witnessed. Lazarus, the soldier, with his wounds and ills, caught the crumbs from the money-master's table.[107]

In the many long debates which dominate the novel, the colonel, war hero turned entrepreneur, is a mouthpiece for the theories of Major Douglas: 'the source of all values is the cultural heritage. The obvious corollary is that such value is not the property of the individual but of the aggregate, that is of the nation'.[108] Usury is 'against the laws of natural increase, and is as repulsive as every similar vice . . . As a general proposition it's infamous that the state should get into debt by creating material wealth. The nation's got to own and govern its own purchasing power'.[109]

Another admirer of Seton Hutchison's literary work was Ezra Pound. They also had close political affinities, on social credit, the Jews and Fascism, which were illustrated in their correspondence between 1934 and 1936. On 13 June 1934 Pound wrote to Seton Hutchison that the British press 'suppressed discussion of [Major] Douglas'.[110] Dismissing 'Moslevy', Pound called for 'volitionist economics'. In his reply of 15 June 1934 Seton Hutchison explained to Pound his political turn and its consequences:

I differ from most of the intelligentsia in that I slogged through the War, and have lived among all kinds of people in every part of the world, and instead of playing class games studied the people I was with; and I learned to love them. Let it be clear that it is not the expression of Italian Fascism to which I am opposed. I have studied this, I know Italy not well but sufficiently and I have good contacts. But I hate Mosley's stupid parody, his music hall fireworks. The true Fascist idea under the name Fascism has been killed in England. I have tried to reorient the word socialism in order to capture these people who have the vision of the new State but who by affiliation must call themselves Socialist.

Monetary reform is at the top of the bill, it is the only thing that really matters. As you say, the bourgeois mind is so filled with Gold Standards and clap-trap that it can scarcely comprehend the simplicity of a common sense financial system to meet the economic and cultural needs of the nation and the world . . .

I've made a close study of Germany for twelve years; and know some of the leaders. There is a crudeness which the best intelligences recognise, but you will see it shape up all right. Among Englishmen, probably none is listened to with greater respect in Germany than myself, especially in Bavaria. They have been deeply impressed by my book *Arya*, mainly philosophic and about the East, India. Remember Germany has been outlawed for twenty years, and now suffers from a terrific (financial) boycott. They want friendship. We can give it. They'll follow our ideas, when they believe we are sincere. But there'll never be peace or confidence so long as Ramsay, Simon, Attlee, Cripps and Co, are at the head.

Germany, he claimed, was not 'militant today. I'm sure of it'. And yet, France and Britain, in cahoots with the Soviet Union, might unleash another war: the 'Stavisky-Litvinoff-National Government crowd may drive Germany mad. If you are interested I could put you in touch with some brilliant minds who have grasped the possibility of a Germany in the Twentieth Century Revolutionary Era and are working for it'. Seton Hutchison reassured Pound that he was 'all for Douglas'. And he stood by his own entry into the political arena:

> Of course I have been boycotted in my profession for more than a year. I was a newspaper darling when I wrote fantastic thrillers. When I deliberately wrote *Meteor* and *Arya* and published *The National Worker*, I committed economic suicide. But I believe these ideas must triumph because they are right; and I have been flogging at them ever since the war.

On 17 June 1934, Pound replied that he thought 'Aryan traitors ought to be LUMPED with Jews'. As for Adolf Hitler, 'I have always thought he meant well/rather pathetic hysteric, best the hun can do/and certainly I am pro/Adolph as against that unadulterated shit and gun-seller von Papen'. In the poet's view, 'the WHOLE intelligentzia would/back a WORKERS' party the moment they thought the workers HAD ENOUGH intelligence to believe in some economics'.

For Seton Hutchison, the reason why so many intellectuals were furious with Hitler was because 'it seems to them that Adolf having debunked so many intellectuals in Germany, insulted English intellectuals. Eyes turned inwards. One of the most virile nations, far advanced in science, medicine, architecture, etc, couldn't almost unanimously support Hitler if he wasn't two thirds right'. There were 'heaps of good fellows in the Blackshirts. Ignorant. They don't like Mosley. They know nothing of Rothermere. But Mosley's clever enough not to allow any man of literary quality to get into his Headquarters. Testimony to his funk and insincerity. BUF ought to demand that all men acting on those lines should be heard. He did it: his darre feder Goebbels highly intellectual should pursue the revolutionary economic lines'. But 'names as you say are dead and clogged. I especially want Cambridge and Oxford'. As for the English working classes, they were 'terrified of employers and labour

bosses'. The Labour Party was 'simply hopeless. They are either innocent or deliberate tools of High Finance'. To fight private credit
and usury, the inevitable result 'must be National ... Socialism, that
is combining best Tory and Labour elements focused in personality'. He added: 'I've written to Germany, General [Karl] Haushofer,
highly intelligent, stupendous worker, adviser of Hess, broadcasters
and orientalists. Deeply interested to read your philosophic basis'.

Seton Hutchison and Pound discussed other possible allies of
their enterprise. On 30 June 1934, Pound wrote: 'I believe ole John
Buchan might be mobilized IF etc'. On 5 July, Seton replied: 'I'm
after John Buchan. He once wrote to tell me I was a gentleman. Most
charming and unusual.' Concerning Germany, 'I've written [Karl]
Haushofer get in touch with you. Both he and his wife read perfect
English. Revolutions throw up gangsters as well as idealists. But even
Röhm had his points'. Back in Britain, 'the war gang are very busy'.

Seton Hutchison was frustrated by the indifference of many to
his political message. On 25 July 1934, he complained of 'the smug
St Albans – cathedral-tennis-party-charity, etc – folk around me
like the plague'. He could 'talk economics to any workman or bunch
of boys in a train or on the roadside at any time. They understand.
The old folk are hopeless'. He had nonetheless continued his public
interventions with *Blood Money*. Noting the BUF's loss of crucial
backers, he told Pound: 'Jew boys went in bunch to Rothermere and
call him off Fascism'. That said, Seton Hutchison kept his distance
from other Fascist movements in Britain: 'I get the *British Lion*
sometimes. Patriotic stuff, but moving. Imperial Fascists, hopeless.
Leese, super director general, an ignoramus. Condemns Douglas.
Knows nothing of economics and Jew crazy.'

Seton was embattled. On 30 July 1934, he recalled to Pound that
Footslogger, *Warrior* and *Meteor* were not published in the USA. He
asserted the rightness of his position and his importance:

> I cannot be too widely known that I have probably more influence
> in Germany than any other Englishman. Since 1919 my attitude has
> been wholly correct as towards a fallen foe. Even as late as 1923 when
> I contested the General Election I was even assaulted and called a
> traitor because I asserted the Versailles Treaty would inevitably lead
> to trouble.

On 14 August 1934, he prophesied: 'the Nazi spirit will never be suppressed by political force, any more than the essence of Hinduism can be exterminated during four thousand years ... Among the masses in England Hitler is far more popular than Mussolini. Make no mistake about that'.

The unsuccessful coup against Engelbert Dollfuss and the failed *Anschluss* of Austria and Germany disappointed both correspondents. On 17 August 1934, Pound described Vienna as 'a pus sack', though the Nazi murder of Dollfuss was 'a damn shame'. Seton Hutchison had, however, found some comfort elsewhere. On 7 September, he wrote:

> Returned from France where I have been painting. French peasants, both in south and north seem fully alive to the fact that finance causes war, and I found them, resulting from the Stavisky affair, strongly anti-Jewish ... I find more sense among Catalan peasants than I hope in my day to find in the nation of shopkeepers. What the hell's the good of keeping shops if there is no purchasing power? But you are a perfect easy if you sell sweeties to school children, whereas if you make something with your hands you are only a common workman.

Blood Money had been 'a strong plea and argument for financial reform', but Britain was 'doped, and I think will have to go Bolshie before there is any chance of resurrection'. So far, *Blood Money* had been 'completely boycotted in the press'.

On the question of Arnold Leese, camel vet turned Führer of the Imperial Fascist League, Pound opined:

> Seems rather a good egg/thirstin' for jew/brew GORE, but rather good on his economics/
> At any rate he don't stall like Mose(s)le(v)y behind a 'committee' and give jewbiguous answers.
> I don't want to stop Leese fox hunting for circumcised furriners/ BUT I think it wastes time and causes unneeded argymint/
> Time to have pogroms is WHEN YOU have the power.

Seton Hutchison somehow failed to share Pound's enthusiasm:

> Unfortunately Leese, though highly courageous, is ignorant. I believe he gets his economics from an excellent Scot who often visits my

house and is a member of Leese's party, because I can't believe that
Leese, who was a camel vet, has any economic concept. I've often
talked with him and he is incredibly dull, but a ferocious Jew hater.
On the East, he is stupidity personified.

Even the founder of social credit was open to criticism: 'Isn't it about
time that someone told the world that Douglas is not an inventor?
. . . Nor does he appear to be the good Scot his name suggests.'

But there were still sources of inspiration. On 23 November 1934,
Seton Hutchison told Pound: 'I have electrified huge audiences in
Dorsetshire by telling them the truth. No Mosley fireworks and now
they're all talking.' At the end of that year, which had seen the Night
of the Long Knives liquidate the Röhm brothers and the Nazi regime reveal its brutal side, he could write:

> No truth in the rumour of more executions of Brownshirts. I've never
> heard Hitler described as *Mädchen* in Uniform. Seems to be part of
> the whispering campaign whose technique is quite familiar. Hitler's
> War record. Front line soldier, Western Front for four years. Twice
> wounded, twice recommended for conspicuous gallantry. And for
> past yes qualities of highest courage.

The following year, Seton Hutchison brought out another call for
action, *Challenge*: 'The spirits of the battlefield on which is fought out
Right against Wrong, in Britain's crisis, will be all the generations of
men of British blood, the hosts who, in some Valhalla of their own,
out of cosmos, come again to make sure the unbroken destiny of
their race.'[111]

And yet, this 'mission of the British race regenerated' could find
no echo. In his last existing letter to Seton Hutchison, on 11 May
1936, Pound wrote: 'Let National Socialist Workers call in the Socialists with slogan: SOCIALIZE the means of EXCHANGE also
communize the PRODUCT. That is what communists don't see in
Douglasism and they OUGHT to see it.'

The National Workers' Party could draw support from neither
the BUF nor the Labour and Communist Left. No documents
offer information on its real membership figures, but apart from
some involvement in anti-Semitic agitation in the East End, Seton
Hutchison's Nazi enterprise seems to have been little more than a

work of fiction. Another setback came in December 1936, when he was successfully sued by Labour leader Clement Attlee. In a pamphlet entitled *Truth*, Seton Hutchison had again outlined the Jewish conspiracy, which included the 'Jew' Attlee. Seton Hutchison was obliged to recognise that Attlee was not of the chosen people he hated, and issued a grovelling apology.

Seton Hutchison would support the *Anschluss* of Austria when it finally came in 1938. But, like many appeasers, he lost most of his illusions when, in March 1939, Hitler ripped up the Munich Agreement by dismembering what was left of the Czech lands. As another world war rapidly approached, Seton Hutchison became more aware of the true nature of, and threat posed by, the leader of Nazi Germany. In 1945 he would recall: 'when Adolf Hitler told the Polish Government quite plainly that the "Corridor" was to be cleaned up ... the Poles very properly refused to be bullied'.[112] In February 1940, in a letter to *The Times* entitled '*Lebensraum* and *Todesraum*', he denounced the 'mendacious propaganda' of 'Lord Haw-Haw' and the 'racketeers performing in the name of what to many, usually in opposed political camps, are most desirable ideals – Nationalism and Socialism'. He contrasted them with British imperialism, which, contrary to the 'depravity' of his former paymaster Goebbels' 'lies', had managed to train leaders among the colonised, from India to the Sudan to Nyasaland.[113]

Retrenchment

In addition to the failures of Graham Seton Hutchison, the BUF had also little to fear from the Imperial Fascist League, Arnold Leese's movement founded in 1929. On 9 March 1936, Special Branch reported: 'It bases its policy on that of the German Nazi Party, is fanatically anti-Semitic in outlook and attacks both the Italian Fascist party and the British Union of Fascists for their toleration of Jews and of freemasonry.' Members wore a brassard showing a Union Jack with a swastika superimposed. Its newspaper, *The Fascist*, claimed a circulation of 3,000 copies, but a third of them were sent to South Africa. A membership of 2,500 was claimed, but active membership did not seem to exceed 150. Present branches were predominantly English, notably Hackney, Kentish Town, Bristol and Newcastle-upon-Tyne, with Glasgow an exception. Certainly, in March 1936,

a report from Jewish representatives in Edinburgh complained that
IFL leaflets were being distributed in the city, purporting to draw
attention to 'the number of Jews concerned in crime, bankruptcy,
fire-raising and other law-breaking pastimes'.[114] Nevertheless, for
Special Branch, the rabidly anti-Semitic outpourings of Leese,
which led to prosecution, seemed only to indicate that 'the influence
of the IFL is infinitesimal, and it has never been strong financially'.[115]

The BUF was therefore the only significant Fascist organisation in
Scotland. But in 1935, as the Olympia debacle kicked in, the Blackshirts had been unable to maintain the dynamism of the previous
year. Already in March 1935, messages from the beyond seemed to
indicate problems ahead for Mosley. On 23 March, Dorothy Mosley wrote from Oban to her mother to report communications with
the spirit of the Leader's dead wife, Cynthia. At a séance in Argyll,
Cynthia Mosley said:

> I fear he never will be able now to manage to move near another
> new policy, while he gives stiffs all the important posts (asked twice
> if 'stiffs' was right, and replied 'Yes'). I have much more I want to tell
> him, when he gets my message. Can you let him know? I must give
> him advice, directly he gets a board.[116]

Nonetheless, in Scotland, as elsewhere, there were attempts to
stop any dangerous drift and rally the legions. On 15 May 1936,
the Leader addressed his second meeting at the Usher Hall. On 23
May 1936, *Blackshirt* announced 'Fascist Triumph in Edinburgh',
with the '"Red Front" thrown out of Usher Hall': 'They came, they
howled and they went'. In reference to the incidents at the notorious Olympia meeting, the paper declared: 'Two years ago Fascists
met and smashed Red hooliganism in London. Last week all the
violence of Communist hirelings attempted to drive Fascists out of
Edinburgh. Once again the Fascist answer and the Fascist method
conquered.' 'Howling, shrieking, yelling Reds' were taken from
their seats and handed over to the police. As ever, the Blackshirts
posed as victims:

> The peculiar structure of the gallery hampers the work of the stewards,
> who were in continuous danger of life and limb. This circumstance
> was taken full advantage of by the violent opposition. A number of

Blackshirts were thrown down over several rows of seats and one of them was saved at the last moment from being thrown over the parapet into the area below.

The anti-Fascists had mobilised to refuse them 'freedom of speech':

> Between last October and the beginning of April the City Treasurer's Committee of the ETC had three times refused to let the Usher Hall for a 'Mosley meeting', and it was only after an appeal had been made to the full Council that the committee at a specially convened meeting, reversed their previous decision.[117]

From the moment it became known, various organisations and individuals – among them the Communist Party, Edinburgh and Leith Trades and Labour Council, Edinburgh University Liberal Association and ministers of religion – combined in an endeavour to secure a last-minute refusal of the hall. There had been protest meetings, flyposting, chalking, literature and loud-speaker vans. A petition to 'Keep Mosley out of Edinburgh' had collected thousands of signatures, while a 'Monster Anti-Fascist Demo' of 800 had been held the day before.

The Scotsman reported 'Wild Scenes': 'The Fascist leader made his speech amid interruption and uproar, and a score or more of people, men and women, were ejected by Blackshirt stewards. Fights and scuffles were seen to be breaking out, especially in the gallery, which was the only unreserved part of the hall.'

A dozen arrests were made and 'there was intense excitement among the crowds outside the hall, particularly after several men had been thrown out with their faces bleeding'.[118] A month later, a communist miner, George Watters of Prestonpans, was fined for his role in the incidents. The accused 'rose to a point of order and asked Sir Oswald Mosley whether his friends, Italy and Germany, allowed freedom of speech'. Also in the dock, but acquitted was a young Yugoslav, Ratibor Djurdjevic, studying forestry at Edinburgh University, who had no previous record of 'extreme opinions'. On the fascist side, Richard Plathen was found guilty of assault: in order to 'take charge of the commotion', he had assaulted a man 'by twisting his arm and dragging him from his seat and along a passage in the hall'.[119]

The 'triumph' at the Usher Hall was therefore yet another example of the disorder associated with the BUF. But the meeting was also significant for the way it expressed the anti-Semitic and pro-Nazi turn of Mosley's organisation. When asked about Jews, Mosley's answer had been unambiguous:

> We shall safeguard the position of the small shopkeepers by eliminating the great chain stores run by American and Jewish capital. . . . Our principle is that any Jew who has abused the interests of Britain will be deported. Those against whom no such charge rests will be treated as foreigners in our midst and therefore will not enjoy the rights of British citizenship . . . Our charge against organised Jewry in this country is that it is organised as a racial community against the interests of Great Britain. My generation fought Germany in a British quarrel; we will never fight her again in a Jewish quarrel.[120]

Shortly after the rally, Bryham Oliver, the Propaganda Officer for Scotland, publicly resigned. In a letter to *The Scotsman* of 13 July 1936 (reprinted in *The Jewish Chronicle*), he attacked 'Blatant breaches of i) BUF promises that there would be no discrimination against Jews, and ii) BUF promises that Scottish affairs would be run by Scots . . . Both of these statements have now been qualified out of existence . . . As a Scot whose interests lie first of all in Scotland, I shall continue to devote myself to the furtherance of the ideal of the Corporate State of Scotland, with no discrimination on account of race or creed, whereby a Scotland, sovereign, free and independent, may enter into full co-operation with England, and with Ireland, too, in the building of the Greater Britain of Fascism.'[121]

The Jewish Representative Committee commented on Nazi and anti-Semitic propaganda at Glasgow and Edinburgh universities and noted that stickers and posters 'most scurrilous . . . of a large size and containing the most insulting epithets had appeared all over Glasgow'.[122] The JRC asked the Chief Constable to do something about it.

To what extent was the real threat of anti-Semitism in Scotland exaggerated? According to Henry Maitles, there are memoirs of Jews growing up in the 1930s in Glasgow and Edinburgh that make no mention of either the BUF or activity by anti-Fascists.[123] The Jewish presence in Scotland was small in relation to that of the East End of London, and, in the case of Edinburgh, increasingly integrated into the middle class. Anti-Semitism was therefore a poor shadow of anti-Irish feeling. Nonetheless, there had been a vitriolic response in certain sections of the Scottish press and political class to Jewish immigration at the turn of the century. In 1899, William Ormiston, Edinburgh's Dean of Guild, referred to immigrant Jews living in the city as the 'Ishmaels of mankind', and warned the Town Council not to be 'dragged at the heels of a Godless mob of Jews and infidels but (...) rise like a wall of fire about their much-loved isle'.[124] *The Scotsman* had described Jewish areas of residence as being typified by the 'dirt and nastiness, the squalor and crime, superstition and vice, which are the salient features of the Hebraic settlements that one finds in the Russian and Polish frontier districts'. Jews arriving at Leith were said to be 'lower, if that is conceivable, in intelligence and resource than those entering by way of the Thames'.[125] As late as the mid-1930s, relations between Scottish Jewry and the Presbyterian churches were tenuous and strained. In June 1934, against the backdrop of public protest against Nazi Germany and the Jewish boycott of German goods, the Church of Scotland's Commission of Enquiry into Scottish Jews reported at the General Assembly that 'the impact of the Jew on the life of Glasgow and, to a smaller extent, of Edinburgh, is stronger than it ever was and it keeps growing stronger (...) The life of the Jew is permeating the life of the city in a host of subtle ways, far more ways than can be seen on the surface. The growing influence of the Jew on the Scottish folk is sufficient in itself to compel us to see a growingly serious Home Mission problem'.[126] It would only be later in that decade, and especially after the outbreak of the Second World War, that the persecution of Jewry would attract the solidarity of Scotland's Protestants.

Contrary to Maitles's assertions, there are memoirs of Jews which do make mention of Fascist activity. Although Muriel Spark grew up in an assimilated Jewish family in Edinburgh, according to Martin Stannard she later 'recalled with distaste Blackshirts strutting around the streets during the 1930s'.[127] In his memoirs, *Two Worlds*, David Daiches recalls that 'Fascist rumblings' in Scotland 'disturbed and angered' his father, Rabbi Dr Salis Daiches.[128] Indeed, Daiches recalls that his father would 'keep an eagle eye open for letters or articles in the Scottish press which showed any trace of sympathy with the Hitlerite position, and he would reply to each with a forceful and eloquent letter to the editor'.[129] The first such letter appeared in *The Scotsman* in May 1936. In an article titled 'Rabbi's reply to

Sir Oswald Mosley', Rabbi Daiches challenged Mosley's recently uttered allegation that 'the Jews were seeking to bring about war between Britain and Germany'.

Nevertheless, in the face of this growing Jewish vigilance, Mosley's legion marched on, reaching as far as Hawick in July 1936. The *Hawick News* reported that the Blackshirt meeting at the Library Hall, addressed by Raven Thomson, was 'of a most orderly nature'. In its report on this 'uneventful meeting', the *Hawick Express* informed its readers that Thomson was 'given a good hearing by a fairly large audience, which included a considerable proportion of young folk'. There was undoubtedly something exotic about this Fascist raid into Teviotdale: 'A small party of blackshirted young men and girls had travelled from Edinburgh and were engaged as ushers and in the selling of Fascist newspapers.' The journalist continued: 'As is generally the case at a Fascist meeting there were no preliminaries, the speaker walking down the centre gangway to the platform, which was draped with a black cloth bearing the Fascist symbol – the fasces of ancient Rome – and beginning his address. Behind him on the wall hung a Union Jack.'

Raven Thomson began by addressing the issue of Mussolini's intervention in Abyssinia:

> Britain had never asked the blacks if they would like us to govern them, but Britain had brought far more good to the people of Africa than any former government had done. Would they rather that the Caliph had gone on ruling in the Sudan, with his barbarous rule, than that Britain should have taken it over? If they thought so, then they had better throw the British Empire away.

Another world war, Thomson continued, 'would mean the collapse of Western civilisation and the triumph of Communism. The only country that was going to get anything out of another world war was Soviet Russia, and Fascist countries could not possibly survive another world war'. They 'must try to restrain those League of Nations lunatics who were going about the world cursing Italy and Germany and urging on war'.

Turning to economic policy, Thomson explained that what the Fascists wished to attack 'was not ownership, but the exploitation of ownership'. It was 'the robber barons they had to get at who were crushing liberty and freedom with their great combines'. The British Empire, the BUF Director of Policy concluded, 'had enormous resources at its disposal and they had men eager for work'.

However, according to the *Hawick News*, after questions, a member of the audience shouted: "I'm afraid you won't get many recruits" (Laughter)'. Indeed, according to the *Express*, the event did not pass off entirely without incident: 'Once or twice during the meeting members of the audience walked pointedly out, while at the end, when the speaker called on those who did not wish to join in the singing of the National Anthem to leave, there was a deliberate exodus from the body of the hall.'[130]

Back in the Central Belt, activity continued. In spite of Oliver's resignation, the *Blackshirt* announced that, in Edinburgh, 'meetings at McLeod Street, formerly occasions for Red hooliganism, now attract orderly audiences. Saunders Street is improving. Larger and more intelligent audiences'.[131] A week later 'Edinburgh Blackshirts under Mr Plathen visited Glasgow and sold many copies of the *Blackshirt* and *Action*. Mr Plathen sold a large quantity of the *Blackshirt* in Cathcart'. Also in September, the Aberdeen branch won the Sir Oswald Mosley Cup for paper sales.

The year ended on an uplifting note. On Boxing Day, seventy-five children between the ages of five and nine were given a 'Fascist Xmas Party' at Edinburgh District HQ. *Blackshirt* reported:

> The Women's Section, ably assisted by a number of Cadets, took great pains to make the afternoon a great success, and there were many contributions in money and kind to cheer the youngsters whose parents are unemployed. After tea, the children were entertained by a conjurer, and played games until Santa arrived with a sackful of good things. Each child was remembered by him, and shrieks of delight and happy faces, when the wrappers had been undone, told their own story. Each kiddie was given a bag of sweets and a badge with the Leader's portrait as he left.[132]

At the beginning of 1937, in 'Scotland – what of the future?',[133] Robert Sheville looked back at a year of retrenchment and forward to the future:

> What will 1937 bring to Scotland? To what forces will the Scots turn? Literally in the past. Submerged, isolated, soaked in tradition

to the complete negation of actual realities. Here mediaevalism rubs shoulders with modernity, clear-sightedness with myopic wool-gathering, culture with the cult of material ugliness, broad-mindedness with hypocrisy, mass intelligence with mass stupidity; but victory must come.

It was in 1936, Sheville continued, that '*Action* assaulted Sloth. Youth moved forwards to end the domination of slippered pantaloon. Age-old prejudices were brought into the battle. Those that did not fall are crumbling into oblivion. In February the Blackshirt Phalanx moved on to West Edinburgh. At the outset, open hostility. Gradually, by the burning enthusiasm of the real Blackshirts, the lofty ideals and the passionate oratory, hostility turned to friendliness. Communism was laughed off the streets. The clenched fist opened and was clammy with fear. The Blackshirts fought on.' Therefore, despite the misgivings of Oliver and his ilk, 'youth continued its crusade': 'The obvious hollowness of the pseudo-evangelists was illumined. Two young Blackshirt speakers had borne the brunt of those attacks.' Another factor in the growth of 'National Socialism' had been 'the tightening grip of the Jew':

> The Jew is throwing from him the mantle of sweet modesty. With Oriental ostentation he waddles to the fore, glorying in what he assumes to be power. His shops and stores are dominating every important thoroughfare. His clutching hands are bedecked with gems . . . The Jew will never learn; always he must show his cards too soon. He has made this mistake in Scotland, just as he has made it through the ages. The people can see for themselves: they don't need to be told now.

Not only in urban areas had this progress been made:

> In Perthshire an active District has been formed. By hard work, it is true, but only by real work can progress ever be made. Soon, thanks to the superlative organising of the Scottish office Perth cannot fail to become the strongest of Scottish Districts . . . In North Scotland, the struggle is just beginning, but the heroism of the local Blackshirts is carrying them through the concentrated violence of the Neanderthals of the Red Front. In the East, in the Borders and in the West, the torch is being handed on.

The very soul of Scotland, concluded Sheville, was crying out for leadership:

> Leadership of the old fighting kind, is essential to the Scot. It is shown in the most glorious chapters of her history. The leadership of courage and of action can again rally Caledonia to the glories of the new age. Not the alleged leadership of the bureaucrat, bound and choked with this own red tape. Not the passionless, test-tube measuring of spineless automation. Not the bullying, prison-camp dominance of the pinchbeck Napoleons, not the posturings of the publicity-grabbing self-seekers. That leadership must be vital, inspiring ... British. With such a spirit Scotland can be won. Scotland is waiting for Mosley, who can measure up to the heroes of the past to lead her from the darkness of the present. The foundation stone upon which is built the renewal of life and of courage, the aspirations and hopes of the new world ... Leadership.

Retreat

In the sales league for *Action* and *Blackshirt*, Perth, Berwick, Dumfries, Edinburgh West and Bathgate contended; but the title belonged to Aberdeen, which in the course of 1937 emerged as the most active BUF branch, and, with that, a focus for street violence. The Aberdeen Führer was a local laird, William Keith Abercrombie Jopp Chambers-Hunter, of Tillery, near Udny. *Blackshirt* offered this short biography:

> [Chambers-Hunter] was a planter in Ceylon before the War, enlisted in the Seaforth Highlanders in 1914, and was seriously wounded, losing an arm in 1915. From 1916 till 1927 Mr Hunter was in Government service on the Cameroons plantations and later in the Gold Coast Agriculture Department. Now, at 43, Mr Hunter is in charge of the British Union in Aberdeen, where he was born. He has had no earlier political attachments, having seen all the old parties' promises broken and British prestige sacrificed by their ineptitude. Aberdeen has made great progress under his capable leadership. [134]

Chambers-Hunter may have been physically impeded from making the orthodox Fascist salute, but was helped enthusiastically in his political work by one Mrs Botha, daughter-in-law of Louis Botha, first Prime Minister of the Union of South Africa, plus two women in their early twenties, Jenny Linton and Jane Imlah. That said, an ominous sign of the limits to their success was the fact that in April, the leader was 'drowned out by Reds' at the Music Hall.

In May 1937, Edinburgh reported that a 'very successful Whist Drive organised by Women's Section brought members and friends together in happy atmosphere which was not disturbed when two stones which Reds had not had time to throw on Sunday came crashing through windows'.[135] The following month, at a meeting at Simon Square, 'Jewish opposition was encountered, but it never took serious form as rain had kept away the Red leaders (recently returned from Spain)'.[136]

The violence escalated. In July 1937, *Blackshirt* reported that 'Reds Riot in Scotland':

> During the past few months, Mr Plathen, Mr Chambers-Hunter and a handful of other speakers, together with a small but gallant band of Blackshirts have been attacked with a planned and intensive campaign of violence reminiscent of the early days of Blackshirts in East London ... But just as the decent working people of East London realised that the 'Red violence' was indirectly directed against them hearing the case for Fascism and so strengthen their determination to hear that case, so will it be in Scotland. Intensive phsyical opposition met courageously as it is by Blackshirts, excites the admiration of all reasonable people, and soon the first stage of the fight for National Socialism in Scotland will be won and the people will turn to the revolutionary creed, the only creed which will offer them release from the twin evils of 'Red violence' and financial democracy.

The Red violence referred to had occurred on a Sunday night meeting at the Market Stance. The speakers were met with missiles, Communist Party songs and cries of 'We want Mosley dead or alive' as the crowd surged towards the Fascist van. Even when the van disappeared up Union Street 'the hostile attitude of the crowd did not relax. Several scuffles took place, and in one of them a policeman's helmet was sent flying. The danger of the situation involved not only those who were directly concerned with the incidents, but others who immediately found themselves in the mob'.

At the same time, in Edinburgh, several Communists and Scottish ultra-nationalist Wendy Wood were on trial at the Sheriff's Court, charged with various offences arising out of scenes at a Blackshirt meeting on the Mound on 20 June. The court was told that the accused shouted, bawled, gesticulated, rang bells, interrupted and threatened. The local Communist leader Fred Douglas even bit a police officer. A witness saw stones thrown and squibs exploding near the Fascist van. The Blackshirt was drowned by chants of 'Down with Mosley' and 'Down with the Baby-Killers'. But the BUF paper concluded combatively: 'Still the struggle for free speech goes on and will be won by the tenacity and courage of the Blackshirts. Carry on, Scotland!'[137]

In July, it was reported that in Moffat, 'a visiting Propaganda Party from Dumfries was received with considerable interest'.[138] But the south of Scotland had not really kept its initial promise. The most active and successful leaders now were George Budge in Perth and Chambers-Hunter in Aberdeen. Together they pursued an increasingly lonely struggle, while the leadership in London concentrated its efforts on the East End and other urban areas, mainly in the south of England.

Later that month Budge gave his support to the Aberdonians:

> For forty minutes Budge addressed an orderly meeting on the Links. Then a crowd of Red Ruffians arrived on the scene and without any preliminaries smashed up the meeting by a wild attack upon our members. As the odds were 10–1 against us and the opposition even resorted to the use of knuckle-dusters, we won much sympathy from decent elements among the audience and some of them eventually put the 'fight' on a more even basis. As our party were driving off a spanner missing them struck and damaged the glass of a passing car. One of our members received facial injuries inflicted with a knuckle-duster.

The incidents on the Links therefore contrasted with a meeting in Nairn: 'An interested audience gave Plathen an attentive hearing and did not appreciate the tactics of the members of the "Yeller Brigade" who, as "camp followers" had come North with the Territorials to do what harm they could.'[139] However, in early August at Fraserburgh, the BUF meeting had to be abandoned: 'The locally not very popular

Reds had received advance information of our intention to speak. Surrounding themselves with imported toughs they "jumped" the pitch'.[140] Later that month, Chambers-Hunter addressed the throng on the beach and promenade. 'Pandemonium' was caused by the Reds, although 'great sales of *Action*' were reported.[141]

However, the 'Red Rabble' in Aberdeen acted most spectacularly in early October, by attacking a Blackshirt rally at the Market Stance. In October 1937, *Blackshirt* reported:

> Aberdeen was chosen this year as the venue for the meeting with which Scottish members always commemorate the birth of the Movement. Last Sunday, whilst out Leader and London contingents were marching to Bermondsey, members of the north of Scotland, from Perthshire, Fifeshire and Edinburgh rallied with their Aberdeen comrades to carry the spirit of the British Union to the 10,000 who had assembled in the Market Stance, filling it to capacity.

With the arrival of the Fascist van, the 'worker's brigade' came into evidence:

> To enable the huge audience to hear the National Socialist message, loudspeakers were then put into operation. After only a few minutes, however, the police requested that they should not be used as complaints had been made by local residents. This ban would appear to have been applied only to the BU loudspeakers, as the ILP continued to operate theirs without interference. It was allowed to blare forth the irresponsible speeches of men like Councillor Fraser Macintosh, and the cracked renderings of the 'Internationale' and 'Hold the Fort'.

Lumps of granite were thrown at the Blackshirts, several of whom were struck about the head and body. The police decided to use batons to restore order. While the crowd was being swept back, a young woman was bowled over and trampled on, and had to be carried away. Later, at a Communist rally in the Music Hall, local organiser T. Baxter denounced 'brutal batoning down of men and women by the police'. There were protests by the Trades Council and NUWM, but no inquiry was ordered by the local council.

At the BUF offices, where Mrs Chambers-Hunter and members of the Women's Section had prepared refreshments, members celebrated the occasion among themselves, singing the Blackshirt songs. With the National Anthem, the day's activities were closed. The article concluded: 'A loud "Hail Mosley" broke the stillness of the evening air as Scottish Blackshirts departed into the night, forward to another day and to continued struggle with Mosley, towards National Socialism.'[142]

On 15 October 1937 the Deputy Chief Constable of Aberdeen made his own report on disturbances at the Fascist meeting:

> In this rush I was carried off my feet and thrown on to the off front mudguard of the Van, my legs being under the wing. At this time there was another rush at the Van and I was struggling to keep my legs from being run over by the off front wheel which was close to them. The Van was still gradually moving downhill and as I was almost exhausted hanging on to prevent myself being run over, I shouted to the men to draw their batons. They immediately did so and chased the crowd back in a few seconds. I got to my feet and by this time there was a space cleared which could have held ten vans, and I then shouted to our men, 'that will do'. While this was taking place the Van moved forward and I held up my hand for it to stop. . . . Had I not given the order for the Police to draw their batons, I certainly would have been seriously injured as the off front wheel would have passed over my legs and I would have been trampled by the mob, while the Van would, in all probability, have got out of control and might have killed or seriously injured some of the large crowd which was behind it, and its occupants.[143]

The 'United Howling Front' also disrupted the BUF's local election campaign in the Canongate and St Giles wards of Edinburgh. In September, *The Scotsman* had reported the launch of this campaign by the Leader himself:

> Sir Oswald, after expressing strong indignation at the action of a Town Council Committee in forbidding the Fascists the use of loudspeakers at a meeting which they had arranged in the East Meadows, yesterday, said that plans were being made for the elections. 'Some of these Socialist Councillors who are so anxious to prevent free speech may possibly find the issue testing,' he declared. 'Incidentally,

in Edinburgh we are hoping to arrange a fight or two in the same wards of some of these Councillors who were responsible for our meeting having to be cancelled.'[144]

The BUF candidates were Richard Plathen and Alexander Young. Young was an Edinburgh man, having been born in the capital in 1897. He was a telegraphist with the GPO until 1915, when he enlisted in the Cameron Highlanders. Wounded and gassed, he was discharged from the army on account of war disabilities. Young was quite exceptional for having gone over to the BUF from Protestant Action in late 1936. He was attracted by the BUF's pronounced turn towards anti-Semitism. By the summer of 1937, local reports from the Edinburgh branch were couched in strongly anti-Semitic terms. In July, *Blackshirt* ran a piece entitled 'Persecution by an Alien Race', detailing the tale of 'Joe the Jew', a slum landlord in Edinburgh, and blaming the local housing problems upon immigration from Eastern Europe.

The local election campaign quickly ran into stiff opposition. In October, *Blackshirt* reported:

> Mr Young and his party were stoned as they left their meeting. But the courageous bombardiers, numbering about 20, made a bolt for safety when one of the Blackshirts turned and moved in their direction. The Roxburgh St meeting was largely patronised by Jews. One of these heroes, after receiving a warning from Mr Plathen on account of his inciting shouts, disappeared and returned a few minutes later with a baby in his arms. Several attacks were made on the speaker and he was thrown off his platform on these occasions.

Nevertheless, curiosity and interest had 'attracted large audiences to our meetings. A large proportion leave at the end impressed by the commonsense argument, disgusted by the exhibitions of hooligan conduct by the would-be church-burners of Scotland'. [145] A week later, 'Red hooligans' had their comeuppance at well attended meetings: 'Attendances at our meetings have been well above those of the other contestants! The united front of Labour, Protestant Action and Communists have been hard at work. They are unanimous in their methods of violence though there is discordance in their factional songs.' Convictions were not shaken: on 28 October, the *Edinburgh*

Evening Dispatch reported that Young advanced the demand that shops should be made to display the proprietor's name, presumably with a view towards focusing upon any incoming Jewish proprietors.

This campaign misfired spectacularly. On 3 November, *The Scotsman* announced 'Fascist Failure in Edinburgh'. Plathen and Young had garnered a pitiful number of votes. In St Giles ward, Plathen received 51 votes, behind the Progressive Alexander Sievenwright with 910, Mary Sellar of Protestant Action with 1,286, and the Socialist Mary Ingles with 2,301. In Canongate, Alexander Young received 41 votes, far behind Protestant Action's George Robertson with 1,968, and the Socialist George Rhind with 2,301. The only consolation for Young was that he came in front of Robert Gillespie of the International Socialist Labour Party, who attracted the support of only 31 voters. On a 51.1% turnout, the Edinburgh Blackshirts had received 91 out of 108,935 votes cast: 0.08%.

The overall results indicated important shifts and inertias in electoral behaviour: the PA share of the vote fell to 25.6%, John Cormack being defeated not once but twice – in North Leith and Gorgie – and only one PA candidate was elected. It was the Labour left that advanced, with the Socialists adding two councillors to their group. At the same time, the majority on Edinburgh council remained solidly Progressive (Tory). John Cormack and his Klan's hour had passed: the leader's *folie de grandeur* had ended up alienating loyal supporters in the city of John Knox. Yet in 1938 Cormack would still be returned for South Leith, a ward he represented without interruption until his retirement in 1962. Nonetheless, Cormack – and, very briefly, Ratcliffe – would struggle in a postwar Scotland where the common war effort, the creation of the welfare state and the return of full employment reduced, without eliminating, sectarian tensions.

On 10 November 1937, Special Branch reported on the BUF's 'mediocre results' at the recent municipal elections throughout Britain. If the Blackshirt candidates had known disaster in the Scottish capital, the two candidates in Leeds could only muster 178 votes, and the candidate in Merthyr 170. The strongest support by far was in Bethnal Green, notably for Raven Thomson. Generally, Special Branch concluded, there was 'an atmosphere of defeat'.[146]

And yet, boasted *Blackshirt*, in Aberdeen the public were 'beginning to see through the maze of misrepresentation',[147] while George

Budge addressed successful meetings in Aberfeldy, Auchterarder, Blairgowrie, Coupar Angus, Crieff, Dunkeld, Pitlochry and Perth. At the end of 1937, there was claimed to be spreading interest in building up membership in Glasgow. Only blizzards and heavy frosts seemed to interfere with outdoor activities in all districts.

In November 1937, at the Caledonian Hotel, Aberdeen, W.K. Chambers-Hunter was presented, by Mosley himself, with the BUF's Gold Award, at a ceremony attended by 100 guests. On 8 January 1938, *Blackshirt* showcased Chambers-Hunter, 'Stalwart of the North'. Two months later, the regular section 'Legions on the March' announced meetings in Edinburgh 'in spite of chilly, stormy weather', while there were leafleting and speakers' classes in Glasgow.[148] On 9 June 1938, 'a very interesting meeting' was held in Aberfeldy, 'which happened to be the same day that the Duchess of Atholl was holding a meeting in the Town Hall. The town was shaken to its foundations by the appearance of "Mind Britain's Business" chalked on all the roads leading to the duchess's meeting'.[149] There were gatherings in Blairgowrie and Crieff, 'ever-increasing friends in Dundee' and propaganda raids on Perth and St Andrews.

In the late summer of 1938, things came to a head for Aberdonian Fascists, anti-Fascists and policemen alike. Increasingly, the disorder caused by BUF meetings was irritating the authorities. On 14 August 1938 Chambers-Hunter wrote a letter of complaint to the Chief Constable.

> I wish to protest very strongly against the action taken by an Inspector of Police in stopping a BU meeting at which I was the speaker at 7pm tonight. This meeting was advertised to take place at 7.30pm at the Square, Miller St. When I arrived there punctually at 7.30pm a Communist called Baxter was pretending to hold a meeting. The Inspector apparently regarded this as a proper meeting and informed me that I could not hold mine as he couldn't have two meetings in the same Square despite the fact that on my arrival Baxter ceased speaking, and all the people came round to listen to me, with the exception of the usual handful of hooligans, who bawled and shouted. He told me that I could go to that part of the Links near the Amusement Park, which I did. The crowd from Miller St and the hooligans followed me to this meeting and while the former tried to hear what I said, the latter kept up a continual bawling and yelling round the car;

during which time I was hit with a potato, stones, and bit of broken glass and phials containing, I think H3 [sulphuric acid].[150]

In the face of orchestrated heckling by the communists, who had also brought along children, the authorities intervened:

The Inspector of Police at 8.27pm told me I was not making any progress, which was none of his business, and incidentally was not true as two ladies comparatively far away have informed me that they could hear every word I said. Only a comparatively small percentage of those present were causing the row and disturbance around the car, and I consider that the Inspector was in no danger himself and that his action in stopping the meeting was not only childish but is putting a premium on hooliganism designed to prevent BU speakers getting free speech, which is supposed to be the right of every British citizen.

On 17 August 1938 Chambers-Hunter wrote again to the Chief Constable, 'with reference to our, or rather, your telephone conversation this morning': 'I would point out to you that having a lot of personal abuse through the phone and then banging down the receiver is of course equivalent to hitting a man unawares and then running away. You called me a coward through the phone. All right! I challenge you to put the WHOLE of your remarks on paper.'[151]

In a letter to Neil Francis-Hawkins, Director-General of the BUF, Chambers-Hunter denounced the 'complicity' of the Chief Constable and the involvement of Labour councillors in disrupting activities. The CC had told him he would get no more advertised meetings, and that 'I was a coward who sheltered behind the police to make provocative speeches'. He would 'have me inside' and declared that 'I was just as much a hooligan as the Communists'. At a meeting at Torry, 4 September 1938, 'our car was overturned. Police made no effort to stop it'.[152]

Mrs Botha also complained to Francis-Hawkins:

On arrival there, seeing no police we however started the meeting, Mr Hunter speaking through the loud speaker. I got out to steward the car on the driving side, Mr Budge the other. We were both kicked assaulted and the car swaying already and still no police, so I decided

I would get in and keep the engine going, but as I opened the door with my hand on the seat, over she went, so I went in head-first with my legs in the air and had to get out through the sunshine roof with my leg bruised and my hands bleeding from the broken glass. The police still did nothing; when Mr Hunter called for volunteers to right the car several came forward but were torn back by the crowd, no police came forward to help. We got her up and proceeded to Lodge Walk to make a complaint and found there was a strained atmosphere for no-one wanted to take our statements.[153]

The *Press and Journal* reported the next day that 'Mr Chambers-Hunter was standing inside the car, with his head and shoulders through the sunshine roof'. Once the anti-Fascists had overturned the car, 'he was helped out through the sunshine roof, followed by his two assistants, and Mrs Botha was assisted out of the car by the window'. The police eventually intervened to help the car back onto its wheels. However, Chambers-Hunter 'could not make himself heard above the shouting ... and drove away, followed by catcalls. Every time a shout was raised he gave the Fascist salute'. It did not stop there. On the evening of 8 September, Chambers-Hunter informed Francis-Hawkins that 'Mrs Botha and myself were assaulted, pushed, sworn at, kicked, etc, also the car tyre was slashed, and the Police made no attempt to preserve order'.[154]

The disturbances reached their climax on 11 September. The *Press and Journal* headlined with 'Wild Scenes in Aberdeen'. The *Glasgow Herald* reported the presence of 6,000 people at the meeting in South Esplanade East:

Mr Chambers-Hunter made an effort to speak through the loud-speaker and he was greeted by a shower of burning fireworks, sticks, stones and pieces of coal, which had been picked up from a nearby coal yard. Part of the loudspeaker equipment was torn from the lorry and thrown into an adjoining coal merchants' yard. One of the Fascist speakers was seen to jump from the lorry and engage in hand-to-hand fighting with a section of the crowd.

On 19 September 1938, Francis-Hawkins wrote to the Secretary of State to criticise 'serious maladministration in the Aberdeen Police Force':

The Chief Constable has failed, by his neglect of duty, to prevent breach of the peace, assaults on our members and interference with meetings lawfully convened and conducted by them. The Chief Constable has neglected to procure, and by his orders or attitude has discouraged his subordinates from procuring, the punishment of wrongdoers who are members of the Labour and Communist Parties[.] The Chief Constable has discriminated between BU members and members of the Labour and Communist parties[.] The Chief Constable has been guilty of unworthy, unjustifiable and improper conduct towards Mr Chambers-Hunter. Immediate action against him is necessary.[155]

Unsurprisingly, the Aberdeen police saw things differently. On 14 September 1938, Superintendent W. Murray reported to the CC:

[Chambers-Hunter's] meetings in various parts of the city have met with little or no success. The Communist Party has always been very bitter against the Fascists, and have created considerable trouble at Hunter's meetings. It was obvious at the outset that Hunter did not want the Police to deal with his political opponents, and although he was molested, and obstructed in delivering his address, and on occasions assaulted, he would report the matter to the Police some considerable time after the incident, when it was almost impossible to trace the offenders. No notice was given to the Police regarding the meetings, and things reached a state that Hunter was practically coerced to give notice of his meetings to the Police.

Mr Chambers-Hunter had failed to exercise his powers under the Public Order Act in a proper manner:

When interrupted in the course of his address he either refrained from pointing out any person or else pointed out a known political opponent who was taking no part in the disturbance so far as the police could perceive. To aggravate the situation, Mr Hunter's demeanour and provocative habit of raising his arm in the Fascist salute on the slightest pretext inflamed the hostile elements in the crowd to such an extent that he lost control of his meetings and they invariably finished in disorder. Children attracted by the commotion gathered to sing and jeer at the speaker, and his meetings eventually became so notorious that huge crowds of several thousand people came to see and hear what was going on.

The police were aware that 'the climax has been reached and that drastic steps must be taken to prevent a recurrence of incidents like these which might well culminate in a riot':

> The only practical method of dealing with the situation would appear to be to debar the Fascists from proceeding to the appointed meeting place, when, in the opinion of the Police, their presence could in all possibility cause a breach of the peace. Mr Hunter is, however, a strong willed man who is not always amenable to Police advice . . . It is regretful to have to suggest taking this course as it may appear like submitting to mob law, but the speaker has no control of the crowd at his meetings; he is decidedly provocative in his manner, and although speakers are entitled to free speech, it is not the duty of the Police to maintain free speech at meetings which create a highly dangerous situation and may end in a riot.[156]

Were the Blackshirts, in Scotland and the rest of the UK, unfairly singled out for punishment? For Stephen M. Cullen, 'a strong argument can be made that the BUF did not use violence as a political tactic, and were far more the victims of political violence than they were the perpetrators of such violence'.[157] Cullen offers the example of George Budge, who suffered several violent assaults and was left with lasting facial injuries. He concludes:

> The Scottish BUF appear not to have attacked any of their opponents, and no attempt at all was made to disrupt non-Fascist meetings, or to prevent non-Fascists selling newspapers. The only occasion on which the BUF used violence was during Mosley's meetings in Edinburgh, and in both cases there were more injuries suffered by Fascists, and of a far more serious nature (including a Blackshirt blinded in one eye), than by anti-Fascists.[158]

This may have a basis in fact, but our sympathy must be tempered by the Blackshirts' violent and provocative rhetoric, the military 'style' of their politics, and their support for anti-democratic, expansionist and eventually genocidal regimes.

By the autumn of 1938, Mosley's legion was very much in retreat. In September, the *Northern Blackshirt* reported a meeting of parents on the Craigmillar estate near Edinburgh. The BUF speaker was repeatedly interrupted by Labour activists. He declared defensively: 'I admit I'm a Fascist. I am not ashamed of it. I am more concerned about conditions for children of Edinburgh than for children in Spain. I am here tonight as a parent who wants facilities for his child, and not as a Blackshirt.'[159]

The Scottish BUF's activity had moved its focus to small, indoor meetings, but the tone of its propaganda had, by 1938, begun to show signs of desperation and failure, with anti-Semitism coming to the fore. During the West Perth and Kinross by-election of December 1939, the remnants of the BUF played on fears that the rural north of Scotland was about to be used as a dumping ground for Jewish refugees from Germany. In January 1939, the *Northern Blackshirt* claimed that 'Edinburgh businessmen are muttering. They want to know why Jewish shops don't carry the names of their owners'. Tony Milligan remarks, with some, if not complete, justification: 'The turn towards open anti-Semitism in the Scottish localities represented the BUF's final abandonment of any real attempt to relate to the peculiarities of Scotland's political terrain.'[160]

In March 1939, Chambers-Hunter and Mrs Botha resigned from the BUF on the grounds that the policy of social credit was not given a sufficient profile in BUF policy. This brought an end to BUF activity in Aberdeen. Richard Plathen left Edinburgh to set up a business career connected with Empire trade. By the outbreak of war, writes Cullen, 'the BUF in Scotland depended entirely on a small number of dedicated and peripatetic activists to spread the word – an almost hopeless task'.[161] Of 1,000 activists interned in spring 1940, only three were from Scotland.[162]

2

Fasci di Scozia

In its 1933 census, the Italian consular authorities estimated that over 40% of Italian-Scots were full members of the Italian Fascist Party. Yet despite this important presence, there seems to have been very little contact between Scottish Blackshirts and expatriate supporters of Mussolini. A senior member of the Edinburgh *Fascio*, Joseph Pia, remembered how some BUF members from Stockbridge attempted, in vain, to get him interested in their activities.[1] That failed attempt at recruitment was the exception that proved the rule.

The first *Fasci* were founded in 1923, and reflected the distribution of Italian immigrants in the British Isles: two out of the six were in Glasgow and Edinburgh, the others being in London, Dublin, Belfast and South Wales. Pia, like other Italian-Scots, remembered membership of the party as being primarily a cultural issue, peculiar to their community, rather than a more general political statement. However, this anodyne description and explanation of *Fascio* membership masks the hegemonic ambitions of the Foreign Ministry in Rome. As Wendy Ugolini has pointed out, 'the tendency within historiography and personal narratives to understate the intended propaganda and political aspects of the *Fasci* reflects a reluctance to address the role of the clubs in light of Fascism's uncomfortable present-day associations'.[2]

In September 1935, a report by MI5 described the network of organisations created by the Fascists to achieve 'peaceful penetration' of the Italian community.[3] The Opera Nazionale Balilla (ONB) organised the youth. Established in Italy in 1926, the ONB sought to provide 'moral and physical education for the young according to the principles and ideals sponsored by Fascism'. It was a conscious attempt to reverse the tide of emigration which had, it was believed, weakened the race. In March 1927, the Under-secretary of Foreign

81

Affairs, Dino Grandi, had asked: 'Why must our race continue to be a sort of human reservoir at the disposal of other countries of the world? Why must our mothers continue to furnish soldiers for other nations?'[4]

Children were received into the ranks of the ONB at six years of age and passed successively through four sections, known as 'Sons of the Wolf', 'Balilla', 'Vanguardista' and 'Young Fascists' according to age until they attained 18 years, when they entered the adult party. Veterans were organised in the Associazione Nationale Combattenti, while the Italian Co-operative Club was a centre of social activity for numerous Italian workers in the catering trade, and offered help with finding work. The Villa Marina in Felixstowe was a place of relaxation for Italian Fascists from throughout the British Isles. The Anglo-Italian Club and Friends of Italy extended the Fascist message into the host community.

Their gatherings could be considerable. *The Scotsman* of 16 August 1932 reported on the annual outing of Italian Fascists. More than 200 members of the Glasgow, Edinburgh and Stirling branches converged on Loch Lomond Park, Balloch. *L'Italia Nostra*, the central organ of the Italian Fascist Party in Britain, gave regular coverage to the various activities of the *Fasci di Scozia*. On 4 January 1935, at the University of Glasgow, the consul-general, Dr Ferrucio Luppis, gave an 'important lecture' on 'Rimini in History and Love Poetry'. On 18 January 1935 at the Scottish–Italian Society, Ernesto Grillo, Glasgow University's first Professor of Italian Language and Literature, spoke about 'the divine message of Dante Alighieri'. There were not only intellectual activities. On 15 February 1935, *L'Italia Nostra* reported on a football match between the *squadra azzurra* and Rutherglen Merchants at Springfield Park, Glasgow, followed by a supper-dance at the Balmoral restaurant. Indeed, the Fascist football teams in Scotland would compete for the *coppa Grillo*. In April, Luppis visited the Italian Fascists of Ayr, while a large ball was organised by the Fascio Femminile di Glasgow.

In this year of the Abyssinian crisis, politics did not fail to make an appearance. In May 1935, *L'Italia Nostra* reported that one Mr McDonald, secretary of the 'Scotch–Italian Society' and 'sincere friend of Italy', 'spoke about Fascism, on its conquests and its beneficial effects not only regarding Italy but also in respect to world pacification'.[5] A fortnight later, the Casa d'Italia at 22 Park Circus,

Glasgow, was solemnly opened. This house was 'one of the most sumptuous in Glasgow', having belonged to the rich McFarlane family. The Casa d'Italia was 'designed to welcome Italian associations of a cultural nature'.[6] The ceremony was attended by numerous members of the Italian community, from schoolchildren to veterans in their uniforms and with their banners. Sir Daniel Stevenson, Chancellor of Glasgow University, offered them his blessing.

An important aspect of Fascist activity was the organisation of holidays in Italy, especially for children. In August 1935, *L'Italia Nostra* announced the departure of a great number of Italian-Scottish *bambini* for a summer camp in the home country: 'the wife of our consul Mrs Wanda Luppis was present at the Central Station, distributing with maternal kindness ice creams to all, who smiled purely in appreciation of her so noble gesture'. The desire of the mothers was that, after a month in Italy, the children would return 'with the spirit for future conquests in life', being educated in the 'purest feelings of the Fatherland and the creed'.[7]

Meanwhile, back in Glasgow, the new Casa d'Italia pursued its hegemonic mission. On 6 September 1935, there was a large meeting on Abyssinia, at which 'All the orators illustrated the contribution brought by Italy to the civilisation of the African peoples, arousing the most lively enthusiasm in the audience who applauded at length and enthusiastically the King of Italy and Il Duce.' At the same time, the reader was informed that the Casa d'Italia, 'which brings together in its bosom all the life blood of the colony', contained 'enormous and splendid rooms which are distributed among the various Associations. The billiard room, reading room, conference room, ballroom and restaurant complete the organisation of the *Casa* which constitutes, for whoever visits Glasgow, a great source of pride'.[8]

A week later, the *bambini* returned for another school year, while comrade Eduardo Palleschi, secretary of the Glasgow *Fascio*, protested at a cartoon in the *Evening Times*, 'Troops for Ethiopia', portraying mutilated Italian ex-servicemen. The community mobilised in favour of Il Duce's campaign, commenced in October, to make Ethiopia part of the colony of Italian East Africa. Mussolini may have violated the League of Nations Covenant and unleashed tanks and mustard gas on troops often armed with spears and bows. Nevertheless, in November 1935, *L'Italia Nostra* boasted that the Italian community in Scotland 'has voluntarily donated gold and silver objects to be presented to the Head of the Government as a symbol of homage and devotion'.[9] The *Fasci di Scozia* and their friends would distribute propaganda in the form of the *British-Italian Bulletin*, denouncing the 'barbarity' of Italy's enemies in Abyssinia, a benighted land of slavery, lepers and public floggings. The natives' use of dum-dum bullets completed the sordid picture. 'Liberated' Tigre was contrasted with 'darkest Ethiopia', while on 18 April 1936, Ezra Pound, in 'The Fascist Ideal', glorified the Blackshirts' 'creative urge'.[10] A fortnight later, Marshal Badoglio's 'March of the Iron Will' ended in Addis Ababa; 10,000 Italians and 275,000 Ethiopians had lost their lives. In May 1936, the *Bulletin* proclaimed that the victory of Italy was 'the victory of civilisation'.[11] On fleeing his country, the defeated Ethiopian emperor, Haile Selassie, told the world: 'It is us today. It will be you tomorrow!'

The Abyssinian crisis marked members of the Italian-Scottish community. According to Joe Pieri, who was born in Italy in 1919 just prior to his family's emigration to Scotland, Italy's invasion of Ethiopia and later intervention in the Spanish Civil War 'created a wave of ill feeling against Italy in the general population. The childhood taunts of "dirty wee Tally" had given way to more frequent and insulting remarks about my nationality from some of the more drunken and belligerent types who made up a good percentage of our night-time clientele'.[12] Carmen Sidonio, who grew up in Invergordon with Italian parents, was 'shocked and horrified' when his classmates at school began 'dancing around me saying "Eyetie, eyetie, Mussolini eyetie"'. Until the time of the Ethiopia conflict, Sidonio had always self-identified as Scottish.[13] Richard Demarco recalls, at the age of seven, attending a Young Fascists' film show at La Scala and being 'ill at ease' as he watched films about the Ethiopian campaign.[14]

During this period of crisis, the authorities began to take a closer interest in both the Italian Fascist Party and the Nazi Party. In January 1936, MI5 reported that, with 3,000 members, the Fascists had trebled in size in the space of 12 months. In Scotland they remained disproportionately strong, with *Fasci* in Glasgow and Edinburgh, but also in Greenock, Aberdeen and Dundee. In September 1936, another report looked at Fascist organisation of children: summer colonies in Italy, but also the seaside colony at

Felixstowe and the fourth Campeggio Mussolini at Maidstone. The author concluded:

We do not know exactly how many of these 572 members of the Youth Organisation were British subjects but we have ascertained that of the Glasgow and Greenock contingent 54 out of 61 were born in the UK and it is not unlikely that the proportions throughout are somewhat similar. The fact that so many British subjects of Italian origin are receiving this form of pre-military training in Italy seems likely to give the considerations raised in the Memorandum on sabotage even greater significance . . . At present there is no analogous organisation for sending British subjects to Germany to join Hitler Jugend camps but with the Italian example before them it is not unlikely that the Nazis will develop something on a similar scale.[15]

Such activities were therefore considered a sinister and growing threat. In a report to the Foreign Office on 27 July 1936, the Italian Fascist Party and the NSDAP were described as 'incompatible with the British way of life and existing institutions. It would not be reasonable to expect that they should be allowed to develop further on British territory'.[16] The NSDAP was engaged in winning over '*Deutschtum*' British subjects and contained a potential for sabotage. Under the leadership of *Landesgruppenleiter* Otto Bene, Nazis in Britain were organised into *Ortsgruppen* in London, Ealing, Dalston and Dublin, and the smaller *Stützpunkten* of Bradford, Doncaster, Birmingham, Liverpool, Manchester, Cardiff and Hull. A reflection of patterns of German settlement, there was no branch in Scotland. As far as the Fascists were concerned, however, five of the fifteen *Fasci* were north of the Cheviots. It was concluded that it would be 'desirable that all the above organisations, German and Italian, except those mentioned in brackets, should be dissolved'.

However, the dissolution of these organisations took time. On 24 March 1937, the Assistant Chief Constable of Glasgow reported to Sir Vernon Kell that the membership of the *Fascio* now stood at 600 members: 'The majority of the members reside in Glasgow, the remainder being resident in Lanarkshire and Ayrshire. The membership of the Italian Youth Organisation, here, for boys and girls between the ages of 6 and 18 years, is 500.'[17]

On 16 February 1937, another report was submitted to Sir Robert Vansittart, Permanent Under-Secretary at the Foreign Office:

> Both the Nazi and the Fascist Party organisations in this country are becoming increasingly active. If they are allowed to continue, their influence over Germans and Italians in this country and over British subjects of German and Italian extraction will inevitably become more powerful, and greater will be their potential danger as ready-made instruments of intelligence and – in the event of war – of sabotage.[18]

The Italian Fascist Party exerted 'all its influence to prevent British-born children of Italian parents from becoming anglicised and to keep them Italian.' During the annual summer camps in Italy 'they undergo training in the Italian youth organisations, including the use of rifle and machine guns. At the same time other similar camps are organised in British territory where the training includes drill but not the use of weapons'. According to the author, Nazi and Italian Fascist Party officials had to be told that permission to remain in the country could no longer be granted. He concluded:

> It is probable that the totalitarian regimes will not disappear in the near future, and the extension of their organisations into British territory is virtually an infringement of sovereignty ... These organisations on British territory are continually developing, and both Germans and Italians have greatly increased their membership during the last year or two. If the present position is allowed to continue, awkward precedents would be created by its tacit acceptance. The power and influence of these organisations over Germans and Italians and over British subjects of German and Italian extraction will inevitably increase. The longer the organisations are allowed to exist, the greater will be the potential danger resulting from their activity in the form of espionage and sabotage.

But such pleas for intervention were not heeded. On 2 March 1937 Willie Gallacher, Communist MP for West Fife, wrote to Sir John Simon, Home Secretary, protesting at the distribution of Nazi leaflets in Edinburgh:

As you will see they are printed in Hamburg and shipped over here by the boat-load. According to the index at the bottom there have been somewhere in the region of 1,000 different leaflets published – for circulation in English-speaking countries. I am certain that the attention of the Ambassador would be drawn to it if Russian ships were being used to flood this country with leaflets produced in Russia and I am of the opinion that the attention of the German Ambassador should be drawn to these.[19]

However, the Home Office concluded on 18 March 1937 that in this literature, produced by the Fichte Association, there was 'little, if anything, directed, against us ... They consist of anti-Semitic, and anti-Bolshevik pamphlets and others designed to show Germany in a peace-loving role – many of them are reproductions of speeches made by prominent Nazi leaders'.[20] At a time of non-intervention in Spain, and appeasement, there was no urgency about clamping down on such propaganda. Indeed, the authorities seemed more concerned about the circulation of *Mein Kampf* in India. Vansittart adopted the *pis-aller* of keeping an eye on the Fascists and Nazis. This would be put back into question only in early 1939, after the arrest of Otto Karlova for spying.

On 23 February 1939, a report on the activities of the Nazi Party, now with 560 members, and the Italian Fascists, now numbering 1,700, declared:

The ostensible object of these organisations is to propagate and maintain Nazi and Fascist ideas among Germans and Italians living in this country and to strengthen the conception that those living in foreign lands still owe allegiance to the Führer and the Duce. In fact, they go beyond this and must be regarded as providing very effective reason for the respective Governments to maintain control over their nationals.

The Nazi Party was considered particularly dangerous. It exerted 'undue pressure on German residents ... There are Gestapo agents resident in this country, and their mere presence is known to terrify or terrorise refugees'. The question to be decided was 'whether on grounds of security and foreign policy the breaking up of these organisations is desirable, and, if so, whether the expulsion of the organisations would take place immediately before a new crisis is expected so as to give as little time as possible for reorganisation by underground methods'. It was only on 21 March 1939, after Hitler's troops had completed their occupation of Bohemia and Moravia, that Vansittart concluded there should be 'no more "appeasement"', and saw no objections to dissolving Nazi organisations.[21]

The *Fasci di Scozia* could therefore continue their activities for more than another year. Despite the declaration of war against Germany, there did not seem to be any sense of imminent danger. The annual general assembly of the *Fasci di Scozia* was held in Glasgow on 30 November 1939. *L'Italia Nostra* reported the success of the film session of the *Dopolavoro* (Fascist leisure organisation), which saw the projection of two important films by the GILE (organisation of Italian youth abroad) of Longniddry and the Biggar Colony on their trip to Ferragusto.[22] On 19 January 1940, it was announced that 'the Fascist Youth have in little less than a year seen their numbers treble'.[23] In March 1940, also in Glasgow, there was a Dante concert, while in Aberdeen, Savoia Athletic had gone down honourably to the *Dopolavoro* of Edinburgh, 3–6, in the *coppa Grillo*. The reporter concluded: 'the Aberdeen squadra continues to improve with tenacity and good will and we can foresee it providing a challenge in future meetings with other teams in our Scottish community'. On 10 April, the final of the *coppa Grillo* at Glencairn Park in Rutherglen brought together the *Dopolovaro del Fascio* of Glasgow and Edinburgh. 'A beautiful day favoured an interesting match' won 6–2 by the Glaswegian Fascists. During the entire game 'a perfect sporting spirit was maintained'. Once it was over, 'the guests were taken to the Casa d'Italia for a delightful and cordial dance'.[24]

Later that month, the *Fasci* celebrated the birth of Rome and the festival of labour. In Green's Playhouse, Dundee, the Italian community had a ball: 'the total number present came to the fine total of 450 and the excellent orchestra directed by the renowned Andy Lothian, and which includes our Glasgow comrade Cabrelli, led a dance which lasted till three in the morning'.[25] Fascists had come from as far as Perth, Arbroath and Aberdeen. At the beginning of May, in Glasgow, Professor Cesare Foligno gave a lecture on the love poetry of Leopardi, while an event was organised on Dante. The *Dopolavoro* gathered in the Albert Ballroom, Bath Street: 'More than

550 were present and lively dancing lasted from eight in the evening to one in the morning'.[26]

But such delights came to a swift and brutal end. From 12 May 1940, all male aliens in Edinburgh were subject to a curfew, had to report daily to the police, and could not make use of any private motor vehicle or bicycle. On 10 June 1940, the lightning progress of the *Wehrmacht* in France prompted Mussolini to fatally declare war on Britain and France. His announcement from the balcony of Palazzo Venezia was broadcast to the 'Italian Empire' and relayed to the rest of the world. Within minutes, Italians in Britain began to be rounded up for internment and deportation.

On 12 June 1940, Major Perfect, head of security for Scotland, forwarded to Sir Vernon Kell a report on the police raid on the Edinburgh Fascist Party headquarters in Picardy Place two days previously. The detective sergeant wrote:

> On entering the premises I found Mario Trudu, the Italian Vice Consul, seated therein examining papers. He was taken to his home and placed under House Arrest. I commenced to search the Conference Hall and found the afternoted documents therein: Sixteen membership cards Opera Nazionale DOPOLAVORO ANNO XVI Peace Organisation, the members of which must, before being admitted to the organisation, be members of the Fascist Party.

The detective found a list of names and addresses of members of the Fascist party in and outwith Edinburgh. What's more, during his search of the Hall, he 'observed a large metal trunk, and on examination . . . found it to contain documents relating to Consular business, and it was apparent that the Consul had removed this trunk to the Hall and had been burning papers taken therefrom'. At 10.20 p.m., he went on, 'I observed that the floor of the Hall had caught fire, due to the overflow from the fireplace of paper and files, which had been destroyed prior to my arrival there. I immediately notified the Fire Brigade.'

Following receipt of a Home Office telegram requesting examination of Italian consular premises for arms, explosives and wireless transmitters, etc., the detective carried this out, but 'did not discover any of the articles referred to. I also examined thoroughly documents and papers therein, but found that the office had been cleared of all important documents that would be of interest from a Police point of view ... With the aid of an interpreter, I examined the contents of the Consular box which had been removed by me to Police Headquarters, and learned that all the documents therein referred to legal, shipping, sport, charity matters, etc., with the exception of several documents relating to the activities of the Edinburgh Fascist Party'.

The documents found were hardly incendiary. Membership lists showed that Fascist membership in Edinburgh had grown between 1935 and 1939 from 79 to 166, out of a community of 800, while membership of the youth organisation had quadrupled in that period. The *Fascio di Edimburgo* was active in offering Italian language courses and promoting Dante Alighieri. The *Fasci Femminili* circulated propaganda, but also engaged in charitable works aimed at large families and sick people. Courses of hygiene were offered for the 'Health and Defence of the Race', creches and orphanages protected mothers and infants, while assistance was given to working women with courses in crafts and housekeeping. Finally, the *Fascio* had its own band and promoted gymnastics and sports. There was therefore little or no sign of a 'fifth column' ready to sabotage the war effort.[27]

Nevertheless, anti-Italian disturbances erupted throughout Scotland, as in other parts of the UK. These were particularly vicious in Glasgow, Clydebank and Edinburgh. A mob of a few hundred gathered in the Paisley district of Glasgow at about midnight on 10 June, moving along various streets smashing the windows of every Italian shop they came to and looting the contents. When the police arrived they had to face intense hostility from the crowds and 20 people were arrested. In Greenock and Port Glasgow, Italian fish and chip and ice cream shops were targeted.

The majority of the looters were young men and women, though children were also prominent. According to Lucio Sponza, a 'specialisation along lines of gender and age characterised looting: women took away smaller pieces of furniture (like chairs, electric bulbs and other fittings); men – their pockets full of tobacco and cigarettes – made off with the heavier items (such as tables, mirrors and cash registers); children went for sweets – though chocolate appears to have crossed gender and age boundaries'.[28]

Despite such venality, there were also 'patriotic' motives for these attacks. Robert Douglas recalls how a crowd gathered around an Italian café in Glasgow, shouting: 'Hey, Eyeties! We're here tae put yer windaes in. You're no gonny get stabbed i' the back like Mussolini would dae it. We're gonny fuckin' dae it right i' front of ye!'[29]

This orgy of destruction was repeated in Edinburgh and Leith, with upwards of 3,000 people attacking Italians and their property. *The Scotsman* reported:

> While the Edinburgh police were busy rounding up Italians, anti-Italian feeling found vent in an orgy of window-breaking and looting in different parts of the city . . . Crowds attacked ice-cream and fish and chip shops in Edinburgh and large reinforcements of regular and special police were called out to deal with the demonstrators.

Fifteen arrests were made, and proceedings were possible against several others. Six persons were taken to the out-patient department of the Royal Infirmary, three of them women who were treated for head injuries caused by stones. In Leith Street and Union Place, there were 'riotous scenes after ten o'clock. A crowd of over a thousand gathered, the great majority of them in the role of spectators. The trouble was due largely to irresponsible youths, who started stone-throwing. There are numerous shops in the vicinity occupied by Italians, and before the police were able to get control of the mischief-makers, many plate-glass windows were shattered'. The police were forced to make a number of baton charges: 'Sections of the crowd showed hostility, and in the course of the exciting skirmishes policemen had their helmets knocked off. Patriotic songs were sung when some people who had been arrested were being transferred to a police van. Stragglers lingered about in the streets till the early hours of the morning. Sporadic outbreaks occurred in Stockbridge, Dalry, Portobello and Abbeyhill.'[30]

According to the *Evening News*, the main streets of Leith 'looked in places as if a series of heavy bombs had fallen. In Italian premises not a scrap of glass remaining in single or double-windows: furniture broken; window frames and dressings destroyed and, in a number of cases, the cigarette machines at the entrances damaged beyond repair'.[31] *The Scotsman* pointed out that 'the occupants of some of the shops were British subjects. The proprietor of one well-known restaurant whose premises were among the most seriously damaged in the city, fought throughout the last war in the ranks of a Scottish regiment. Another man, whose premises were subjected to considerable damage, is understood to have two sons at present on active service in the Black Watch'.[32] But this did not dissuade a mob which seemed to have forgotten its previous ties with the Italians in its midst. An eyewitness of the attacks in Ayr recalled how he 'stared in horror as large jars of sweets and bulky packs of cigarettes were handed out to accomplices, who made off with guilty haste. My heart was sick as I saw onetime neighbours, and even friends, sneaking off into the growing darkness of a summer night'.[33]

It was also reported that during the evening the police were engaged in rounding up Italians. At the headquarters in Picardy Place there was constant coming and going of motor cars and between 80 and 100 were detained. Again, *The Scotsman* was sympathetic to their plight:

> A large number of the Italians have spent many years in the city, and have families born and brought up in Scotland. Numerous Italians have become naturalized and are respected British citizens. It is understood that only those who have been resident in Scotland for a comparatively limited period have so far been detained.

Secretary of State Tom Johnston 'strongly deprecated the mob violence'. But still, more than 200 Italians were rounded up in Glasgow, and women and children carrying suitcases crowded the passages of the Central Police Station. Dundee police were also busy rounding up Italians. Regular and Special Constabulary mobile squads were utilised, and most of the Italians were taken from bed. Cameras and other items were confiscated. A number of men and women were conveyed to prison, and a large batch of men who had been arrested were taken to an internment camp.

Anti-Italian demonstrations took place outside shop premises in the principal streets of Falkirk. In Glasgow, 38 people were charged for the disturbances, 13 of them in Govan. Lord Provost Dollan declared: 'Citizens should refrain from unlawful acts involving disorder and damage to property. These attacks do not injure Mussolini, but involve the city in expense. We are not going to tolerate hooliganism masquerading as patriotism'.[34]

It would be wrong, therefore, to portray anti-Italian feeling as universal in Scotland. Primo Bosi, restaurateur and member of the Italian *Fascisti* but registered for National Service, may have been fined £1 for possessing an automatic pistol and rounds of ammunition. However, the following exchange in court showed his case was treated with understanding:

> Depute-Fiscal – there is nothing to connect the revolver [*sic*] with his membership of the *Fascisti*. The accused usually held large sums of money in the house, and he may have had it for protection.

> Sheriff Jameson – Oh yes, protection. The poor Italians need something of this kind after these cowardly assaults of last week.[35]

Three days of correspondence in the *Evening News* expressed disgust at the 'hooligans'.

Nonetheless, correspondents also pointed out that the local Fascists had sent money and gold to support wars of aggression in Abyssinia and Albania. According to Lucio Sponza, the social research organisation Mass Observation had found widespread ambivalence about the aliens in their midst: 'The Italians were quiet, peace-loving, hence likeable, even charming, individually; but that quality is also the result of their innate laziness, which at time of war means cowardice, hence they deserve contempt.'[36]

In fact, anti-Italian sentiment was not a recent phenomenon. The memoirs of Eugenio D'Agostino, who ran the Royal Café in Edinburgh, relate incidences of drunken violence from his customers, including one infamous occasion just after the First World War (when Italy was on Britain's side), when a crowd of sailors appeared outside the café 'armed with sticks, stones, bottles and some with bricks'. Renzi Serafini, who was born in Hawick in 1915, refers to 'the hammerings that our fathers had before the war when we had fish and chip shops and people used to come in and knock the hell out of you'. Wendy Ugolini writes: 'The wartime aggression focused on the Italian population did not emerge from a vacuum but was rooted in a pre-existent antagonism towards and categorisation of Italians as "dirty" foreigners.'[37]

In Scotland, contempt had turned to hatred and outright violence. For Sponza, 'the intensity of violence was less related to the number of Italian shops, and Italian presence generally, than it was to the economic and socially depressed conditions'. Added to this was the virulence of John Cormack's sectarian boot boys: 'One element which was considered instrumental to the viciousness of the Edinburgh mob was the fierce anti-Roman Catholic sentiment which had been bellowed for some time by the Protestant Action Society'.[38]

There thus had begun a dark period of internment and deportation whose greatest tragedy was the sinking in July 1940 of ss *Arandora Star* by a German U-Boat, with the loss of nearly 700 lives, many of them German and Italian internees. Those Italian women left behind in Scotland were victims of discrimination. A woman relocated to Peebles recalled: 'I don't think the Italians were allowed to walk about the streets at night after eight o'clock. Even my sister and the rest of the Italian girls, we were never allowed to go out and play in the streets or anything like that. We were kept indoors. Because we were getting a lot of verbal abuse even in Peebles, of course.'[39] Other women recalled being ejected from their cottage in Blair Atholl.

That said, the myth of 'good Italians' fallen victim to geopolitics does hide the reality of the *Fasci di Scozia*. Terri Colpi provocatively remarks that in many cases, those who expressed the view 'I had nothing to do with Fascism' or 'My father had nothing to do with Fascism' were 'the sons of *Fasci* leaders, often men who were lost on the *Arandora Star*'.[40] And there were those Italian Scots who had resisted 'peaceful penetration'. Charles Forte, born in Italy in 1908, recalled: 'Although close members of my family were still living in Italy, I knew perfectly well whom I wanted to win the war.'[41] A small number of Italian Scots even died fighting Mussolini's troops. Others who could not fight their brothers – sometimes literally – served in the Pioneer Corps, which provided what Ugolini calls 'an alternative site of Italianness in Britain during the war'. She concludes thus on the place of this Italian contribution to the anti-Fascist war: 'The general negativity surrounding the pioneers is linked again to the concept of the good Italian, whereby those who helped support the British war effort in any form have since been criticised or diminished within dominant discourse.'[42]

3

Scotland for Franco

Daniel Gray's book and TV series, *Homage to Caledonia*, have confirmed the image many have of Scotland and the Spanish Civil War: the uplifting story of a relatively large number of deeply committed and courageous Scots who volunteered to fight for democracy and socialism against General Francisco Franco and his Fascist allies.[1] Here, we do not wish to deny or denigrate such commitment: if 549 Scots volunteered for the Republic (including a former Blackshirt from Dumfries), we know of only one Scot, a Seaforth Highlander from the Black Isle, who ended up fighting in Franco's Moorish *regulares*.[2] But more light remains to be shed on that smaller, yet still vocal, minority in Scotland who chose to support the Nationalist side. Gray's brief chapter on 'Scots for Franco' does not draw on archival sources or recent secondary literature. Moreover, his book passes over the crucial, albeit not universal, connection between religious background and Scottish attitudes to Spain. To help rectify this, I have chosen the case of Professor Charles Saroléa and his campaign against the 'Red' Duchess of Atholl (who is herself only mentioned twice in Gray's book). The case of Saroléa offers insights into the network of Francoist sympathisers in Scotland and the limits of their influence in a country deeply divided on religious lines. The anti-Bolshevik professor's intervention in the debate on Spain must also be considered in relation to appeasement and the ultimate fate of Fascism.

The Wraith of Saroléa

Charles Saroléa was born in Belgium in 1870 and went on to study philology at various European universities. In 1894, he became the first lecturer in French at Edinburgh University, and in 1918, its first

Professor. Between 1901 and 1953 he was consul for Belgium in Scotland, although in 1920 he adopted British nationality. Saroléa claimed to know more than 20 languages. His huge apartment at 21–22 Royal Terrace held a private library of over 200,000 volumes: the largest, he typically claimed, in the British Empire. G.K. Chesterton marvelled at the 'Wraith of Saroléa':

> Dr Saroléa, that fiery Flemish professor of French, is certainly one of the most striking men I have known. Dr Saroléa is one of the most learned linguists in Europe; he learns a new language every week or so. His library is one of the wonders of the world, not to say the monstrosities of the world. When last I saw him he gave me the impression of buying the neighbouring houses right and left to find room for his library.[3]

Saroléa became editor of *Everyman*, a journal devoted to international understanding which promoted the 'third way' economic doctrine of distributism. An avowed cosmopolitan, Saroléa was in favour of European co-operation and the prevention of war at all costs. With the outbreak of the Great War, he was a vocal opponent of Prussianism, militarism and the Lutheran Church: in 1915, he published *The Curse of the Hohenzollern*. Paradoxically, he defended small nations against aggression rooted in the principle of nationalities.

He was an active propagandist for Belgium, making a long speaking tour of the United States. He promoted the cause of Czech and Slovak independence from Austria and struck up an acquaintance with Edvard Benes and Tomaš Masaryk. He was also a vocal supporter of Poland. But, as his biographer Sam Johnson points out, at the apex of Saroléa's affections stood Imperial Russia, a state he long regarded as his spiritual home: 'the only state capable of safeguarding Europe's spiritual integrity'.[4] In 1916, he published *Europe's Debt to Russia*.

Saroléa welcomed the defeat of the Kaiser and the liberation of Belgium, but he denounced the injustices of the Versailles diktat, which, in his view, only reinvigorated national rivalries and prepared the way for German revenge. After October 1917, the professor was convinced that the foundations of civilisation faced an even greater threat from communism than they did from a Prussianised Europe.

A visit to the land of Lenin only confirmed his worst fears. In *Impressions of Soviet Russia* (1924), this devout Catholic denounced 'the Kingdom of the Anti-Christ'. In a glut of letters to *The Times* and *The Scotsman*, Saroléa attacked the Bolshevik threat and supported those radical right-wing regimes and movements ready to stand up to it.

In 1931, Saroléa resigned from Edinburgh University in protest at what he considered to be its lamentable decline in pedagogical and human standards. He would now devote his apparently inexhaustible energy, wealth and contacts to the geopolitical struggles of the 1930s, establishing very friendly relations with the authorities in Rome and Berlin. For example, in the mid-1930s, Saroléa supported Mussolini's invasion of Abyssinia. In a pamphlet, 'The Case against Sanctions', and a series of letters, he attacked the League of Nations as an instrument of war. His work in the Scottish press was deeply appreciated by the Italian ambassador and, in February 1936, Saroléa was guest of honour at a dinner hosted by the *Fascio di Edinburgo*.

Around this time, Saroléa began a rich correspondence with Lady Marie-Louise Maxwell-Scott, wife of General Sir Walter Maxwell-Scott, great-grandson of the author of *Ivanhoe*. American by birth, Lady Maxwell-Scott had spent much of her life in Europe. Her first husband had been French, which contributed to her keen interest in continental affairs. Her second husband had a vast array of political and personal connections which included the British ambassador to Rome, Sir Eric Drummond. The Lady of Abbotsford seems to have been dazzled by Saroléa's cosmopolitan intellect; she adhered wholeheartedly to his bracing views on Abyssinia and the failure of the League of Nations, and distributed offprints of his letters to *The Scotsman*. In a letter to her on 21 January 1936, he wrote:

> I have embarked on a campaign which is bearing good fruit. And curiously enough, in that campaign I have some of my best fellow workers in the Conservative Party. I also find that ladies are most efficient propagandists and liaison officers. One very influential Conservative lady politician, the Duchess of Atholl, is in daily contact with me.[5]

Indeed, it was on the advice of Lady Maxwell-Scott that the professor sent the Duchess of Atholl his critical examination of the League of Nations Covenant. In his covering letter of 6 January, he wrote to 'my dear Duchess': 'If you ever happen to be in Edinburgh I would be delighted to discuss these matters with you. I would always be delighted to put you up and you would see the largest private Library in the British Empire – some 250,000 volumes, filling 26 rooms'.[6] On 16 January, the duchess replied: 'I shall send it to those Conservative MPs who I believe see things as I do because I feel the letter gives most useful information which very few of us have got'; however, she feared that his criticism of the allocation of mandates would 'play into the hands of those who wish to restore the German Colonies'. The duchess sent copies of his *Scotsman* letters of 8–9 January to 180 MPs, half the Conservative group. On 17 January, Saroléa wrote appreciatively:

> I hope you will not relax in your efforts to fight the policy of sanctions with true Scottish and Highland determination. And please do not forget that just as in this country the driving force behind the policy of sanctions is the hatred of Fascism and the propaganda of the Trade Unions, so the driving forces at Geneva behind sanctions is Comrade Litvinoff and Bolshevik Russia. It was an evil day when Germany left the League, but it was a worse day when the Soviet entered it.[7]

On 24 January, the duchess let him know that 'when I was in the House yesterday, several Members to whom I had sent your letter of January 9th came up and thanked me warmly for it'.[8] That said, even Lady Maxwell-Scott expressed private doubts on the efficacy of Saroléa's interventions. On 26 January she wrote to Paul Morand, the French writer-diplomat and future Vichy ambassador to Bucharest:

> I am very frightened by this English affection for the League of Nations, which will end in driving Italy out of it, if not into the arms of Germany. Can you not begin preaching the reform of the League? We must get something started, we who believe that Italy is useful to us in Europe ... They live on the Moon these dear English, and would not recognise Europe if they met her. You can do so much because you do it lightly. I can send you learned works by a professor of the University of Edinburgh but no-one will read *him*. But his idea is the right one, and could be put otherwise.[9]

It is unsurprising that Saroléa found common ground with the Duchess of Atholl. Born Katherine Stewart-Murray, and Conservative MP for Kinross and West Perthshire since 1923, she had previously been known for her campaigns against slave labour in the Soviet Union, notably through her 1931 book *The Conscription of a People*. She was also alarmed by anti-clerical violence in Spain. For example, on 11 January 1933, she wrote on this subject to her friend the Earl of Glasgow:

> I feel it would be rather inconsistent if our Movement said nothing about what had happened in Spain though fortunately there the Communists do not seem to be actually in power. The Government, however, appears to have taken a very weak line about this burning of churches, in that they have allowed them to take place ... I should, therefore, like to feel that we could talk about what is happening in Spain as an indication of what Communists do all the world over if they are given the chance but I should suggest that it be not too much emphasised for fear that we should be regarded as too much identified with the Roman Catholics.[10]

The duchess confirmed her right-wing credentials by repudiating, in 1935, the National Government whip in protest against the India Bill, which prepared the way for that country's independence. She was also, as we have seen, initially opposed to confronting Mussolini and receptive to Saroléa's robust critique of the League of Nations.

Birth of a Red Duchess

However, in the course of 1936, the duchess moved towards a position of anti-appeasement which would strain to breaking-point her relations with her local Conservative Association as well as occasional allies such as Charles Saroléa. After the remilitarisation of the Rhineland in March 1936, Nazi Germany replaced the Soviet Union as what the duchess considered to be the main threat to British interests. In May, after close study of an unexpurgated version of *Mein Kampf*, she wrote to Prime Minister Stanley Baldwin that 'Germany is the only serious danger to peace in Europe'.[11] On 6 August 1936, the duchess wrote to Saroléa:

> Surely liberty is so precious that we must be ready to fight for it if we cannot preserve it otherwise? It is inconceivable to think that our people would submit to living under Nazi rule if they had any idea

of what it meant. And if liberty can be preserved, civilisation need not be destroyed as people are so ready to say, surely so long as there is liberty, the human mind can restore civilisation, but if liberty goes, everything goes?[12]

In his last extant letter to the duchess, on 17 August, the professor expressed his concern at the content of her letters to *The Scotsman*, *Daily Telegraph* and *Morning Post*: 'You are treading on very dangerous ground and you are expounding views which are not only dangerous, but which I think to be erroneous ... You do an injustice to the Soviet government in comparing their propaganda to that of the Nazis. The Moscow propagandists are incomparably the greater artists'.[13]

The outbreak of the Spanish Civil War in July 1936, and the involvement of Nazi Germany and Fascist Italy, confirmed the duchess in her views on the threat to peace in Europe. At first, her involvement was humanitarian, concerned mainly with the plight of refugees, and in the autumn she joined the All-Party Committee for Spanish Relief. Early in 1937, she made a tour of Republican Spain, surveying the havoc caused amongst the civilian population by Luftwaffe bombing. This visit led her to criticise the one-sided effect of the Anglo-French policy of non-intervention in the conflict. As Stuart Ball points out, 'her concern thus evolved from the charitable to the political, and from the particular case of Spain to the wider issue of the appeasement of dictators in general'.[14]

Her pro-Republican sympathies earned Katharine Atholl the sobriquet of 'Red Duchess' and outraged erstwhile friends. On 23 June 1937, Arnold Lunn, a pioneer of alpine skiing who had just reported from 'White' Spain for *The Tablet*, reproached her for accepting 'the hospitality of the persecutors of the Catholic Church'.[15] She also attracted the ire of a fellow Conservative MP, Captain Archibald Maule Ramsay, who wrote on 6 September 1937:

You are espousing the cause of the Reds in Spain. The Communists, and other homicidal extremists in the 'Government' (which does not govern), are a small fraction as the Socialists are in our National Government, – BUT whereas our Socialist fraction keeps its proper place – in Spain the Red minority seized the whole machine by murder and terrorism.[16]

Ramsay failed to convince the Duke of Atholl to join his United Christian Front Committee, 'formed to co-operate with the Roman Catholic Church to present a United Christian Front against the Red Menace to Christianity'. On 4 October, the duchess rebutted Ramsay's version of events in 'Red' Spain:

> My opinion is that it was Anarchists far more than Communists who were responsible for the violent acts committed on the Government side in the early days and if you know anything of the Anarchist creed you will know that it is diametrically opposed to the Communist one and that Anarchists can therefore never be under the domination of Moscow which I know is what the word 'red' is intended to convey.[17]

On 10 November 1937, Ramsay wrote to the duchess:

> I fear there is little use in my discussing any of these subjects with you as I regard all your sources of information as tainted, and the foreigners to whom you look for information, as the scum of Europe ... As long as you run with that pack, I fear there is so great a gulf between us that you are not likely to listen to my advice and I am certainly not likely to listen to you.[18]

In her last letter to Ramsay, on 12 November, she asked: 'Can you not see that a new and much more immediate danger has arisen to threaten the peace of Europe than the days when you were sitting under my Chairmanship on the Russian Trade Sub-Committee?'[19]

The Francoists Riposte

The 'Red Duchess' also came up against the opposition of the Friends of National Spain (FNS), an association formed under the leadership of Lord Phillimore to 'combat the flood of propaganda emanating from Valencia and Moscow'. On 6 May 1937, a Nationalist representative in London, Alfonso de Olano, informed Jacobo Fitz-James Stuart, the Duke of Berwick and Alba, then residing in Seville, that this grouping of businessmen, journalists and peers of the realm would provide 'rapid and effective information to counter Red propaganda, which becomes more and more tendentious and calumnous with each passing day'. De Olano urged *querido Jimmy* to join this battle for British minds 'as soon as possible'.[20]

In its founding statement, signed by, among others, the travel mogul Sir Henry Lunn and Conservative MPs Sir Nairne Stewart-Sandeman and Henry Page Croft, the FNS declared:

> Every cause for which Englishmen of all classes and all creeds have fought in the past – liberty of conscience, the sanctity of human life, the maintenance of public order, and the freedom of lawful trade – are being fought for in Spain by the armies of the Nationalist forces ...The conditions of normal and decent life disappeared in July 1936 and no effort has been made to restore them.[21]

In a letter to Croft, the duchess refuted their claims:

> I can only say that in April I was in Valencia, Madrid and Barcelona, and that though in the first streets and hotels were crowded on account of the many refugees who had poured in from the insurgent territory, and in the second selling was pretty continuous, perfect order prevailed in all three towns without any display of force.[22]

The Protestant churches in government territory, she claimed, had not been interfered with and many masses were now being said daily in the three principal towns. Franco's advance was thanks to the help of Moors, Foreign Legionaries, and Italian and German aeroplanes. She contrasted this with the robust health of Republican territory: around Valencia there were good harvests and steady production of munitions. In conclusion, she pointed to the dangers posed by Nationalist guns at the gates of Gibraltar, and the occupation of Majorca: 'Are these the acts of a friend? Those who ignore them, as do the signatories of the letter may indeed be the Friends of National Spain, but are they quite acting as the Friends of Britain?'[23]

Her vocal support for the Spanish Republic would also trigger war with Saroléa. The professor had supported the Spanish Nationalist cause from the outset. In January 1937, he organised a meeting of 150 people at his house for Eleonora Tennant, the pro-Franco Scottish author of *Spanish Journey*. He then lent his support to the Scottish branch of FNS, whose honorary president was Lady Maxwell-Scott. In early 1937, Saroléa made an ill-fated tour of Nationalist Spain, falling seriously ill in Algeciras. But this did not shake his convictions.

Saroléa's sympathies were by now explicitly pro-Fascist. He cultivated close ties with the Nazi authorities. On 7 March 1934, Rolf Hoffmann, of the Nazi Party's propaganda department in Munich, wrote to Saroléa:

You will remember me in the 'Brown House', Munich, where I intend to come over to England end of March and most likely, if time permits, I shall go up to Edinburgh, for 2 or 3 days as I wish to see Scotland. I found our conversation most useful and I think we could have more talks in peace. I want to hand over to you some very interesting books about our movement for your library.[24]

On 20 August 1936, after the triumph of the Berlin Olympics, Baroness van der Goltz wrote to the professor:

We have so much work to do in our country that a war would be only suicide for us. During the Olympic Games one felt here everywhere the ardent desire of the Germans to make their foreign guest feel confident and the best way to understand each other is to learn to know each other? We hope therefore that the Olympic idea will survive and that these past days will have helped the 'Youth of the World' to come to a good international understanding and to serve by it the great cause of peace.[25]

Saroléa would become a willing host for such members of the Nazi elite. On 21 July 1937, T.P. Conwell-Evans, secretary of the Anglo-German Fellowship, wrote to Saroléa:

Frau Schlitter, the wife of the the First Secretary of the German Embassy, and Baroness von Puckler are motoring to Scotland on Saturday next and will be touring the country for about ten days. They may be accompanied for the first three days by Baron von Hadlen, a young German who is ADC to Herr Himmler, Head of the Police and of the Black-Unified Guard in Germany. Frau Schlitter is most charming and is the daughter of a large land-owning family in East Prussia. It would be nice if they could see you when they come to Edinburgh.[26]

In August 1937, Saroléa attended the Nuremburg rally – he was given 'the best seats in the house' – and was introduced to Adolf

Hitler. On his return to Edinburgh, he gave a series of lectures on the new Germany. One of them, entitled 'The Scottish Origins of the Nazi Religion', was hosted by the Edinburgh University Scottish Nationalist Society. Professor Saroléa told his audience:

The philosophy of Nazism, the theory of the dictatorial state, was discovered and formulated a hundred years ago by the greatest Scotsman of his time, namely Carlyle. Subsequently, it was elaborated and developed by another famous Scotsman, the descendant of an illustrious line of Scottish forebears, namely Houston Stewart Chamberlain. There was not one of the doctrines on which the Nazi religion has been built up which was not found either in Carlyle or in Chamberlain.[27]

Ideas of enlightened despotism and aristocratic race, he claimed, had roots in the Scottish genius. However, the Saroléa papers also indicate that these lectures were 'boycotted' by parts of the Scottish press.

In January 1938, it was the turn of the Maxwell-Scotts to visit behind the Francoist lines. Already, in *The Border Telegraph*, Lady Maxwell-Scott had informed the readers of Red terror in Barcelona:

The fact can no longer be denied that all the bodies of those citizens killed by the Marxist committees were horribly mutilated before death. Quantities of knitting needles alone, to mention only one form of torture, have been removed from the eye-sockets of the victims in the presence of this crowd.[28]

A week later, A.L. Cochrane of the First British Ambulance Unit, replied: 'Did Her Ladyship really see those knitting needles? . . . It is difficult in England to see through the "Red Gold" mist, and too easy to take one's own conclusions ready made from Unionist bazaars.'[29]

This time, the Maxwell-Scotts could see Spain from themselves, or at least behind Nationalist lines. On arrival, Lady Maxwell-Scott sent Saroléa a postcard from the Rock Hotel, Gibraltar: 'It is simply *heavenly* here. Bright warm sun. We start for Seville on Friday and I'll write you later on. If you kept a clipping of any of the Red Lady's speeches do save them for me until I come back.'[30] However, General Maxwell-Scott would also fall seriously ill during this sojourn.

Pro-Fascist activity continued unabated. In the January 1938 issue of the *Anglo-German Review*, Saroléa again stoutly championed the Scottish origin of Nazism. Like Hitler, Thomas Carlyle had never wavered in his hatred of the parliamentary system and always believed in the saving virtue of dictatorship, as seen in his *Shooting Niagara* and *The Nigger Question*. Like the Nazi leader, Carlyle had never ceased to challenge the economic interpretation of history, while remaining a demophile and socialist. Finally, Carlyle believed in 'Divine Mission of the German Race', as illustrated in his biography of Frederick the Great and especially his book on the Kings of Norway.[31] He was joined as one of the major prophets of the Nazi Religion by another famous Scotsman, Houston Stewart Chamberlain. (That said, Saroléa's theory did not receive the complete support of the Nazis. In reply to the question, 'Was Carlyle the first Nazi?', the *Deutsch-Englische Hefte* replied: 'National-Socialism is our own original creation in spite of Carlyle, or, rather, because of him').[32]

As part of the pro-Nazi cause, Saroléa also played host to Douglas Chandler, an American journalist ruined by the Wall Street crash who had eventually settled in Germany, becoming a Nazi and correspondent of the *National Geographic*. On 5 October 1937, Chandler wrote to Saroléa: 'I suppose you are now back in Edinburgh, installed in that beautiful library of yours, remembering the *Parteitag* at *Nürnberg* as an early-autumn phantasie!' In November 1937, Saroléa replied to Chandler: 'I am sure that the Scottish and the London Press would listen to the evidence of a distinguished American.' On 4 January 1938, Chandler informed Saroléa that he would be taking the boat from Hamburg to Leith to counter anti-Nazi propaganda:

> I have visited Labour Camps in various quarters and talked with their happy, healthful inmates. I have visited Concentration Camps and have observed that those incarcerated there are far better cared for than the occupants of most places of detention in outland countries. I am in a position to refute most of the current lies that are being broadcast by Jewry and its non-Jewish team-mates.

Chandler's meeting in Royal Terrace seems, however, to have been a rather mitigated success. On 18 January, Saroléa informed Rolf Hoffmann: 'Unfortunately, public opinion in this country is terribly poisoned and prejudiced by the hostile propaganda especially in

106   FASCIST SCOTLAND

Scotland'.[33] On 26 January, the professor wrote to C.E. Carroll: 'Mr Chandler is an ardent Nazi, but he soon discovered that the majority of his audience, which pelted him with irrelevant questions, had not been by any means convinced or converted, although Mr Chandler was a very persuasive speaker.'

Nevertheless, on 30 January 1938, Chandler was upbeat in a letter from Germany:

I am happy that some of your guests of the 19th have experienced satisfaction with my address on Naziland. If it should chance that there were seven in the audience, who received good impressions regarding Germany, and these seven should pass on the good word to seven others ... and that geometrical progress of good influence were to be carried forward seven times, the total number of those brought around to the truth would amount to 823,543 (not far from a million). Such are the responsibilities of the spoken word ... and on this principle is based the subversive work of our highly intelligent and organized enemy!

On 9 February 1938, he wrote again:

One great 'booster' for Germany (and a recent convert to the ASIATIC-TERMITE-DANGER) is Sir Alexander Walker – *der Besitzer von dem weltberühmten Johnnie Walker'*. I had always pictured whiskey-magnates as purple-jowled bailiffs of Beelzebub. Imagine my surprise in finding this man (whom you probably know, as he is a Scot with a most gorgeous Scottish accent) a highly cultured, distinguished person with charm galore. We were entertained in their home, and found both Sir Alexander and Lady Walker militant defenders of poor, abused Germany.[34]

In March 1938, Saroléa was back in the Third Reich. But, as the postcard from the Maxwell-Scotts in Gibraltar indicated, the declarations of 'Red Kitty' worried her former friends. After all, the Duchess of Atholl's noisy activism had continued that summer with the publication of her short book, *Searchlight on Spain*, a Penguin Special dedicated 'to all those Spaniards who are fighting or toiling for national independence and democratic government against tremendous odds'. The book dealt with the extreme poverty and intransigence of the ruling classes which had led to the Popular Front's electoral victory. It then demolished Francoist propaganda about the beginning of the rebellion and the conduct of the war: the coup had, she argued, been planned since 1934 with the connivance of Hitler and Mussolini. The duchess concluded by describing the threat posed by a Francoist victory to Britain's strategic interests. She demanded that the Spanish Republic be allowed to buy arms to defend itself. The book was an immediate bestseller, its three editions selling over 300,000 copies. It would also be translated into French, German and Spanish. This publishing sensation incensed the Francoists. On 23 July 1938, Arnold Lunn wrote to the Duchess of Atholl, denouncing the 'inaccuracies' in her account of the Spanish situation:

> It will be difficult to reach all those who have read your sixpenny book, but you owe it to your Father, whose prestige you have attempted to exploit for propaganda purposes, to make public amends for these breaches of a code which historians respect and which propagandists too often defy.[35]

The Scots for Franco joined the propaganda war with varying success. On 7 April 1938, FNS held a meeting at the St Andrew's Halls, Glasgow, on the theme 'The Truth About Spain! The Truth About Intervention!' Already, the socialist group on Glasgow Town Council had been bitterly split over letting out the hall. On 21 March, Bailie Thomas Kerr, Labour representative for Fairfield, had moved that the hall not be let, arguing that 'the point you are considering is whether or not you are going to give an opportunity to an association who are avowedly out to justify the brutalisation of Franco in Spain, his butchery of the non-combatant population – a man whose hands are reeking with the blood of innocent women and children'.[36] The opposition to Kerr's motion showed that the left–right dividing line when it came to Spain could become blurred. Among his fiercest opponents was Bailie Alexander McGregor, Labour representative for exchange and father of the Scottish treasurer of the FNS. He declared: '"If I did not believe that Franco was a democrat I would not be supporting him"... Several interjections ... "Away with you." ... "He is a murderer" ... "Baby-killer"'.[37] The meeting was eventually authorised in the name of freedom of speech: among those approving of the meeting was the very Catholic, and Labour, Patrick

Dollan. At St Andrew's Halls, 1,500 packed in to hear Arnold Lunn. He was confronted with continuous interruptions, clenched fists and attempts at singing the 'Internationale'.

The FNS could therefore attract a crowd, but not necessarily a friendly one. On 12 May, they took the battle to Perth, with a well-attended meeting organised by Captain Luttman-Johnson. James Barrie, of the *Courier*, sent the Duke of Atholl an account of this meeting.[38] The first to speak was Sir Nairne Stewart Sandeman MP:

> They used to hear – and still heard – a great deal about Nero and his murders, etc. He had made a very careful investigation and had discovered that Nero certainly had not murdered more than 500 – there were many more savage persons in the world than Nero had been.
>
> A voice: What about the priests of the Spanish inquisition?
>
> Yes or the way they did things in Russia. They murdered them there in tens of thousands and very little was said about it.

When challenged on civilian victims of the bombing of Guernica, Stewart-Sandeman retorted that they had been killed by land-mines left by retreating Reds. As for the drama of refugees: 'He had been talking to a holy father in London about some of the Basque children and the holy father had told him that every one of the nurses was frightened because they had broken every window in the place.'

The next speaker was Sir Walter Maxwell-Scott, who began by saying that 'he and General Franco had attended a senior officers' course at Versailles some years ago. He never thought that in those three weeks that he associated with Franco that a civil war would come and that General Franco would take a leading part'. He then referred to a three weeks' visit he had paid to the war-front in Spain: 'He had had a very good time. He simply went where he wanted . . . What prevented him getting to Madrid was the arrival of the first International Brigade – 15,000 splendid men from all over Europe.' In Spanish Morocco, Maxwell-Scott had found that 'Franco was adored by the Moors and that they called him the Holy Man.' As for accusations of Moorish atrocities, he said: 'Possibly Moors liked a bit of loot. He had also known British soldiers who liked a bit of loot.' There was, he argued, 'no colour bar in Spain': the use of Moorish troops against the Republic was akin to 'the Welsh coming to the aid of Northern England against the South of

England'. Nevertheless, hecklers demanded answers on Francoist atrocities:

> The interruptions continued for nearly five minutes at the end of which the speaker lost his temper and referred to his hecklers at the back of the hall as 'scum'. There was another outcry and one black-shirted member of the audience advanced towards the platform asking for an apology.

Maxwell-Scott apologised for his language and finished his intervention soon afterwards.

The last speaker was Arthur Loveday, former president of the British Chamber of Commerce in Spain. He explained to his audience that 'in 1931 there began in Spain a revolution organised for years by the efficient and careful work of the Comintern of Russia. This Revolution had been aided very much by the organisation called the Oriental Freemasonry of Spain ... In 1936 the people of Spain rose in a counter-revolution led fortunately by General Franco'. Loveday recounted his own trip to Spain: 'He had also travelled by air for many hundreds of miles. Why? Because the roads were not safe. Soldiers were holding up tourists and relieving them of their cash and valuables. Wherever he looked he saw the sickle and the hammer (cheers)'. Franco's war was against those whose only religion was the principles of Karl Marx and class warfare. The Reds, he said, had confiscated British property, which provoked 'Shouts of whose money? And serve them right!' 'You have no compassion' said Loveday. 'You fill me with disgust.' After a number of questions had been asked, a resolution approving of the views of the Association was passed by a majority.

On 17 June 1938, three arrests followed a meeting at the Usher Hall in Edinburgh. According to *The Scotsman*, it attracted 600 people including several opponents: 'A large number of stewards, who wore red and yellow badges – the Nationalist colours – were in attendance and these pounced upon the interruptors and ejected the most persistent of them.' One of the speakers, Sir Henry Lunn, declared: 'Would to God we had a Gladstone today to rouse the nation to the enormity of what had happened in Spain. Nero's persecution was a light thing compared with what had happened there.' Dr Denzil Batchelor, a journalist just back from Spain, remarked on the destroyed churches and disappeared nuns and priests in Red territory, and refuted accusations of massacres in Franco territory. At the end of the meeting, one Commandant Mary Allen, in police uniform, moved a resolution supporting 'Franco and the Spanish people' that was carried with only 20 hands held up for the contrary. Meanwhile, at the Mound, the Labour Party and Trades Council had organised an assembly against the supporters of Spanish Fascist brutality. There was also a Communist procession outside the Usher Hall: demonstrators carried placards reading 'Franco, Hitler, Mussolini: enemies of religion'. This procession linked up with the Mound protestors to form a crowd of 800.[39]

Such events pointed to the numerical superiority, as well as the aggressiveness, of Republican supporters in Scotland. On 24 July 1937, the Republic's London ambassador had reported to Valencia that 'the only individual, according to all my information, who behaves in Glasgow like a true adversary of the Republican Regime is called Rafael Jorro'.[40] This contrasted with five in Cardiff, three in Newcastle and four in Liverpool. Scotland was therefore seen as one of its securest bastions of support. The Glasgow consulate was active in intervening to stop the departure of ships carrying fuel and food for Nationalist-controlled ports such as Las Palmas and Seville.[41] At the same time, it worked closely with the numerous aid committees which had sprung up across Scotland.

Solidarity with Republican Spain was not immune to the stresses and suspicions of the Civil War. This was illustrated by a conflict in Dundee's Basque Children's Committee. The Republic's consul in Dundee, Villa, was accused of 'disturbing work' at the Montrose home for Basque children. Villa was a road haulier who had lived for 22 years in Dundee, but seems to have been loathed by a young Communist schoolteacher, Kathleen McColgan. Villa was accused of being a Francoist agent: Fascist newspapers had been left lying around the children's home; the *Courier* had photographed *los niños de Montrose* making the Fascist salute; Villa had decorated one of his cars with Nationalist colours; and he had even expressed the desire to go the Basque country now occupied by the enemy. The Glasgow consulate launched an investigation and, on 22 December 1937, could report to William Roberts, leader of the Basque children's relief campaign:

Mr Villa only left a Fascist newspaper with the children so that they could look at the photos, contained in it, of places familiar to them. The photo published in the *Courier*, of the 21 October, has no Fascist significance whatsoever. The children are only holding out their hands for sweets. Mr Villa desires to go to Bilbao only for the purpose of seeing his mother, who is 80 years old, and has been taken ill in this city ... He has never flown the Fascist colours on his car. Many people who know Mr Villa well, testify that he is a Liberal and loyal republican and have not the least suspicion of his sincerity.[42]

Miss McColgan was asked to leave on a majority of votes by the committee.

During this period, the FNS recognised the influence of the Duchess of Atholl and maintained contact with her via the Duke of Alba, now senior Nationalist representative to London, on the issue of the repatriation of Spanish children, notably to the Basque country. Nevertheless, the iconic Red Duchess was a woman that the FNS had to stop. On 19 June 1938, Lady Maxwell-Scott exerted her 'friendly tyranny' on Saroléa: 'Last year you said you would show up the Red Duchess and that she would lose nothing by waiting. Please do it at once. Her book is a filthy collection of red propaganda.'[43] Saroléa concurred: 'I think the book of the Duchess of Atholl is very important and will do infinite mischief.'[44] He informed one O'Neill of the press office of the Nationalist legation in Victory House, London: 'I have started at once my answer to our Scottish Tory Bolshevik and I have interrupted a book on Czechoslovakia which I am trying to finish.'[45] In July 1938, he wrote of the Red Lady and *Searchlight on Spain*:

That book is all the more mischievous and dangerous because instead of being published at the usual price of 10/6, she has published it in a Bolshevik series at the price of 6d which is being circulated in hundreds of thousands of copies ... I shall try to have my book published as soon as possible as, in the meantime, the Red Duchess is doing an enormous amount of harm. She has also been addressing Mass Meetings in London, in Paris and in Madrid. Indeed, it seems to me that the dear Scottish Duchess is completely losing her balance of mind ... Alas! The anti-Franco propaganda in Great Britain is terrifyingly active and efficient, whereas the pro-Franco propaganda is lamentably inefficient.[46]

In September he wrote: 'I hope that my book will help to get "Red Kitty" unseated.'[47]

Saroléa's chance would come with the Munich crisis. Since the outbreak of the Spanish Civil War, the Duchess of Atholl's relations with local Conservatism had deteriorated dramatically. On 1 May 1937, the Association secretary, James Paton, had written to her: 'You have had, I am sure, a very interesting time in Spain, sometimes rather exciting and performed a very humane duty. Unfortunately, I hear rumours of very strong objections from constituents.' The duchess replied that 'I think public opinion down here is turning a good deal since the destruction of Guernica', although she did make some acknowledgement of the opposition: 'You have to remember that Catholics are strongly against the Spanish Government. Is opposition coming from any other quarter?' Paton informed her that powerful opponents were Colonel Rupert Dawson, a Roman Catholic, who was 'very bitter' about her letter in the *Glasgow Evening News*. Another grandee, Sir Kay Muir, was 'a strong supporter of the Insurgents in Spain, as he says he would rather have Spain under a Hitler or Mussolini than under Communistic rule . . . I would humbly request you to restrict your activities and support of the Spanish Government meantime'.[48]

Indeed, her views on Spain had alienated the Roman Catholics in the Association, notably executive member Colonel Rupert Dawson, who were receptive to Francoist propaganda. Dawson was helped in his oppositional efforts by the Archbishop of Edinburgh and John Campbell, secretary of the Catholic Union, who played an active role in distributing pro-Franco propaganda published by the Spanish Press Service. Indeed, as Tom Gallagher has shown, the Catholic Church in Scotland was active in support of Franco: *The Glasgow Observer and Catholic Herald* was an unquestioning mouthpiece for Nationalist propaganda, while, at the shrine of Carfin, near Motherwell, up to 70,000 people attended masses of reparation for the crimes committed against the Church in Spain.[49] On 1 June 1937, the archbishop asked Campbell to provide Dawson with information on the civil war: 'He certainly will have sufficient ammunition to make an impression on the Red battalions. Whether he will be able to use the information with sufficient skill to silence the unbalanced Duchess in Perthshire remains to be seen.'[50] This information was used for a pamphlet rebutting her *Impressions of Spain*. On 26

June, Campbell congratulated Dawson: 'I think your publication has served a very useful purpose and, so far as I can see, the Duchess of Atholl and other kindred spirits have a monopoly of Press and platform so far as Spain is concerned.'[51] However, opposition to the duchess's foreign policy stance went beyond Catholic circles to include the anti-Bolshevik right. What's more, writes Stuart Ball, 'her identification with foreign affairs, her overseas missions, and her political and social sojourns in London had the effect of eroding her local links, so that in some eyes she took on the appearance of an outsider, careless of local interests and indifferent to the concerns of the parish pump'.[52]

On 22 February 1938, after Anthony Eden's resignation as Foreign Secretary, the Duchess of Atholl had abstained in the vote of confidence. In April 1938, she had resigned the government whip 'on account of the failure of the Government to take adequate steps to secure the withdrawal of Italian troops from Spain before the signature of the Italian pact, or to take action with other Powers to safeguard the peace in Central Europe and on the shores of the North Sea'.[53] Chamberlain replied to her: 'I am satisfied that the interests of fair play have not suffered through the policy of non-intervention in Spain.'[54]

This was a decision which placed her outside the party. Her position was further weakened when, on 15 May, she spoke at a large rally of the International Peace Campaign in support of 'Arms for Spain' in Kelvin Hall, Glasgow. This rally, attended by 4,000 people and chaired by Alan Boase, Professor of French at Glasgow University, concluded with the singing of the 'Internationale'. Such details were reported by pro-Franco sympathiser Helen H. Strachan to Colonel Dawson as evidence of 'the great harm that is being done by your MP'.[55] On 27 May, the executive council of the Conservative Association voted overwhelmingly not to re-adopt the duchess at the next general election.

On 27 September 1938, at the height of the Munich crisis, Saroléa wrote to Lady Maxwell-Scott: 'The future is very dark. It is almost fantastic to think that at the bidding of international Jews and Bolshevism, Europe is going to be driven to war in defence of a Czechoslovakia which has ceased to exist and which no French or British Army can possibly save.'[56] For Saroléa, as for the vast majority of political opinion, relinquishing the Sudetenland to Germany was the only means by which European peace could be guaranteed, and the world saved from a hideous catastrophe.

The duchess's outspoken views on the 'shameful surrender' of Munich, issued in a leaflet on 7 November, did nothing to permit the reversal of the Association's decision, which was confirmed at its annual general meeting. The Duke of Atholl resigned from the presidency of the Association, and, on 24 November, his wife announced that she had also resigned and would fight a by-election as an Independent, saying: 'this is supremely a moment in which country must come before party'.[57] In order to provoke a by-election, she applied for the Chiltern Hundreds, and on 1 December the writ was moved in the House of Commons. Reluctantly, the local Liberal candidate, Coll MacDonald, who had polled a creditable 10,000 votes in 1935, agreed to step aside to avoid splitting the anti-government vote. The recent victory of an Independent in the Bridgewater by-election seemed to show the potency of a 'popular front' electoral strategy. But there were limits to the breadth of the front and the 'Redness' of the duchess. Certainly, on 28 November, the Soviet ambassador to London, Ivan Maisky, sent a message of goodwill: 'Congratulations on your courage in applying for the Chiltern Hundreds! I hope very much that such a determined and straightforward attitude will reap the victory it so richly deserves.'[58] At the same time, the duchess declined the Communist offer of support: 'I have no sympathy with the principles of the Communist Party.'[59]

The Unionist candidate, William McNair-Snadden, a prominent breeder of pedigree Shorthorn cattle, robustly defended the foreign policy of Neville Chamberlain:

> The peoples of the world want peace. After Munich a universal sigh and prayer of thankfulness rose. The policy of Mr Chamberlain may take years to bear fruit, but some time the effort must be made, and now, when the minds of men, having glimpsed the awful horrors of war, are receptive to the idea, is the time to plant the seed of collaboration, and to hope that as the years pass it will grow into a fine flowering plant of lasting peace in Europe.[60]

It was with this by-election that the Spanish Civil War seemed to be transposed to Perthshire and part of the Scottish aristocracy. Lady

Maxwell-Scott was aware of the weakness of her forces elsewhere in Scotland. In late October, she wrote to Saroléa:

> In Glasgow it has been a terrible struggle for, except for the Catholics, there is no support; on the contrary, a very well organised opposition which does not stop at violence. We were lucky last night, on the Rectorship platform, to have only celluloid balls and lumps of sugar thrown at us, as we expected tomatoes at least![61]

Nevertheless, the struggle continued. Saroléa's counterblast, *Daylight on Spain*, completed in August, was guaranteed against loss by the Marquis of Bute. To rival the Penguin cheap edition, it was published in Hutchinson's sixpenny series. Hutchinson had rejected the title *Searchlight on a Duchess* as 'offensive'. The initial title, *A Scottish Duchess lost in the Jungle of Spain*, was not considered snappy enough. The cover proclaimed: 'One of the greatest authorities on Spain gives a complete and crushing answer to the statements and views of the Duchess of Atholl'. This denunciation of a 'Comintern conspiration' was graced by an introduction by the Comte de Saint-Aulaire, former French ambassador to London and Madrid, now a supporter of the far right *Croix de Feu*. Saint-Aulaire wrote of the conflict:

> It is a gigantic duel in which, under the Sign of the Cross and the Spanish colours on the one side, and the Sign of the Sickle and the Hammer on the other, Order and Anarchy, Humanity and Barbarism, Good and Evil, Christ and Antichrist, are brought face to face.[62]

The retired diplomat expressed alarm at the 'epidemic' of aristocrats like the Duchess of Atholl converting to the cause of the 'Reds', while praising Saroléa's book as 'an excellent preservative from this strange disease'.[63] The professor was not just a great scholar and philosopher, but an apostle.

In *Daylight on Spain*, Saroléa endeavoured to subject the facts and conclusions of the duchess's book to 'the generally accepted tests of historical criticism and to the more acid tests of plain common sense and political realities'.[64] With her, he argued, the Conservative flag merely covered Bolshevik merchandise. The former enemy of the Reds had become their ally, a useful 'decoy duck'. The triumph of the Spanish Republic she defended and misrepresented would be one further step by the 'Revolutionary Demagogue' towards its ideal of oriental despotism. On the deadly menace of Communism, Saroléa concluded with typically apocalyptic verve: 'there is no possible recovery from an insidious deadly poison, from persistent loss of blood, from the inoculation of a virulent microbe. Death may be slower, but it is absolutely certain'.[65]

According to Sam Johnson, 'Saroléa's omissions from the text of *Daylight on Spain* are of far more interest to the historian'.[66] On reading the manuscript, Sir Walter Maxwell-Scott suggested that he add 'Jewish to Bolshevik influences . . . Jewish influence in Washington is very strong. Much stronger than the Bolshevik.'[65] However, Saroléa advised the Maxwell-Scotts of the political disadvantages of being publicly labelled an anti-Semite: 'I do not think it would be wise to add "Jewish" to Bolshevik . . . In our country it would be fatal even in conservative and much more in liberal and radical circles'.[67] Johnson remarks: 'such a label would immediately disqualify him from his self-appointed role as an impartial political commentator. It would also exclude him from the cosmopolitan circles he frequented. The Edinburgh rabbi, for example, would have been none too impressed'.[68] What's more, 'Jewish' and 'Bolshevik' had, in his mindset, long since become one and the same thing.

This polemical intervention was well-received in influential circles. On 6 December 1938, the Archbishop of Edinburgh wrote to Saroléa:

It is full of interest, and I can only hope that it may meet with an even wider circulation than the Duchess's pestilential book on Spain. It is amazing how effective the Russian propaganda has been in blinding even those who ought to know so much better as the real issue is at stake. I congratulate you on this production, and trust that it may do much to avert the very real danger which threatens this country at the moment through Communist propaganda.[69]

On 15 December 1938, the Duke of Alba told Saroléa: 'Its issue in such a cheap form should go far to neutralise the damage done by the Duchess of Atholl's effusion, though I fear it is always more difficult to catch up with a lie than to start one!'[70] That said, there is no mention of *Daylight on Spain* in the diplomatic archives of the Spanish Republic.

Although they could not make it to Perthshire, the Maxwell-Scotts continued the fight from Abbotsford. On 6 December 1938, *The Border Telegraph* reported a meeting of the FNS at the Ex-Service Club Hall in Galashiels. Lady Maxwell-Scott and her fellow speaker, Captain Henry Scott, the laird of Gala, sought to 'disabuse minds of the great wealth and power of the Catholic Church'. The Church had been the victim of 'liberal confiscations' that had created the 'economic evils of modern Spain'. The dictatorship of Primo de Rivera had been a brief parenthesis of 'prosperity, peace and progress', followed by the Republic's 'mis-rule' since 1931. To complete the local elite's solidarity with the Nationalist cause, the vote of thanks was given by Major Scott Plummer of Sunderland Hall, who promised: 'We shall be a majority in Great Britain who shall welcome the victory of that great Christian gentleman, General Franco.'

Despite widespread interest in the Perthshire and Kinross by-election, it was, according to *The Scotsman*, a rather low-key campaign:

> There appears to be little danger of the electoral waters rising in common with the turbulent waters of the Tay and the Tummel . . . Election addresses and leaflets are doubtless providing solid reading for the long evenings in remote cottages and elsewhere, but, apart from notices posted about meetings, there is an almost entire absence of flamboyant bills which might jar upon the senses of those who like the rural scene unspoiled by glaring displays. An emphatic and unfamiliar tone has been struck for the Duchess of Atholl, however, by loudspeaker vans. The glens have been echoing for a few days with the booming voices of the Lloyd Georgian Council of Action.[71]

An important factor was the weather: heavy snowfall disrupted campaigning and offered an advantage to those who could get the vote out.

It became clear that Snadden was a formidable opponent. His campaign was buttressed by the logistical help of Scottish Central Office and the oratorical support of a flood of National Government MPs. It was also helped by the influence exerted by sympathetic lairds on their tenants. In contrast, the duchess's supporters were enthusiastic but lacking in practical experience; meetings were badly advertised, and on polling day, cars were lacking. Moreover, her campaign spent too much effort on the villages and not enough on the towns in the more populous south of the constituency. This indicated how much ducal influence was limited to the Highland region nearer to Blair Atholl, and even there it was waning. At the meetings themselves, the duchess's charisma showed its own limits. Her otherwise sympathetic biographer Sheila Hetherington writes: 'Her voice was a rather monotonous drone, her speeches were too long and her appearance was uninteresting.'[72]

The campaign showed the duchess's isolation from the Conservative Party, which was increased by her decision not to stand as an 'Independent Conservative', and as Stuart Ball points out, she made a tactical error by devoting much of her attention to the Spanish issue. This 'ensured the continuance of Roman Catholic antagonism. Although the "scarlet woman" of Rome was a more deeply entrenched bogey than the "red duchess" of Atholl, the latter did not benefit from any Protestant backlash'.[73] A son of the manse, Snadden was palatable to Presbyterian and Catholic alike.

But it was still a surprise that on 21 December, 'a day of wild winter weather and heavy snow',[74] Snadden prevailed over the Duchess of Atholl, by a narrow majority of 1,300 votes. The crucial element in his success had been the 'solidarity' of the Conservative vote, which had held up better on a lower turnout. The defeated duchess thanked those 'who share my views, and long to see this country return to a foreign policy more consistent with our great traditions and our immense responsibilities'. Snadden told a reporter: 'This is not a victory for me; it is a tremendous victory for Mr Chamberlain; against an established member and all the natural prejudice in favour of a well-known Perthshire personality, the cause of Mr Chamberlain has triumphed in an almost overwhelming manner.'[75] Indeed, as *The Scotsman* reporter pointed out, despite the 'popular front' triumph at Bridgewater, in the eight by-elections since the Munich Agreement, the total number of votes cast for the government candidates had been 200,000, against 180,000 polled by opposition candidates. According to Ball, Conservative leaders and voters were both 'fed up with the Spanish wrangle, and either did not understand the issue or feared that the duchess's policy would lead to British entanglement and defeat the hope of localising the conflict'.[76] During the campaign, a working-class Crieff woman had told Mass Observation: 'I am voting for Mr Chamberlain, he saved war.'[77]

On 22 December 1938, Saroléa could therefore crow to Lord Phillimore:

> We have done it and the Red Duchess has been ignominiously beaten. I must confess, until the last moment, my only hope was that we might reduce her majority. A displacement of 650 votes in her favour would have given her the Seat. We may flatter ourselves that it is our little book which has made all the difference and influenced, in our favour, those 650 jurymen good and true.[78]

After all, in the week of the by-election, *The Glasgow Observer* (under the headline 'The Battle of the Books') had declared: 'Professor's *Daylight* dims Duchess's *Searchlight*'.[79] The following day, Lady Maxwell-Scott expressed both joy and wariness: 'Never in our wildest dreams could we have expected such a result in such a feudal part of Scotland. . . . But her energy has become diabolical now, and she has no more idea of giving up fighting for the Reds of the whole world than Stalin has.'[80] A reply from Saroléa reasserted the importance of his intervention, though it also indicated other, perhaps more mundane, factors explaining the duchess's defeat:

> 2,000 copies sent to Scotland have done much good. In fact, they have been the cause of the Red Duchess losing many votes. It was indeed a splendid victory . . . The opinion of the public was also very clearly shown in the fact that in spite of her territorial influence, she could only muster 60 cars against the 500 for Snadden.[81]

Blair Castle had been receiving telegrams of both support and abuse. Sylvia Pankhurst had sent her best wishes for the ill-fated campaign. At the same time, one 'Stalin' informed the duchess: 'Moscow is proud of Katharine the even greater'. Masks fell after her defeat. On 28 December, the BUF branch in Las Palmas telegraphed: 'words cannot express the delight of the British Colony here on hearing of your defeat at a recent by-election. Your presence in the House of Commons was a danger to the peace of the world'.[82]

On 3 January 1939, the duchess was at least consoled by Pablo de Azcarate, the Republic's ambassador to London:

> On my return from a short visit to Barcelona, I hasten to offer you the expression of my heartfelt sympathy, and tell you of the deep regret

with which the Spanish people learned the result of the West Perth-shire by-election. We must never forget, however, that the noblest aspect of the struggle is the risk of losing.[83]

The success of *Daylight on Spain* did not let up. On 11 January 1939, Alex McGregor Jr wrote to Saroléa: 'I understand the book is going very well in Catholic circles. I sent copies to the Catholic Press and it has received very favourable reviews.'[84] A week later, the director of the Institute for the Study of the Jewish Question wrote from Berlin: 'You are a true friend of ours in the struggle against Jewish insolence and Bolshevic imperialism.'[85] The following day, Saroléa addressed a meeting in London of the Link and the Anglo-German fellowship, and declared, 'the Axis saved the world' – though he opined to the Lady of Abbotsford: 'I am waiting to see what further mischief our "Red Duchess" is preparing to do'.[86]

These were heady times. Barcelona fell on 26 January, and sorry streams of Republican refugees made for the French frontier or the port of Valencia. That day, Glasgow Trades Council may well have sent the embassy a message of 'encouragement and support, never doubting the victorious emergence of Spain's fight for freedom'. On 27 January, pro-Republican Aberdonians collected £400, a 'shop-full of fruit' and even a car.[87] However, on 2 February, at a celebratory dinner of the FNS held in the Grosvenor restaurant, Glasgow, Saroléa proposed the first toast to Barcelona: 'The conquest of Barcelona has not only meant the liberation of thousands of misguided Catalonians, who received that liberation with such enthusiasm, but it has been a powerful blow to world Communism.'[88] *The Glasgow Observer* reported:

A large portrait of General Franco, framed in the Nationalist colours, in the place of honour; the menu card printed in Spanish; the Nation-alist colours everywhere; a musical programme consisting entirely of Spanish songs, and a regular chorus of 'Arriba España, viva Franco', – members of the Scottish branch of the Friends of National Spain were celebrating the liberation of Barcelona at a dinner in Glasgow last week. While the chief speaker, Professor Charles Saroléa, author of the book, *Daylight on Spain*, which helped to unseat the Duch-ess of Atholl in the West Perth by-election recently, was telling his audience that it was beginning to dawn on the British public that the Nationalists did represent the Spanish nation, a crowd of very ardent Valencia supporters gathered outside and loudly demanded arms for Spain. Several of the more foolhardy spirits rushed into the hotel, created pandemonium among a party of dancers who had nothing to do with the Spanish dinner, careered round the corridors shouting slogans and dodging the police. Six of them were taken into custody.[89]

Outside the restaurant, which held 200 guests, a crowd of about 2,000 demonstrated, waving red flags and shouting: 'Child Murderers Dine To-night!' But it should be pointed out that opposition to Saroléa and the FNS was not limited to the Reds. From the outset of the Spanish Civil War, a vocal opponent of 'Franco the Baby-Killer' had been Alexander Ratcliffe. Already, in the *Vanguard* of June 1937, Ratcliffe's Scottish Protestant League had denounced 'The Vatican Arch-Hypocrite!':

Spain continues to hold the eye of the world, and as we write there does not seem to be an end to the terrible and mad slaughter which has continued in Spain for months without stop. It is to be hoped that the ultimate result of the struggle will be the end, once and for all, of Papist domination where the opportunity of spreading the True Gospel of Jesus Christ is rich indeed.[90]

In August 1937, John McGovern MP was praised for 'kicking' the Pope: 'Hail McGovern, the Reformer. But note how the deluded Papists booed and hissed as the Doughty John sat down!'[91] In October 1937, a dispatch on 'The Crisis in Spain' contrasted the Francoist execution of evangelists with the tolerance now prevailing under Republican rule: 'In the Government area conditions remain the same. Protestants are treated everywhere with respect and, in some cases, with special favour. I understand that the Barcelona churches, which had been closed through fear of mob riots, have now been re-opened'.[92]

It was therefore natural that Ratcliffe rallied to the duchess's cause. In January 1938, the *Vanguard* portrayed her as the victim of the 'Bigoted Action of Papist Unionists': 'Slap-dash Her Grace gets it for daring to air her opinion on the Spanish situation, and seemingly because of her siding with the Spanish Government against the unlawful propaganda of Franco and his Papist rebels'. The Perthshire Conservative Association was riddled with 'Papist aristocrats', firstly, Sir Alexander Kay Muir, Second Baronet of Blair Drummond: 'not a Roman Catholic yet, but his wife is' – then Colonel Rupert Dawson: 'educated at the Papist college by name of Stonyhurst'. The Duke and Duchess of Atholl were 'to be congratulated on the firm stand which they have taken. After all, it as not the Papists of Kinross and Perth that returned the Duchess to Parliament. It was the Protestants'.[93]

In April 1938, the *Vanguard* raised the alarm about the Friends of National Spain:

> Protestants are warned against financially or otherwise helping a new body called the 'Friends of National Spain' whose Presidents are Roman Catholics. The Treasurer also is a RC. This body is to help the Pope-blessed Franco in his hellish work of bombarding innocent and helpless Spanish citizens because they will not toe the line to Popery and its mongrel offspring – Fascism.[94]

In May 1938, Ratcliffe issued a challenge to debate Arnold Lunn, 'A pervert from Protestantism to Popery'.[95]

Already in November 1938, Ratcliffe opined: 'If the Rebels should win, the same men believe that it will be the end of all Protestant work in Spain'.[96] So as the fall of Barcelona was celebrated in Glasgow by Saroléa and his friends, he lamented:

> We are not told that the King was 'toasted', or that the Union Jack was hoisted up. But we are told that the colours of National Spain draped the walls and tables and that the menu card was in Spanish, and that Spanish songs were sung. To our mind the fall of Barcelona and with it the evident success of Franco is a blow to world Protestantism.[97]

It was a sign that the end was nigh when the Republic's ambassador informed Provost Dollan that he could not make the *mercado Español* in Glasgow on 25 February 1939.

Saroléa boasted to McGregor: 'Only a few days ago a Clerk at one of the three bookstalls at the Waverley Station told me that the sales were going strong and that at his one Bookstall they had sold over 1,000 copies.'[98] The ultimate accolade came on 14 March 1939, in a letter from the Marques del Moral:

Mr Robert Sencourt, who was in Spain and who followed the troops into Barcelona at its capture, and has visited many of the towns and villages of Catalonia and Castille, told me that in his conversation with the people in the villages and towns he found a matter of enormous importance to them was the defeat of the Duchess of Atholl. People in Spain can understand a Duchess, but they cannot understand a Duchess who is Red! Her defeat was a momentous event in their opinion and created a great impression.[99]

Subsequent events seemed to vindicate Saroléa and his friends. Two weeks later, Madrid and then Valencia fell. Triumphant, the Friends of National Spain renamed themselves the Friends of Spain.

A Bitter Victory

But, despite the confident declarations of Snadden, Europe was indeed slipping rapidly towards another world war. In March 1939, Hitler's troops had invaded what was left of the Czech lands, tearing up the Munich Agreement and destroying the last illusions of appeasers such as Graham Seton Hutchison and badly shaking those of the Marquis of Clydesdale. Nonetheless, *The Anglo-German Review* reported that on 21 March, when Professor Saroléa addressed The Link in London, the Assembly Room of the Army and Navy Hotel was 'packed and members overflowed into the corridors':

> Professor Saroléa, one of Britain's most distinguished historians, said that appcasement had never really been tried (. . .) They were told that Germany murdered the body politic of a free nation. Czecho-Slovakia had collapsed, but it was not a question of murder, it was a question of suicide. German dominance in Central Europe might be a danger. In that case they only had a choice of evils. Did they prefer a world war?[100]

The free city of Danzig was now in the sights of Hitler, and Saroléa and his friends were keen to appease him. On 19 June 1939, General Maxwell-Scott had no truck with any intervention against Nazi Germany:

> If we have to fight with Russia we shall be fighting alongside the Reds and Pinks of the world, with the Jews and with the Grand

Orient and with all the Anti-Gods. But what can you expect from a country in which Christianity is dying, in which easier divorce and abortion are on the increase, and where contraception is used more and more to stop an urgently needed increase of the population![101]

Saroléa wrote to *The Scotsman* on the issue of Danzig, supporting 'peace'. In the June issue of *The Anglo-German Review*, an anonymous article focused on 'Danzig and her Scots', recalling that, in 1575, when Danzig rejected the Polish claim for possession and declared for Germany, 700 soldiers, under Colonel William Stuart, hurried to Danzig and helped repulse the Poles: 'according to German scholars the stubbornness and shrewdness of the East Prussians is largely due to the Scottish blood that flows in them'.[102] The following month, Saroléa graced the pages of the *Review* to show, 'as an old and loyal friend of Poland', that Danzig was 'a thoroughly German city whose purely German characteristics have been surprisingly well preserved'.[103]

But the professor's appeals for a 'wise compromise' seem to have fallen on deaf ears. On 22 June 1939, he informed C.E. Carroll, editor of the *Anglo-German Review*:

Nobody, so far, has taken my side except a Ukrainian nobleman. That is where the mischief lies. I had two enthusiastic letters from the Duke of Buccleuch and from the leader of the SNP, Mr Gibb, who informed me that they agree with every word I said. But why do these gentlemen who agree with me in private fail to express their agreement in public?[104]

Indeed, at the SNP conference of May 1939, Andrew Dewar Gibb had declared:

The people of this country are being stampeded into war. The press, the BBC, so called responsible ministers by their inflammatory utterances are all working up a will to war as though in a sacred cause. There is only a threat, actual or imaginary, to the supremacy of British imperialism. We indeed as nationally minded Scotsmen may well condemn recent rapine and conquest. But it requires a fit of brass indeed for imperial England with her long record of rapacity and cunning to criticise the actions of any other country.[105]

Gibb's public silence on the Danzig issue notwithstanding, Saroléa told the SNP leader on 30 June:

> Of course neither you, nor I, nor anybody can reveal the substantial truth. The driving forces behind our policy are, first, the Jews, which means France, Big Business and the Press, as well as the Cinema and the BBC. The second most powerful driving force is the Church, for this will be partly a Religious War.[106]

On 22 October 1939, nearly two months after the declaration of war, Gibb would tell Saroléa: 'I feel everyone among us who feels the pinch of the Communist threat, with the three great powers insanely weakening themselves, should strive to do all in his power to counter it. What service can we render?'[107]

In July, the professor participated in the Link's last tour of Germany. On 20 July, their Lufthansa plane left Croydon Airport, stopping off at Cologne, Munich, Nymphenburg and Salzburg. After attending a production of the *Rosenkavalier*, conducted by none other than Richard Strauss, Saroléa presented a copy of *Daylight on Spain* to Josef Goebbels. Then there were trips to Berchtesgaden and Obersalzburg, a motor tour to Mundsee, lunch at the Wolfgangsee, and *Much Ado about Nothing* in the Felsenreitschule, Munich.

The Nazi–Soviet Pact of August 1939 tore apart those anti-Fascists who had rallied to the Spanish Republican cause and the Communist Party, but also caused considerable confusion and soul-searching among pro-Fascists. Certainly, in early 1940, Lady Maxwell-Scott and Saroléa were united in their support of armed intervention in Finland against the invading Red Army. She told him: 'I have 60 women working for the Finns, knitting hard, and work-parties all up Yarrow and Ettrick are working for me too, so we send a steady stream to London every week.'[108] However, during this period, there were terse exchanges between the lady and the professor. Her profoundly Catholic and Latin affinities led her to prefer the cause of Franco or Mussolini to that of the godless 'Prussians' in Berlin. On 8 February 1940, with Poland partitioned in the wake of the Molotov–Ribbentrop scandal, she wrote: 'Nothing can exceed the horrors in the German half of Poland. Not even the Bolsheviks. There is *no longer* anything to choose between them. So I hope you will drop their defence once and for all ... We want to *add* Stalin to Hitler as the *Enemy*.'[109] Maxwell-Scott denounced the invasion of Belgium and France. On 20 August 1940, she wrote: 'have been so crushed by grief for France that I have seen hardly anyone. Life doesn't seem worth living without France'.[110] She would go as far as expressing her support for De Gaulle's Free French.

Over the course of the war, the activities of the Friends of Spain were reduced to the absolute minimum, and its supporters became troubled spectators of the conflict, especially after the Axis invasion of the Soviet Union in June 1941. One of Saroléa's correspondents during this period was the eighth Duke of Buccleuch, who had been among the peers most involved in pro-German sentiment and activity. A frequent visitor to Nazi Germany, he had accompanied Lord Brocket, in April 1939, to the celebration of Hitler's fiftieth birthday. Buccleuch's position of Lord Steward of the Royal Household caused official embarrassment, and he was ordered by Buckingham Palace not to attend the festivities. Nevertheless, on 11 September 1939, after the declaration of war, he had attended a pro-peace meeting at the Duke of Westminster's house. Along with other peers, including Lord Halifax, he had responded positively to Hitler's 'peace offer' of 6 October 1939. In December 1939, he wrote to Buckingham Palace, tendering his resignation as Lord Steward, but also remarking: 'How much better to have allowed Germany to come up against Soviet Russia instead of pushing them into that alliance'.[111] The Palace would not reply to him until May 1940. Even as late as July 1940, after the replacement of the French Republic with the collaborationist Vichy regime, Buccleuch had put his signature to 'The Salvage Corps (Darning Needles) Memorandum', which expressed fear of the effect on European stability of disturbing the power structure by war: 'If we succeed in bringing about the overthrow of Hitler by force, the result may well be a Communist revolution. The thing that Weygand and Pétain are trying to prevent is a Communist revolution in France.'[112] According to Richard Griffiths, even after the outbreak of war, Buccleuch 'believed, above all, that the King and the Government had been taken in by sinister forces, consisting of Jews, Americans, and the pro-war party in Britain'.[113]

On 14 July 1941, the duke wrote to Saroléa: 'I do not like our too warm embrace of the Soviet, and fear our war leaders, or some of them, would readily bring our countries into any form of international provided they are in power.'[114] Two years later, after the balance of power had shifted decisively in favour of the Allies, the melancholy duke declared: 'Germany was not entirely to blame for the war'.[115] His sympathies were now with thousands of Polish officers massacred near Smolensk.

As for Saroléa, he had to be consul for a nation, Belgium, whose king collaborated with the Nazi occupier, but whose exiles were most often on the side of the Allies. On 14 May 1943, he wrote: 'The morale of the Belgian forces is very low and as Belgian consul I have had to deal with many cases of theft, mutiny, desertion and even murder.' Many of the Belgians held 'pro-Bolshevik opinions'. He added: 'One can't help feeling sorry for the all the Poles. Most of them tell me that their only hope is that the Germans may succeed in defeating the Russians, before they are themselves finally defeated by the Allies.'[116] This, of course, would not come. On 10 August 1944, the Duke of Buccleuch told Saroléa:

> The end of the present war in Europe with Germany is coming very quickly. What then in Europe? Moscow will presumably decide terms for Germany and many other countries, and where there is no annexation, 'suitable' governments will doubtless be installed. Will the Peace justify the War?[117]

It can be said that, in her remaining years, the Duchess of Atholl effectively moved back towards her erstwhile friends, as a prominent member of the Scottish League for European Freedom and opponent of Soviet control of Eastern Europe. As far as Spain was concerned, the Saroléa papers for 1943–45 contain standard letters from Katharine Atholl asking for donations to the National Joint Committee for Spanish Relief and Basque Children's Trust Ltd, accompanied by an annual report and financial statement. For example, in October 1945, she wrote: 'We are all hoping that the situation in Spain may make it possible for the Spanish refugees here and in France to return soon to their own Country and that the end of our responsibilities as the NJCSR, is at least in sight.'[118] There are, however, no replies from Saroléa to the duchess, or indications of money being donated by the professor to this humanitarian cause.

However, barely six years after the triumphant entry into Barcelona, there was little hope among the pro-Francoists. In late August 1944, her beloved Paris may have been liberated, but the Lady of

Abbotsford wrote to Saroléa: 'I weep with you over the Atheists, but as most of the world is with them in their firm determination to prepare the ground for the arrival of Anti-Christ and his Materialism, they ride the crest of the wave.'[119]

Saroléa, suffering from the inevitable problems of advanced old age, withdrew from the public debates he had once constantly participated in. Certainly, he did not abandon anti-Semitism, becoming a close friend of Link founder and anti-Semitic conspiracy theorist Admiral Sir Barry Domvile on the latter's release from internment. There is no mention of the Holocaust in Saroléa's last writings, although he continued to obsess about Bolshevism, noting on 1 January 1948 that Stalin was 'the master dictator of the world'.[120]

Sad Professor

In 1946, Saroléa made one last trip to the continent, visiting Belgium, Germany and France, but not Spain. Nevertheless, he retained sympathies for a Franco regime which was very much a pariah state: politically and economically isolated, excluded from the United Nations. On 9 July 1946, Lord Phillimore wrote to Saroléa: 'I regret to say that we find that there is more bitter opposition to the Franco regime today than there was even in the days of the Civil War.'[121] Saroléa was also bitter in his reply, indicating the weight of the religious divide in his chosen home, as well as his own isolation:

> I admit that propaganda for Spain in a Protestant country is a somewhat difficult proposition … I made a free gift of my little book to the Committee of the Friends of Spain. I made two costly and fatiguing journeys to Spain at my own expense. I succeeded in getting my friend Comte de Saint-Aulaire, a former Ambassador to Spain, to write an inspiring Introduction to the book, but I did not see a single article published in the London press on my book. Nor did I receive a single letter or postcard from Spain.[122]

He wrote thus to the press attaché of the Spanish embassy:

> Unfortunately Spain has been hidden away from us for so long behind the Iron Curtain of hostile propaganda that it is very difficult to see for one's self and even more difficult to make other people see

the facts of the Spanish situation ... It is obvious to me that Spain is the victim of a sinister political conspiracy whose wire-pullers are in Moscow as well as in Paris, London and Washington.[123]

On 28 November 1946, the Spanish ambassador in London cabled to Madrid that the Friends of Spain had been 'reorganised and rejuvenated'.[124] There was no longer any place for the professor.

In fact, Franco's Spain would, with the Cold War, soon find a role in the Western alliance against 'Godless Communism', welcoming US air bases as early as 1955, while becoming a popular destination for holidaymakers, both Protestant and Catholic, from as far away as Kinross and West Perthshire. But Saroléa would not live to see that, dying on 11 March 1953, six days after Joseph Stalin. The many obituaries of Saroléa found themselves alongside copious details on the funeral of his nemesis. The authors concentrated on his passion for languages and books, and skirted around his political affinities, although *The Times* declared that the professor 'found it difficult to adapt his thought to the new values created by the quickening tempo of the modern world'.[125]

On 5 May 1944, Saroléa had written to his good friend the Duke of Argyll: 'I have tried to specialise in political prophecy for the last thirty years.'[126] There was certainly a time at which the professor seemed to have the gift of insight into geopolitical developments. In 1915, on the appearance of the US edition of *The Anglo-German Problem*, the *New York Times* hailed Saroléa as a 'seer' who had predicted with 'rare perspicacity' the Kaiser's aggression against Belgium, France and Britain.[127] However, the professor's obsessive fear of the Bolshevik threat blinded him to both the aggressive character of Fascism and the limits of Soviet influence. To this was added an exaggerated sense of his own importance. These faults illustrate themselves in his campaign against the Red Duchess which, while in touch with pro-appeasement opinion and buoyed by Catholic sympathies, was of marginal impact. Sam Johnson rightly remarks: 'if there were individuals who were swayed by Saroléa's advice and knowledge, they were confined to the lower echelons of politics and international affairs. The prime example here is Lady Maxwell-Scott'.[128] In the light of Saroléa's endless, and often fruitless, battles – which echoed the quixotic adventures of the Red Duchess herself – it is worth quoting as an epitaph his 1931 lecture on 'Thomas Carlyle, a Scot lost to Scotland':

> It was precisely because Carlyle failed in all his endeavours, because he fought a losing battle, because his life was a tragedy from beginning to end, that his work became infinitely more interesting and infinitely more instructive and his personality infinitely more fascinating. The common saying, 'nothing succeeds like success', was the sordid motto of the shopkeeper.[129]

4

The Nazis and the Nats

In January 1939, Douglas Young, future leader of the SNP, wrote to his fellow poet George Campbell Hay: 'If Hitler could neatly remove our imperial breeks somehow and thus dissipate the mirage of Imperial partnership with England etc he would do a great service to Scottish Nationalism.'[1] Young thus showed the ambivalent, to say the least, attitude of Scottish Nationalists towards Fascism. Hatred of the English led to the downplaying of the Fascist threat to freedom and peace, while more radical Nationalists could be attracted to the authoritarian and xenophobic solutions offered by the Führer and the Duce.

For a Scottish Fascism

C.M. Grieve, alias Hugh MacDiarmid, had been a member of the Independent Labour Party since 1908, and of the Scottish Home Rule Association since 1920, when in June 1923, after Mussolini's Blackshirts marched on Rome, he called for a Scottish species of Fascism. In 'At the Sign of the Thistle. Programme for a Scottish Fascism', published in *The Scottish Nation*, he wrote:

> Scotland is not Italy and the political, social, and industrial traditions and conditions of the people of Scotland, and their psychology differ entirely from those of Italy. Nevertheless there is need for a Scottish Fascism just as there was need for an Italian Fascism – and the first plank in the programme of the former would be precisely the same as the first plank in the latter – 'Scotland First' for us as it was 'Italy First' for them.

The Fascist example therefore inspired the reinvigoration of both Labour and Scottish Nationalist movements:

Upon what does the development of such a force depend – upon the intensification of everything in contemporary Scottish life that sets the spiritual above the material – that is to say the majority of the motives that activate Scottish Labour organisations; of the spirit that is seeking to revive the Gaelic and the Scots vernacular; of the instincts that are responsible for the contemporary efforts towards a Scottish Literary Renaissance and Scottish National Theatre; of all the associations concerned to preserve distinctive Scottish traditions and tendencies from absorption and obsolescence.

For MacDiarmid, it was of special significance that 'the saltatory development of the Labour movement in Scotland, the intensification of Scottish Home Rule propaganda, the awakening of the Churches to a new realisation of the moral and spiritual values of Scottish nationality and the need to conserve them, and the recreation of distinct tendencies in Scottish Literature when almost on the verge of complete submersion in English literature, should synchronise'. The new Nationalism would incline to the left and meet Labour half-way in the interest of 'Scotland First'. It would also create a socialism which respected or revived traditional, rural-based culture:

The desuetude of the Vernacular was one of the consequences of that Industrialism of which State Socialism may be the apotheosis; but a Scottish Nationalist Socialism will be a very different thing and will restore an atmosphere in which the fine, distinctive traits and tendencies of Scottish character which have withered in the foul air of our contemporary chaos, will once more revive.

Citing Pietro Gorgolini's *The Fascist Movement in Italian Life*, MacDiarmid claimed: 'Italian Fascism needs most urgently to be almost exactly reproduced in Scotland in so far as agrarian policy is concerned. Its agrarian policy is summed up in the maxim, *the land for those who work it*'. The entire Fascist programme could be 'readapted to Scottish national purposes and is (whether it be called Fascist or pass under any name) *the only thing that will preserve our distinctive national culture*. Mere Parliamentary devolution and every association interested in anything Scottish can only ensure the success of the particular aim in view by being joined with every other individual and every other association interested in anything Scottish'.[2]

Also in 1923, MacDiarmid declared that Mussolini represented 'an experiment in patriotic socialism' and that 'we want a Scottish Fascism which shall be ... a lawless believer in law – a rebel believer in authority'.[3] Another link to Italian Fascism was MacDiarmid's admiration for Pound: 'Of all the men I have known, I loved Ezra Pound.'[4] Both poets were influenced by A.R. Orage's review *The New Age*, which, in addition to publishing modernist verse, promoted Major Douglas's theory of social credit. Peter Crisp explains thus the politico-economic affinities which, as we have seen, were shared by Graham Seton Hutchison:

> It was not only Pound and MacDiarmid's poetic forms and meta-physics which were moulded to a large degree by *The New Age*, but also their politics, or at least economics. The economics of Social Credit, an underconsumptionist doctrine which saw economic salvation as lying in the abolition of private banking, were introduced to Orage by its inventor Major Douglas in 1918. Social Credit was quickly taken up by both Pound and MacDiarmid. It was the basis of their correspondence in the early thirties, when Pound, in a letter of 1934, cited MacDiarmid to show that you could be both 'Douglasite and Communist'.[5]

MacDiarmid may well have eschewed the British Fascists, whose British patriotism, imperialism and anti-Communism were absolute anathema. He would leave the ILP only in 1928 to join the National Party of Scotland. It can also be argued that, in 1923, the Fascist regime, as it is now historically understood, had not been fully established. Nevertheless, in the *Scots Independent* of May 1929 he unquestionably sought the type of leadership which Mussolini practised in Italy: 'What I have said about the need for aristocratic standards, for a species of fascism applies equally here. I feel we will never make any real headway till we cease to imitate English organisations by running the Party on democratic lines or want-ing anything similar in organisation or programme to the English parties.'[6] In 1930 he said of a secret Scottish nationalist society to which he belonged, Clann Albain, that 'the whole organisation is on a militaristic basis, and in this resembles the Fascist movement'.[7] This 'organisation' would, however, only count six members. That said, MacDiarmid had great plans for it. In the *Scots Independent*, he imagined the Scotland of 1979, whose path to independence had been opened by Clann Albain:

> No longer confining themselves to English precedents, [young Scots] availed themselves readily of the examples of Italy and Ireland, and, powerfully re-enforcing the transitional organisation of the Scottish Nationalist Party (up till then still deplorably liberal and Anglophile) with their militaristic neo-Fascist auxiliary Clann Albain, carried the Movement to the successful conclusion we know of by 1965, and re-established the ancient Gaelic Commonwealth in Scotland on a modern basis.[8]

In 1931, in *The Modern Scot*, MacDiarmid favourably reviewed Wyndham Lewis's book on Hitler. Scotland, too, needed some *Blutsgefühl* ('blood feeling'):

> Scottish nationalists – especially in view of the ascendancy in Anglo-Scottish politics of a Labour-cum-socialist electoral majority in Scotland, or, at all events in the more densely populated and commercially and industrially important centres, and the particular hatred which Scottish nationalism inspires in Labour-cum-socialist circles – ought to consider carefully the principle which Hitler and his National Socialists in Germany oppose to Marxism. Hitler's 'Nazis' wear their socialism with precisely the difference which post-socialist Scottish nationalists must adopt. Class-consciousness is anathema to them, and in contradistinction to it they set up the principle of race-consciousness.[9]

The struggle of the Scottish race had to be situated in a new geo-political context that provided both dangers and opportunities. But, like Ruaridh Erskine, MacDiarmid rejected the anti-Irish prejudice shared by Scottish Nationalists like Andrew Dewar Gibb:

> The importance of the fact that we are a Gaelic people, that Scottish anti-Irishness is a profound mistake, that we ought to be anti-English, and that we ought to play our part in a three-to-one policy of Scotland, Ireland and Wales against England to reduce that 'predominant partner' to its proper subordinate role in our internal and imperial affairs and our international relationships (not to go further

for the moment and think of a Gaelic West of Europe as essential to complement the Russian idea which has destroyed the old European balance of north and south and produced a continental disequilibrium which is threatening European civilization, and, behind that, white supremacy) are among the most important practical considerations which would follow from the acceptance of Blutsgefühl in Scotland.[10]

Further on in this essay, MacDiarmid linked up social credit, nationalism and socialism: 'Those in the SNP who are attracted to Douglasism as the only economic policy for the party may also be recommended to peruse with care Mr Lewis's chapters on Hitler's economics which naturally follow from the principle of social solidarity.'[11] But it was a peculiarly Scottish fascism that was still in the making: 'Whereas Hitlerism, being German, had developed both a philosophy and an organization, in the Scottish case the latter is still embryonic and immune to anything in the nature of the former.'[12]

MacDiarmid began to call himself a communist in 1932, and in 1934 would join the party, thus submitting himself to the new anti-Fascist line of the Comintern, before being twice expelled by 1939. But his National-Communism was not without its fascistic residues. The 'First Hymn to Lenin', footnoted as coming from a work entitled 'Clann Albain', showed MacDiarmid's attraction to exceptional men of action, the ultimate artists, among whom he also counted Il Duce. An ardent social creditor who detested usury, MacDiarmid would, like Seton Hutchison, strike up correspondence with Pound in the course of the thirties.

A Nazi Perspective on Scottish Nationalism

If *Blutsgefühl* inspired MacDiarmid, there seemed little optimism in Germany about the prospects for Scottish Nationalism, at least at the beginning. In *Mein Kampf*, Adolf Hitler had been concerned with 'England' and how that imperial power could be emulated and dominated: Scotland did not figure. Confirming this after Hitler had come to power, one Gert Antonius gave, in the leading Nazi theoretical journal *Volk und Reich*, a pessimistic assessment of chances for Scottish home rule:

[The] movement is achieving unimpressive results in its attempts to elect Scottish nationalist representatives to parliament. The old parties beat their candidates in all cases, who do not even manage to achieve a respectable minority vote. Most of the time their votes account for less than 20% of the overall vote in the constituency.[13]

That said, according to the author, it would be wrong to dismiss the efforts for regional autonomy in Scotland as meaningless:

For about ten years the demand for Scottish self-administration and self-government has become audible and credible. Scotland has been affected more seriously than the rest of Great Britain by the post-war economic crisis. It is furthest from London, where since the war industrial, commercial and financial management of the British economy has been increasingly concentrated.

Nevertheless, Antonius pointed out that the home rule movement began in the cultural sphere:

In literature, in drama, in the arts, the beginning of a conscious renaissance has begun in the last ten years. Names such as Compton Mackenzie and Eric Linklater, who also have followers outside the British Isles, are at the same time leaders of political Scottish nationalism. In these intellectual origins lie a strength and a weakness for modern Scottish nationalism. A strength in so far as the whole movement draws a strong idealistic momentum from this source. A weakness as all existing political powers unite against them. This is all the more so as nationalism in Scotland has always been a non-partisan movement and had representatives among the Conservatives, the Liberals and the Labour Party.

The movement was 'inspired by an idea but has no firm political programme. Under the leading personalities we see next to literati like Compton Mackenzie, the highly conservative Duke of Montrose and the left-liberal Sir Alexander MacEwan'.

The practical problems facing a *Reich* for the *Volk* were considerable, if not insurmountable:

Scotland itself only accounts for a small part of the Scottish people. Millions of Scots live in all parts of England, are in places of leadership in politics, in the economy and as intellectuals. Scots have played an important role in the making, building and preserving of the British empire and are still playing an important role. For centuries the young Scot has considered the whole world or at least the whole Empire as his natural field of work and birthright and it is unlikely that Sir Alexander MacEwan's desire for a small, independent and self-sufficient Scotland will have much chance against that idea and be able to recruit young Scottish men.

The home rule movement faced a further difficulty: the conviction that a parliament and government in Edinburgh would be more beneficial to the country than the current arrangement was in no way a common outlook:

Especially the thinly-populated Highlands fear that, in an independent Scotland, they will be neglected even more in favour of the overpopulated industrial regions around Glasgow and Edinburgh than they are in the current arrangement. Behind such material differences of the moment lies hidden a more important fact, which is that the Scots are in no way a racially or emotionally self-contained nation. As much as all Scots tend to stick together against other people over the border – and this is undoubtedly one of the secrets to their success – so strongly do their differences show as soon as they are amongst themselves in a common homeland.

These differences were not limited to the Highland–Lowland divide:

Let's start in the North, where the population of the Shetland and Orkney Isles do not wish to be considered part of the Celtic Highland population; they consider themselves of Scandinavian origin. The same goes for the Nordic county of Caithness. So what's generally considered the Highlands does not cover all of the North. The Eastern counties, south of the Moray Firth that is, for example the prime minister's home county of Elgin, cannot be counted among the Celtic Highland population either, even though the Celtic element is relatively strong here with a people originating mostly from the Scandinavian 'Norsemen' ('Norsemen', in comparison to the 'Normans', who came from the north coast of France, where they adopted the French language, and invaded the South of Great Britain). In the whole southern part of the country, which contains the majority of the population, the Celtic element is comparatively unimportant; the inhabitants are mainly of Anglo-Saxon and Scandinavian origin and are generally used to seeing the Highland population as inferior and antiquated, which does not hinder their enthusiasm for the costume, bagpipes or Highland games of these bumpkins, especially as these things are Scotland's most important 'invisible export', of which the enterprising 'Lowland' inhabitants probably derive more practical advantages than the Highlanders themselves.

Hence it did not look to the Nazi academic as if the advocates of a Scotland fully independent from London were likely to fulfil their desires. Despite this, a practical impact of their aspirations was already visible: 'the Government, at least in order to eliminate some of the stress caused by the nationalist agitation, is starting to govern Scotland more and more from Edinburgh'. It was also important to bear in mind that Scotland had maintained a degree of autonomy thanks to the Kirk, and the legal and education systems. There were also special offices for health, agriculture and fisheries. 'Here,' concluded Antonius, 'in the area of design and improvement of the existing Scottish self-administration lies undoubtedly a promising area for the Scottish nationalist movement to act. Here the movement can reap as much success as it has undoubtedly already achieved in the area of awakening a cultural national consciousness. Home Rule for Scotland in the full sense of the word appears to lie still in the distance.'

Scottish Ambiguities

This lukewarm prognosis from the new Reich was not shared by a noisy and fractious fringe of Scottish Nationalism, which, like Mac-Diarmid, had an at least ambivalent relationship with Fascism. In search of a Caledonian palingenesis, the ultras would be tempted by both a pacifist stance on the growing possibility of another European war, and political organisation along military lines.

One of the most militant and visible nationalists at this time was Wendy Wood, founder of the Democratic Scottish Self-Government Organisation (DSSO). From her early days in Cape Town, Wood was marked by both racism and nationalism. In *Yours Sincerely for Scotland. The Autobiography of a Patriot,* Wood recalled the black burglars that plagued white middle-class lives. She was therefore no opponent of apartheid: 'Later events have proved, not the need for integration with the blacks, but the need for the wide conception of allowing him to be himself.'[14] Wood was also influenced by 'cradle tales of my mother', notably about William Wallace. A tour of the Highlands in 1913 converted her to the Nationalist cause. Already in 1916, she was a member of the Scottish League, before joining the Home Rule Association and the National Party of Scotland. Her outlook was also influenced by social credit.

In 1932, she founded the DSSO, which soon attracted the attentions of a Special Branch wary of a Sinn Fein–IRA equivalent emerging north of the Cheviots.[15] On 27 July 1933, it was reported that the Irish Republican movement had been invited to a DSSO meeting at Central Station, Glasgow, on the evening of 18 July 1933. As about 25 persons attended (more than expected), the meeting-place was transferred to a room at the Ivanhoe Hotel. The meeting went ahead despite threats from both Communists and Billy Boys. At the Ivanhoe, the DSSO leader combined virulent nationalism with pacifism:

> Miss Wood said that a plebiscite of the East of Scotland had been taken, which had resulted in a decision to remain neutral in any war England might engage in, except the one against Scotland! ... She asked for volunteers and suggested that each member in attendance should get nine young men who would 'stand up to all opposition'. She said that 'they must prepare and go out and do what Ireland has done; they must be prepared to make sacrifices'. She again referred to the neutrality of the Scottish nation. War in the very near future was inevitable; it might materialise in a year or two. America was the present antagonist, but France would prove to be the next enemy.

In a *coup de théâtre*, Wood 'introduced a man known as Mr Douglas, wearing a McKenzie tartan kilt, described as an ex-Army officer, who had left his job in London to come and render assistance'. Ronald MacDonald Douglas addressed the audience:

> Now I will spit this out to you. I have started a Defence Corps in connection with the DSSO. I have some experience as an ex-Army

Officer. I gave up my job as a journalist in London and went to Edinburgh at my own expense. I know it is a serious matter. Nothing will be got from England without fighting for it . . . We will have war in a year or two, but they will see that Scotsmen will fight for their own country the next time and set up a Government.

This attempt to create a nationalist paramilitary organisation was pursued. On 4 August 1933, at the Mound, an appeal for recruits was made by Wood. 'Captain' Douglas then formed those present into ranks and marched them along Princes Street. On 9 August, Wood was reported as 'abusing all things English, speaking disparagingly of His Majesty the King; describing the Union Jack as "a filthy rag"'. Such outpourings continued in her weekly bulletin *Smeddum*. On 12 August, she asserted the need for both Scottish neutrality and a Scottish Defence Force (SDF): 'The embroiling of Britain in the next European war will mean that Scotland, as ever hitherto since the Union, will bear the brunt, unless a definitive plan for the securing of national neutrality is put into action immediately'.

That said, clear conflicts of personality and strategy rapidly emerged between the DSSO founder and the 'Captain'. According to a Special Branch report of 26 September 1933, Wood was at odds with the 'extremist' Douglas, and resented his advocacy of force. The SDF was 'practically non-existent' in Edinburgh, limiting its activities to drilling in the Pentland Hills. As for the mysterious figure doing the drilling, 'he is stated to have been connected with Sir Oswald Mosley's movement at one time but to have left it'.

Differences between Wood and Douglas displayed themselves spectacularly at an SDF meeting at the Trongate, on 14 October 1933, attended by 40 people:

> The former excitedly attacked Douglas for deprecating her after all her efforts on behalf of the DSSO and the SDF. She called Douglas an 'English spy' and completely lost control of herself. Douglas in turn attacked her and termed her 'a dangerous woman'. After a display of violent temper by both they individually appealed for the support of the meeting. Douglas, who in his appeal engaged in a virulent attack on England, eventually burst into tears, which induced the majority present to exclaim emotionally: 'A Douglas! A Douglas!' (this having reference to ancient history).

The DSSO, which held regular open-air meetings at the Mound, claimed 1,200 members. The SDF also had extravagant pretensions. On Sunday, 17 December 1933, the Glasgow section of the Force held a parade in the form of a route march from Hillfoot, Dumbarton, to a place called the 'The Deil's Loch', near Strathblane, Stirlingshire. Douglas proceeded by motor-car, and addressed his troops in a field by the loch:

> Douglas said it was the first time since the '45 rebellion that Scotland had its own army and he was delighted to command such troops since they reminded him of their cousins, the IRA. He also said he was prepared to lay down his life for the cause of Scottish freedom.

The 'Commandant-General' was expecting great things from the Scottish army:

> It is a great country in which an army could be hidden, such as Bobbie Burns would have liked. You know, he was a great patriot and hated England. I heard you as you marched along singing Irish patriot songs, 'The Soldier's Song', etc. it is more appropriate if you will in future sing the patriotic songs of your own country . . . We are going to do great things, and I am prepared to give my life for my country.

Douglas suggested a uniform of Douglas tartan trousers and a green shirt. Brigade HQ Staff would be in Bruce's Cottage, Killearn, near Glasgow. Gaelic was used as the drill language, and bayonet exercises were done with Boys' Brigade rifles, while instruction in the use of revolvers proceeded by use of an air pistol.

It was therefore a parody of the Irish Republican movement that haunted the British security services. Wendy Wood continued her radical nationalist activities, which led her to fight alongside Communists against Mosley's Blackshirts, while supporting the peace movement as another war approached. On the other hand, Douglas's own hard-line nationalist agenda would, as we will see, lead him much closer to the Fascist cause.

Douglas and Wood can be seen to represent an extremist fringe of Scottish nationalism, on the edge of illegality. However, *The Scots Independent*, main organ of Scottish nationalism, also showed an ambivalent attitude towards issues of race and continental fascism. In December 1926, it had criticised obsession with 'the Irish menace', but only because 'the Menace to Scotland is unrestricted and excessive immigration, *whatever be the country of origin of these immigrants*'.[16] In November 1927, the paper responded to remarks by John Buchan on 'the decay of Scotland', arguing that 'Mr Buchan, in common with most of the Anglicised gangs of self-seekers sent to represent Scotland in the English parliament, are stout defenders of the present position, which means the political eclipse and national extinction of our country'. Only freedom and independence could prevent the 'dying of a race'.[17]

An explicitly racial perspective was provided by one of the key founders of Scottish nationalism, the poet and folklorist Lewis Spence. In his manifesto, *Freedom for Scotland*, he declared: 'The salient feature of racial difference between the English and Scottish races is the presence in Scotland of a preponderantly large Pictish stock, from which the majority of its inhabitants are descended.'[18] Spence therefore rejected any miscegenation: the 'Anglomaniac' was 'usually of the same weakly and degenerate character, held in contempt by both Scots and English, and really of cosmopolitan tendency'. Measures had to be taken to 'protect the Scottish race from being overwhelmed by the swarming millions of England, who will shortly absorb her unless protective measures are resolved upon forthwith'.[19] That said, Spence considered the Scots to be a British race, capable of harmonious relations with their immediate neighbours.

Among Scottish nationalists other than MacDiarmid, the Italian example could inspire rejuvenation: 'Mussolini points the way', headlined the *Scots Independent* of November 1928, referring favourably to *Il Duce*'s land reclamation scheme.[20] In March 1933, J.A. Russell, in his essay 'The "State" of Scotland. A comparison with Bavaria', wrote of recent political developments: 'That federal government is far from obsolete is shown by the political reconstruction of Germany, which perhaps affords the best parallel to Scotland'. In August of that year, the paper reacted thus to the Scottish Fascist Democratic Party's 'curiously mixed programme':

> The first article in its creed is excellent: 'absolute independence and self-government for Scotland'. If that were Fascism we could all be Fascists. There is even a case to be made for the establishment of what is called the Scottish Corporate Commonwealth, and a self-governing Scotland might even learn something from Musso-

lini without adopting castor oil methods. But the main part of the programme seems to consist in the stirring up of religious rancour against Roman Catholics. The first number of 'The Commonwealth', the monthly organ of the movement, has more to say on this than on self-government for Scotland. We recognise that the problem of the Irish in Scotland cannot be brushed aside as of no importance, and a self-governing Scotland would have to deal with it as the present Scotland cannot; but that problem will not be solved along the lines of religious hatred and malice. The chief significance of the new Party is that it illustrates further the rapid disruption of the English Labour Party. Mr Weir Gilmour, the leader of the Scottish Fascists, is an ex-Labourist. Scotland is steadily casting off the English parties and learning to think Scottish in politics.[21]

The rejection of London rule led nationalists to be split over the threat posed by Nazi Germany. In 'Scotland in the World', published in November 1933, J. Gregory bemoaned the 'utter lack of a Scottish view of foreign affairs'. For Gregory, Scotland had to face the world 'as a small nation – and as a European small nation'.[22] Therefore, so long as the League of Nations continued to show the smallest sign of effective life it had to be supported and used to the full.

The official policy of England, 'abjectly dependent' on the United States, was 'opposed to that of the small countries'. France was 'the one Great Power which, by interest as well as political conviction, is permanently bound to the support of the smaller nations'. In the name of small nations, Gregory also denounced the 'recent outburst of barbarism in Germany'. The highest ideal of Scottish foreign policy had to be that of 'making this country a mediator, cultural and political, between its neighbours and friends'. In a following article, Gregory denounced German rearmament and supported a 'short, preventative war' led by France and Poland, but not England.

However, in November 1936, Lewis Spence made a number of comments in relation to the number of Jewish students at Edinburgh University. Spence declared that 'an enormous number of foreign Jewish students are invading Edinburgh; the present figure is 18,000. A lot, of course, have come from Germany. They work like slaves'.[23] The *Jewish Chronicle* demonstrated that there were, in fact, no more than 60 Jews of German origin at Edinburgh University. The *Chronicle* also pointed out that Spence had publicly complained that 'the great majority of the leading fifteen names of successful students in the examinations are Jewish-sounding'.[24] The same complaint had been made by Mosley and the BUF.

In December 1936, as the Spanish Civil War raged unreported in the Scottish nationalist press, Russell gave a much more positive assessment of the Third Reich:

> Germany is held in a tight Fascist grip; Scotland is free – or will be free. Germany inclines towards militarism; Scotland is eminently pacifist. The German mind is mass-moving; that of Scotland is intensely individualistic. From these contrasting effects we might argue, therefore, that Germany is terrorised and enslaved – Scotland well-off and happy ... The strange paradox is that, in practice, it is much more the other way around. Germany under dictatorship gets things done – constructs roads, bridges, swimming-baths, strives to make its people fit and healthy, calls for sacrifices in the national interest, maintains the morale of its unemployed by local schemes of work, and uses its native resources to the fullest extent ... Admittedly, in achieving these things, many individual considerations have been set aside – in the case of the Jews, Trade Unions, Socialists and Communists – quite ruthlessly so. Nevertheless, in ridding itself of all supposedly 'subversive' elements, Germany can be said to have achieved a national spirit and unity of purpose that in many directions might well be the envy of 'free' Scotland, with its rejected appeals for road-bridges and other essential communications, its disregarded fishing and agricultural needs, its unrecognised 'Plan' for the Highlands, its toll of ill-health, its discouraged and disillusioned unemployed given nought to do but hang around the local 'cross', given nought to hope for but an occasional march to London.[25]

Of course, admirers of Fascism and Nazism were in a minority, albeit a significant one. Thus, in May 1937, the SNP conference resolved that 'the party is alive to the significance of the growth in Fascism in England as manifested in the last County Council elections in London, and declare that unless self-government is achieved Scotland might find herself against her will forced by English votes into a British totalitarian state'.[26] But the final words of the resolution reiterated the founding obsession of the SNP: to get rid of the English and be a nation again.

In April 1938, in 'Scotland and Peace', Archie Lamont wrote:

> Scotland cannot afford to go into a war along with England. It would
> mean the final destruction of our national personality. It would mean
> the annihilation of the Scottish National Movement, and the sub-
> mersion of everything democratic and distinctively Scottish . . . We
> must refuse to fight, refuse to pay taxes or advance loans, refuse to
> handle munitions, and if we are forced into the army, refuse to carry
> arms.[27]

In July 1938, Oliver Brown, a socialist nationalist and French
teacher, tried to distinguish between 'good' and 'evil' nationalism,
the latter illustrated by German and Italian imperialism. To offset
these two examples of 'pathological' nationalism, 'the Scandinavian
countries provide convincing examples of a Nationalism which is
healthy, peaceful and progressive'. Nevertheless, Brown's paean to
good nationalism was itself not far from fascist rhetoric. For the
author, 'when national impulses are replaced by alien interests
and influences, the nation concerned loses its power to make any
contribution to the creative thought of Civilisation'. This had been
illustrated by the 'degeneration' of Edinburgh in the late nineteenth
century. Brown quite logically concluded on the dangers of intermix-
ing: 'The eventual results may be estimated in the cosmopolitan parts
of London, Cairo, Marseilles and New York where members of every
nationality freely exchange and acquire one another's vices. In those
cesspools of humanity nothing suffers so much from standardisation
as human personality!'[28]

However, the sacrifice of Czechoslovakia at Munich could be
denounced in the name of small nation nationalism. In November
1938, the editorial of *The Scots Independent* attacked the British
government which had 'abandoned the League of Nations, having
exploited it. It has wrecked collective security, having used that name
for electioneering purposes'. The big-power behaviour of London
contrasted with the 'sane neutrality' of the Oslo Powers. England was
'guiding us to war – a war of which Scotland cannot approve, if she
is to be accounted sane'. The 'moment of Scotland's opportunity' had
come. It was imperative to 'resist all propagandist efforts to march
our people to an imperialist war in the name of those human ideals
which have been betrayed'.[29]

In November 1938, at the Central Halls, Glasgow, John MacCormick reaffirmed 'an unwavering belief in the League of Nations and in collective security as the only possible guarantees of the safety of the small nations and the rule of law in the world'. But the nationalist mindset allowed for all sorts of potent amalgams. The London government, claimed the SNP leader, was 'casting envious eyes on Fascist methods of government, and yearning for the opportunity to introduce them at home'.[30]

In January 1939, as Barcelona fell to Fascist forces, Arthur Donaldson argued for Scottish neutrality in any future conflict:

> Everything that Hitler has done and is said to have done against humanity and democracy will be done here by our dictators within a month or two after the first gun, and worse before it is over. The only good way 'to kick Hitler in the pants' is to establish in Scotland a real political, social and economic democracy which will set the totalitarians a standard of achievement and individual well-being beyond anything they have achieved and can achieve. And that cannot be done by falling for the propaganda of our rulers.[31]

In April 1939, a month after Nazi troops invaded what remained of the Czech lands, destroying all illusions of 'appeasement', John Macdonald was warning the readership about 'The English in Scotland': their country was threatened by 'ever-increasing English immigration', with 'southerners taking top jobs'. Also in that issue, Andrew Dewar Gibb offered 'The True View' on nationalists and war:

> Scotland has good reason to hate all this war talk, in a far deeper sense than England. And the normal Scotsman does not find easy consolation in naval twaddle about 'England's' might and the moral need in the world of a strong (not to say belligerent) Britain. He will be quicker to recognise in all this the revival of the spirit of Imperialist aggressiveness and empty jingoism.[32]

A Visitor from the Third Reich

Given such virulently pacifist and anti-English views, it was not surprising that, on 18 February 1939, Andrew Dewar Gibb received a very warm letter from one Dr Gerhard von Tevenar in Berlin.[33] Von Tevenar was both a Celtic scholar and an agent of the *Abwehr*, Nazi military intelligence. In the case of von Tevenar we see the extent of Nazi penetration of Celtic nationalist movements, as well as attempts by the SNP to exculpate itself.

Gerhard von Tevenar was born on 10 January 1912 near Danzig. In 1929, he travelled around Denmark, Hungary, Ireland and Scotland before returning to Germany to study law. In 1934–35, he researched the problems of minorities in frontier regions. In parallel to this, he did research on Celtology and Celtic migrations. The Breton nationalist and future Nazi collaborator, Olier Mordrel, would later recall a meeting with his friend Gerhard, one day in his architectural studio in Quimper. The latter 'was a slender boy, with pale eyes, and an angular mask filled with a curious expression of grave willpower and mutinous mischief'.[34] He was, continued Mordrel, 'one of those who believed in a renaissance of the Celts, and the study of the past would not have interested him if he had not found there reasons for the race he loved to believe in and to live for'. This bore fruit in 1936, when von Tevenar published *Volk und Raum der Bretonen*. He was also instrumental in founding the *Deutsche Gesellschaft für keltische Studien*.

In 1936, von Tevenar was appointed correspondent of the *Berliner Borsenzeitung* in Holland and Belgium. It was then that he met Werner Best, assistant to the head of the SD intelligence service, Reinhard Heydrich, future architect of the Final Solution. He was then involved in developing a vast network of relationships formed between the numerous autonomist movements of Europe. In the 1970s, Mordrel recalled that 'this travelling salesman of ethnic revolution . . . this idealist who told us of a mystical empire of the North, which would renew against the Latin and Anglo-Saxon world the old barbarian brotherhood, in which he did not hesitate to include the Finns, that people so admirable and close to us'.[35]

Georges Cadiou writes that 'very soon the Nazi circles in power in Berlin began to take an interest in the movements of national minorities in Western Europe. Not through sympathy as you might think but in order to use them for the expansionist politics of the Third Reich'.[36] Von Tevenar's centre for Celtic studies was linked to the information section of military espionage (Abwehr II) and more particularly to a sub-group led by one Major Voss. Dozens of agents and spies would be recruited and trained in Germany before being let loose in numerous countries to fan the flames of revolt on the western periphery.

Scotland was one of the nations of the Celtic race that von Tevenar would visit, study and aim to convert to an alliance with the Third Reich. In 1936 and 1937, he visited Scotland as part of a tour of the Celtic fringe. But the Germans found few co-conspirators in Scotland. According to Daniel Leach, many nationalists 'were not only repelled by the notion of Nazi assistance but also realised such contacts would be extremely damaging if revealed to the public, and would likewise prove useful to British intelligence in its efforts to discredit them'.[37]

Von Tevenar's letter to Dewar Gibb, 'Lieber Herr Professor', displays common commitment to the nationalist cause, but without any explicit reference to subversive activity:

> It is a great pity that you have already got a young German girl this year. In any way, I would be very much obliged to you if you would kindly look round about after a family for 'exchanging' Fraulein Seeland . . . She would like to go and see Scotland through a good Scottish family. With a formal invitation from there she will get here the necessary tourist visa and a few shillings or pounds for pocket-money purposes. She is very keen on tennis and swimming.

But the political and the cultural were never far away:

> Glasgow must have seen recently very stormy receptions of the Air Minister; on the occasion our big papers mentioned for the first time, I know, 'schottische Nationalisten, die als Protest gegen die Versammlung für National Service ein schottisches Kampflied anstimmten' [Scottish Nationalists, who as a protest against the Parliament supporting conscription start singing a Scottish combat song]. I would be delighted to write a book about your country and Scottish Nationalism if I can find time and rest enough this year.

Von Tevenar dreamed of a return to Caledonia:

> It is a great pity, indeed, that the difficulties in going abroad for my countrymen are still growing. Otherwise I would not hesitate to

Left. The Deputy Führer's 'peace mission' to Scotland in May 1941 still provokes speculation. (© Mary Evans Picture Library)

Below. The Duke of Hamilton denied all acquaintance with Hess, but had been a prominent friend of Nazi Germany. (© Scran)

Above. North of the Cheviots, Mosley's Blackshirts came up against religious sectarianism and the Scottish national question. (© Getty Images)

Right. Thomas Carlyle was an inspiration to Fascists and the bunker bedtime reading of Adolf Hitler in the twilight of the Third Reich. (© Getty Images)

Left. Nazi turned SNP supporter, the warrior-writer Graham Seton Hutchison enjoys some Alpine air with nordic youth.

Below. Already in 1923, the Scottish Renaissance poet Hugh MacDiarmid was calling for a native 'species of Fascism'. (Andrew Paterson; courtesy of Gordon Wright)

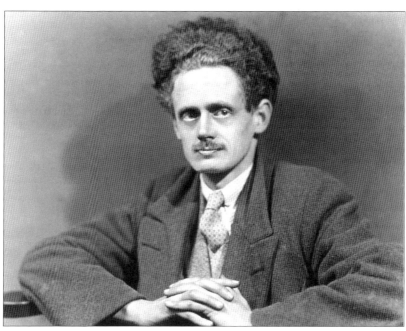

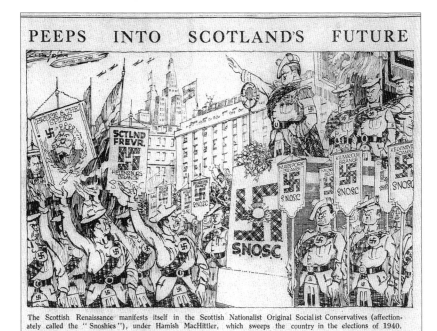

PEEPS INTO SCOTLAND'S FUTURE

The Scottish Renaissance manifests itself in the Scottish Nationalist Original Socialist Conservatives (affectionately called the " Snoshies "), under Hamish MacHittler, which sweeps the country in the elections of 1940.

As early as May 1931, the Glasgow *Evening Times* drew parallels between Scottish nationalism and the Nazi Party on the rise in Germany.

The Scottish Protestant League's hatred of all things 'Papist' led it to support Hispanic anticlericalism before rallying to a latter-day Martin Luther, Adolf Hitler.

Right. Charles Saroléa, Edinburgh University's first Professor of French, was an outspoken supporter of Fascism and a mortal enemy of the 'Red' Duchess of Atholl. (University of Edinburgh Fine Art Collection)

Below. The Duchess of Atholl paid heavily for her support of the Spanish Republic and opposition to the politics of appeasement. (© Getty Images)

Above. In 1938, the affair of Mrs Jessie Jordan, Dundee hairdresser and German spy, became a sensation in the Scottish press.

Left. After a hapless career as a spy, Norman Baillie-Stewart served the Nazi cause on radio.

The rabidly anti-semitic Captain Archibald Maule Ramsay was the only MP to be interned during the Second World War. (National Portrait Gallery, London)

Propaganda for the Wood Elves (collaboration with Harvey Dwight). Ian Hamilton Finlay's use of Nazi imagery attracted the wrath of 'anti-totalitarian' French intellectuals. (© Tate, London 2013)

choose May and June for another journey all over Scotland which I continue to love as *verzauberte, zweite Heimat und geheimnisvolle heroische Landschaft* [an enchanted second homeland and a landscape full of secrets]. As you know, I had the chance to drive all over Alba from John o'Groats to the Mull of Galloway and from Skye to Dunedin, and to catch some very beautiful views of land and men. I do not know if I told you that we were lucky enough to listen to some Gaelic songs which a shepherd sang while driving home his cattle, one evening near Stein (this sounds as German) on the isle of Skye. We were sitting down between some hills, covered with heather, and looking west to the thin lines of the Hebrides, with the great red sun disk behind; as the boy did not perceive us, he sang quite undisturbed – and this evening will be always one of our most beautiful impressions of the Gaelic Scotland.

He recounted his continual struggle in favour of Celtic studies:

As you will remember perhaps, I helped start in '37 at Berlin a *Deutsche Gesellschaft für keltische Studien*; the war had destroyed most of the research and publishing activity on Celtic countries and languages. This work is terribly difficult to push forward for people do not quite understand why to put money on so far [sic] a subject.

He then turned to the prospects for the Nationalist movement:

I wonder if really your 'cautious' (as you say) countrymen will realise one day that prosperity does not necessarily depend on complete union with England; the foreign observer often asks himself why the prosperity-viewpoint seems still to prevail against the national sentiment, in Scotland of today. It seems to me that in Ireland, too, there was and continues to be this awful struggle between 'money' and 'idealism'; since '16 however the Irish proved that their idealism grew stronger than the egoism-mentality of their rich people. You will certainly pardon my frankness, but I must tell you that I found amongst the young Irish more idealism and preparedness for sacrifice (*Opferbereitschaft*) than amongst the young Scotsmen. When I showed a lot of books and paper-cuttings on Scottish problems and even Scottish nationalism to a friend of mine, a young historian, he said to me after reading all this: '*Ich habe ein Eindruck, als ob es in Schottland heute nur noch ein wirtschaftliches und soziales Problem gibt, aber kein nationales mehr'* ['I have the impression that in today's Scotland, there is merely an economic and a social problem but no longer a national one']. And here I think lies the very importance of your action, and, for instance, of a thing like the Covenant of Scottish Action: to shift the whole question from the economical onto the national base. I do not know if you can understand this terribly styled argumentation; but certainly you will imagine round about the idea I tried to explain you in my English. If it means not wasting time to you, I would be delighted to read your opinion on this last question: 'Scotland – an economical or a national problem?' Perhaps I am wrong to compare all your problems with those in Ireland which I know a little better?

Von Tevenar also cited the article by Gert Antonius as an example of pessimistic assessment of the chances for Scottish home rule. But he concluded on a hopeful note:

I would be delighted to discuss all this with you personally and I do regret very much that I had no chance to meet you again in August '36, after that Wallace commemoration at Elderslie. Please do not think me very ambitious and annoying because I am still talking to you on questions which are no more questions to you; I just try to understand your country a little better than most of my countrymen and most of the English do.

Such an encounter would, however, never come to pass. Indeed, the declaration of war against Nazi Germany seemed to finally shake Andrew Dewar Gibb out of indulgence toward the new enemy threatening not only England but Scotland herself. In *The Scots Independent* of October 1939, Dewar Gibb tried to reconcile anti-Englishness with opposition to Nazi aggression.

The war is being fought because Hitler was becoming a menace to the imperial position of Britain. Poland was merely a pretext and a particularly rotten pretext ... The path was smoothed for them by the complaisance of an opposition bitterly hostile to Hitler on 'ideological grounds' ... There are far more Scotsmen today who have doubts about the justice and inevitability of the war than would have had those doubts ten years ago ... The difficulty of Englands' is not Scotland's opportunity – not yet. If the German planes come over, Scotland, equally with England, is threatened with death and destruction. A Scottish life was the first British casualty of the war. In the interests of Scotland we have to save what can be saved for her.

Elsewhere in that issue, 'S.D.' tried to claim the conflict for the nationalist cause: 'After fighting in this war for freedom and the right of small nations to live their own lives, she must claim her share of the victory – the right to control her own affairs.'[38]

In April 1940, Dewar Gibb wrote in praise of 'True Nationalism':

The natural exemplar to which Scotsmen should turn with humility and admiration today is Finland ... If the world is to be the better place after the war which we all rather hopelessly are hoping for, there must be no place for nationalism of the German or any similar brand. The greater the decentralisation, the fewer swollen nations and empires and lands of hope and glory on which the sun never sets, the better for the prospects of a lasting peace. It would be post-war policy of the new Scotland to 'work in friendly collaboration with Europe' – but in *free* and friendly collaboration.[39]

The following month, as the Nazi threat turned towards the last remaining Western democracies, Wilson MacCulloch unmasked 'Hitler's conspiracy in Scotland. The activities of Dr von T–':

The chosen agent for the German penetration of Scottish life was Dr von T–, an intelligent and agreeable young man, a native of Dantzig, who (as later turned out) had played an important part in stimulating the 'Rex' party in Belgium, a now discredited semi-Fascist organisation whose leader, Degrelle, once came within an ace of staging a coup d'état in Brussels. Von T– was also in close touch with the extremer wing of Flemish separatists at the time when he was nominally a research student at Brussels University. Needless to say his interest in these movements was simply for the purposes of furthering German political designs – separating Belgium from France and promoting disruption of the Western democracies.[40]

But, revealed MacCulloch, 'Von T–'s activities were given a wider scope. He became an ardent student of Celtic affairs and culture. He visited Brittany and soon afterwards, the Breton movement received a remarkable access of financial strength. It also became more extreme in its tactics.' According to his own story, 'Von T–' 'studied' the IRA in Ireland and the Welsh Nationalist movement. He also paid a visit to Scotland, travelling about the country, questioning, meeting leading Scottish personalities, and displaying an intelligent interest in all he saw and heard. But his mission was thwarted:

> He was loud in his surprise that the Scottish Nationalist movement had not developed a 'youth movement' which was his agreeable Teutonic way of hinting at a storm troop organisation. Strange to say no Nationalist ever displayed the slightest desire to fill this lamentable gap in the movement. Scottish Nationalism remained staunchly democratic. Dr Von T– must have listened to many a word of abuse of the Nazi system (of which he professed to take a detached view).

After this preliminary exploration, 'Von T–' had returned to Scotland in the summer of 1937:

> This time he was accompanied by three young German friends, two of which were to the observant eye typical Nazi thugs. The four made an extensive 'holiday tour' of Scotland by motor car, a remarkable feat at a time when no German was allowed to take more than 20 marks out of the Reich. Equally surprising was the completeness of Von T–'s dossier of the names and addresses of influential Nationalists. Not only persons prominently identified in the public eye with political nationalism, but many sympathisers on the fringe of the movement as well, were called on and interviewed. But the report to Scotland that went back to Dr Goebbels in Berlin must have been an unfavourable one. Although Scotland was not dropped entirely from the Nazi list of work in progress, the assiduous Dr Von T– does not appear to have visited our shores again. He retired to Amsterdam where he no doubt remains in close touch with Dr Mussert, the Dutch Nazi leader.

The author reported the SNP's receipt of 'curious publications' including *Breiz Atao*, a 'Breton sheet violently hostile to the "Jewish, negrophile" government of Paris'; *Stur*, 'promoting sympathy for Hitler [and] supporting destruction of Czechoslovakia'; and *Peuples et frontières*: 'much scientific jargon.'

The single personality behind them all was Gerhard von Tevenar, 'Goebbels' viceroy to the Celtic and Teutonic West':

> Maybe he is busily qualifying at the moment for the post of Gauleiter in Hitler's Scottish Protectorate. He has earned the job! Unless, of course, he has given Scotland up as a bad job. For it must be acknowledged that our nationalist movement has been a grave disappointment to the doctor and his friends. When the destruction of Czecho-Slovakia was arranged, the SNP denounced it in a memorable declaration of policy. And that declaration was bitterly attacked in the pages of the 'Breton' review *Stur*. A strange chapter in the history of Scottish politics is closed. The Nationalists refused steadfastly to be diverted from the methods of democracy and the goal of freedom. They were not Hitler's dupes. When the Day came, it was to another party that the Führer was forced to turn for his accomplices in our midst!

The SNP thus publicly cleansed itself of any possible taint due to the activities of this Nazi agent and stood up to the new threat. This threat was real: if Scotland may still have seemed far from the front-line and the Battle of Britain raging over Kent, it nevertheless was included in German plans. The central security office ran by Reinhard Heydrich, second in command of the Gestapo, envisaged the immediate creation of headquarters in London and five *Einsatzgruppen* working in Bristol, Birmingham, Liverpool and Manchester, but also Edinburgh. It produced the *Sonderfahndungsliste GB* (Special Search Lists, also known as the Black Book), including the names of nearly 3,000 British politicians, writers, artists and intellectuals. Among the Scots listed for arrest were the Duchess of Atholl, Communist scientist J.B.S. Haldane, Balkanist R.W. Seton-Watson, novelist Naomi Mitchison and James Maxton MP. Willie Gallacher MP would be immediately imprisoned by the Gestapo.[41]

In the *Scots Independent* of June 1940, E. Marischal outlined a 'Nazi Plan to Invade Scotland', involving bombs on aerodromes, small landing parties on the Fife and East Lothian coasts, and small patrols in British uniforms or civilian clothes. London had to be warned: 'Until the British military authorities understand the ingenuity of the German methods, they will not be able to meet them successfully'.[42] In July, the headline was 'Fortify the Cheviots!': Scotland had to be made strong against invasion by the raising of a Scottish Home Defence Army, and the rapid transfer to Scotland of sufficient arms-making equipment, planes and personnel. With Norway in the hands of the Nazis and their puppet Vidkun Quisling, a 'diplomatic correspondent' of the *Scots Independent* asked: 'Who will rule the North?' The war brought possible changes to Scotland's 'living space'. Norway would take Orkney and the Shetland Islands, 'and they will be the bridle with which she holds us in her power'. Conversely, if Scotland emerged victorious from the war, she would find her place in 'a free federation of the Western Scandinavian democracies', including the Faroes and Iceland.[43] In September, the SNP compared its map of Europe with Hitler's. Those Breton nationalists, led by Olier Mordrel, who had been recruited by von Tevenar and Berlin, stood discredited: 'Herr Weyer is nominated governor-general with his capital at Rennes. This is the hideous farce in which the labours of Breton poets and dreamers have ended!' It was the 'Commonwealth idea' that would save the West for civilisation and freedom.[44] In October 1940, *The Scots Independent* described the present conflict as 'a war of nations against the would-be destroyer of nations. It is a war "for" the Commonwealth idea, the idea of a co-operation of peoples, and "against" the idea of a super-race ruling its enslaved sub-races'.[45]

Lewis Spence went further, in his typically lyrical and left-field way. In 1940, he revealed the 'occult causes' of the present war. Nazism and its leader were 'Satanic', the most recent expression of a devilish genealogy that included witchcraft, freemasonry and Illuminism. In the face of the demonic frenzy of the Germans, 'a race suggestible to the powers of evil', the former president of the Scottish National movement rallied to Britishness:

This mystical and serenely beautiful island of ours awaits the ordeal of battle with the legions of a hell-inspired multitude with manly calmness and resolution. The certainty of His triumphs is ours. Tried we may be to the uttermost, but victory is assured by our alliance with Divine virtue and destiny. The Hand that shaped this planet will not permit its deflection into the dark and terrible paths which lead to the abyss. Britain, the sea-borne Ark, bearing the symbols of truth and righteousness, will pass unscathed through the tempest to the haven of that victory which is peace.[46]

Spence would have felt vindicated when, in November 1940, 'from a secret source in occupied Norway', it was announced by the *Scots Independent* that 'the invasion of Scotland is off!'[47]

The success of von Tevenar's mission therefore seems to have been limited largely to Brittany. At the end of August 1939, he had introduced Olier Mordrel into certain influential circles in Berlin. Mordrel's men would devote themselves to political, cultural and even military collaboration with the Nazis that would never lead to real autonomy, and would tarnish the image of Breton nationalism for decades after the war ended.

Von Tevenar's star rapidly waned and was extinguished. Certainly, in December 1940, he married Erika von Seidlitz-Kurzbach, daughter-in-law of Otto von Stulpnagel, German military commander in France, and had two children with her. Yet von Tevenar was already considered suspect by the Nazi Party. One ideological error was his faithful friendship with a former professor, Julius Pokorny, who had to quit his chair because of the racial laws and whom von Tevenar had warned of a pogrom, giving him time to flee the country. The *Abwehr* agent was also compromised by his close relationship with Friedrich Hielscher, founder of the pagan cult, the *Hielscher Kreis*.

Von Tevenar's movements as he carried correspondence for his friend and guru Hielscher – who had baptised his children – were soon under surveillance. Already in June 1938, von Tevenar had been arrested with a forged passport by the SS at the Dutch frontier. He would be expelled from the Nazi Party. In wartime, von Tevenar was arrested again, on charges of homosexuality, and sent to Moabit Prison for four months. He was then regularly tortured by the Gestapo in Berlin before being sent to Sachsenhausen. He was eventually released but, on 15 April 1943, died of a heart attack in Strasbourg.

Gerhard von Tevenar does not figure again in SNP literature or Andrew Dewar Gibb's papers. But Olier Mordrel remained attached to this agent of the Celtic renaissance, declaring in *Stur*: 'I have often dreamed of a garden that we would construct in Brittany for elevated souls, [and] I think of this garden when I think of the man who was Gerhard von Tevenar.'[48]

An Unwanted Brother

Commitment to the Scottish Nationalist cause could lead to exile. In September 1939, a yacht put in at the Irish town of Athlone. On board was a striking man of theatrical bearing, along with his wife, sister and adult daughter. The party maintained they were on their way to the French Riviera, but had been taken by surprise by the declaration of war and had decided to put in at Shannon. Their desire to stay was confirmed when they purchased a cottage in Bray. The head of this family was none other than Captain Ronald Mac-Donald Douglas, former Commandant-General of the Scottish Defence Force.

Although the SDF, a tiny organisation non-existent outside Irish-Catholic areas of Glasgow, had been infiltrated and smashed by the Special Branch, Captain Douglas had not ended his quixotic campaign for independence and pan-Celtic solidarity. In 1936, he published *The Irish Book: A Miscellany of Facts and Fancies, Folklore and Fragments, Poems and Prose to do with Ireland and her People*. It was light and folkish, but with a deadly serious objective: 'To do whatever I can in a small way to re-unite in some fashion the related but severed people of Ireland and Scotland is one of my ardent desires.'[49]

His book was conceived as a 'literary claymore': 'the names of Eire and Alba closely entwined in the metal of its hilt, and ... engraved in the Gaelic with "Repeal the Union" on the one side of its blade, and with "Remember Arbroath" on the other'.[50]

In 1973, in *Catalyst for the Scottish Viewpoint*, the ultra-nationalist journal of the 1320 Club, Douglas recalled his activities after the break with Wendy Wood in the early thirties:

> My abortive gun-running attempts from Switzerland, my invitation and visit to the Brownhaus [*sic*] in Munich, and my meeting with Rudolf Hess. From that moment onwards I was marked, and followed all over Europe and homeward through England, by members of the Special Branch – or, as I prefer always to call them, the Secret Police.[51]

In a sequel, 'The Mad Nationalist', Douglas recounted his persecution at the hands of the Scottish authorities: 'Everyone knows what the Russians do with revolutionary writers. They do what the

Americans did after the war with one of their most sane poets, Ezra Pound. They don't just imprison them. They put them in so-called mental homes'.[52]

While in Versailles in late 1938, Douglas was informed that Scottish PEN had presented his *Miscellany* to George VI's queen. Douglas had replied furiously by telegram: 'I am very conscious of the honour my fellow authors thought of me; but I still remain the incorruptible republican Nationalist and enemy of the British Empire.' The 'secret police' then followed him to Paris, Strasbourg and then on to England where he sought refuge with some friends: 'unfortunately, some of Sir Oswald Mosley's Fascist party "literature" was found in their home'.[53] The action moved to an Italian restaurant in Inverness, where Douglas got caught up in a fight with some drunken English RAF officers. He was then taken to Porterfield Jail, beaten by the police, and falsely accused of wielding his *sgian dubh*. Then, on the orders of the Lord Advocate, he was detained for six months in a mental home in Morningside Drive, Edinburgh. In spring 1939, Douglas dared to breach the 15-mile radius imposed on him. He made for Rosyth to launch a yacht he had purchased and ran the Saltire from the ensign staff. The following day, described as cold and sunny, the Lord Advocate issued an ultimatum for Douglas to leave Scotland: 'He was not to return for over six years. He suffered, but he is very conscious of the fact that in a way he was fortunate, for all over the world millions of innocents suffered far more.'[54]

On arrival in Athlone, Douglas was immediately put under surveillance by the Irish Free State's security service, G2, which reported in November 1940: 'He hopes to do for Scotland what Padraig Pearse did for Ireland.' In fact, the vigilance of G2 showed that the Irish authorities took a very dim view of this 'brother' in their midst. Daniel Leach writes:

> Unlike the post-war asylum granted to Breton nationalists and others, the presence of Scottish nationalists in Ireland was entirely a product of the enduring constitutional relationship with the UK, and in no way an expression of pan-Celtic solidarity. Indeed, Irish agencies regarded resident Scottish nationalists with unease, keeping them under close surveillance, arguing for their deportation and, in several cases, taking direct action to curtail their activities.[55]

In November 1940, G2 remarked of Douglas: 'He is clearly an adventurer and intriguer and potentially dangerous, and his deportation is recommended.' There was a probability of his enthusiasm in this connection linking him up with subversive organisations in the country. According to Leach, 'the prospect of an IRA-backed Scottish rising supplied from Ireland while Britain faced possible Nazi invasion clearly sent alarm bells ringing in Dublin'.[56] That said, no evidence could be found of subversive activities.

As G2's personnel dug deeper, they found allegations relating to the real nature of Douglas's relationships with the women in his household. If he was not an active subversive, G2 concluded, he was, at the very least, an 'immoral adventurer'. Ronald MacDonald Douglas was not even his real name, but the stage name of one Ronald Edmonston. What's more, he was not unknown in Ireland, having previously run a theatre in Dun Laoghaire for two years from 1930. In the face of this immoral adventurer and fascistic fantasist, the attitude of the Scottish authorities toward him at the time 'appeared to be that they would be glad if he stayed out of Scotland'.[57] The Irish did not want this 'brother' either.

Against the 'Fifth Column'

Back in Scotland, there was among some Scots antipathy to any war against continental fascism. On 25 January 1939, Douglas Young wrote to George Campbell Hay: 'To me the cold-blooded financial stranglehold of London on the coolie and semi-coolie peoples under the aegis of democratic Westminster is quite as repulsive as the hooliganism of the Nazi storm-troopers.'[58] Young expanded on these views in a letter to Hugh Seton-Watson:

> The British Empire seems to me a worse institution than the *Staaten-bund* Hitler is trying to erect. We live in as it were a genteel suburb of it, but the real empire consists of Jamaica, and the rand, and the coolie *ergastula* of India and Malaya; if democracy be representative and responsible government for the benefit of the governed, then I should be prepared to maintain that Nazi Germany with all its pogroms etc. is more concretely democratic than our hoary plutocracy, and, what is near a virtue, much less hypocritical. I believe a Nazi boss, and certainly an ordinary SA man, to be a more honest creature than

a typical British bourgeois; at any rate the difference is so slight as not to be worth fifty or even five million lives. The values on which Nazism is based are not altogether my values, but neither are the cash values of our social and economic and political system; anyway it is pretty clear from history that values are spread mainly by precept and example and scarcely at all by war.[59]

George Campbell Hay saw in the possible German invasion of England a form of historical revenge. In May 1939, he wrote to Young: 'Of course there will be starvation – in England. It will be an interesting thing for Ireland to watch.'[60]

When war was declared in September 1939, there was opposition on the far-from-inconsiderable margins of Scottish politics. With the Molotov–Ribbentrop Pact, the Communists had toned down, if not buried, their anti-Fascist passion of recent years. If John Ross Campbell had resigned as editor of the *Daily Worker* in protest at the pact, the majority of the CPGB leadership, including the erstwhile scourge of appeasement, Willie Gallacher MP, had fallen in with the Comintern line. In October 1939, the Communists told the workers: 'The rulers of Britain and France are using this war to declare heavy blows against their own peoples . . . employers have launched a sweeping attack on workers' standards and conditions. The workers must organise to resist the combined attacks of the employers and the Government.'[61] The MP for West Fife opined:

The Home Front – your Front, reader – the Front of wages, trade union conditions; of one Friday night after another – is not so quiet. On this Front there have been ceaseless bombardment, constant raids, incessant attacks. No sparring for position, no reconnaissance flights. But war – and war. Unceasing, deadly, and carried out by the ruthless general staff of British capitalism.[62]

What's more, the arrival of largely nationalist and anti-Communist Polish soldiers caused considerable bad feeling in the coalfield towns of Cowdenbeath, Kelty and Lochgelly. Such hostile feelings would be reinforced with Hitler's invasion of the Soviet Union in June 1941. Trevor Royle writes: 'it did not take long for existing in-difference to be transmuted into outright hostility towards the Free

Poles who came to be regarded in west Fife not as gallant allies but as potential enemies of the Soviet Union'.[63]

Gradually, under the impact of events, the leadership of the SNP moved over to a pro-war stance. Where conscription without the assent of a Scottish parliament had once been considered a violation of the 1707 Treaty of Union, as war neared in May 1939 the party relaxed its stance, provided that conscripts would be used only for the defence of Britain. In October 1939, a manifesto declared Scotland's willingness to fight alongside England and the Commonwealth for ideals appealing to the Scottish people. In December, the SNP conference had agreed a policy of 'acquiescence' in the war, arguing that Germany had trampled on the freedom of three small nations already, and that a free Scotland would 'inevitably' have declared war against it anyway. However, this stance caused splinters – notably, with Douglas Young disaffiliating his Aberdeen branch. It appears that Young even entertained the possibility of collaborating with a future Nazi occupier. In August 1940, he would write to R.E. Muirhead: 'The Germans will look around for aborigines to run Scotland, and it is to be wished that the eventual administration consist of people who have in the past shown themselves to care for the interests of Scotland.'[64]

The poetry of Hugh MacDiarmid showed how anti-Englishness and anti-imperialism – the two inextricably linked – could lead to a downplaying, if not downright denial, of the threat emanating from Berlin. In 'On the Imminent Destruction of London, June 1940', the bard of Langholm wrote:

> Now when London is threatened
> With devastation from the air
> I realise, horror atrophying me,
> That I hardly care.
> [...]
> For London is the centre of all reaction
> To progress and prosperity in human existence
> Set against all that is good in the spirit of man,
> As Earth's greatest stumbling block and rock of offence.[65]

There seemed to be anti-Scottish bias in air defence, as in 'The German Bombers':

> The German bombers came up the Forth
> And unchallenged all day o'er Edinburgh flew
> While not in Edinburgh but only in London
> The air-raid warning siren blew.
> [...]
> The leprous swine in London town
> And their Anglo-Scots accomplices
> Are, as they have always been,
> Scotland's only enemies.[66]

In 'Surely It Were Better', Labour ministers in the National Government were singled out for opprobrium:

> Is a Mussolini or a Hitler
> Worse than a Bevin or a Morrison?
> At least the former proclaim their foul purposes
> The latter practise what their words disown.[67]

Similar sentiments were expressed by George Campbell Hay, for example in 'War or Peace, I care not':

> The war will come in Spring, they say;
> And if it comes I bet, my friend,
> They'll find some 'Belgium' to defend.
> (...)
> Weeping through Scotland, shore to shore,
> And pipers puffing, red and wudd,
> And Donald choking in his blood –
> The 'little Belgiums' matter more.[68]

The poets' sentiments were echoed by Harry Miller (a.k.a. J.H. Miller-Wheeler), leader of the Scottish Socialist Party, whose socialism seemed markedly shorn of internationalism. On 4 January 1941, he wrote to MacDiarmid: 'The latest racket is in sending Scots girls to Coventry, refusal means their dole is stopped while English wenches are arriving in droves and walking into jobs. Glasgow is crawling with prostitutes from London, Birmingham and Coventry. The same thing applies to men, there seems to be a deliberate transference of population.'[69]

That same year, in his pamphlet, *Hitlerism in the Highlands*, Oliver Brown was happy to tar the English oppressor with the Fascist brush:

> You have, so far, been presented with a one-sided view of Scottish history, the 'pacification' of the Highlands, the increase of material prosperity subsequent to (although not necessarily consequent on) the Union of 1707, and the careers offered to Scotsmen through the seizure of that land now known as the British Empire. You have been diligently shown the credit column (containing some assets of dubious value), whereas little or nothing has been said about the debt side. To rectify this omission you will find listed in these pages some of the evil consequences of the *Anschluss* of 1707, whereby the former nation of Scotland was incorporated in the English Reich. It is hoped that you will thus be enabled to strike the proper balance and reach the ultimate truth of which the following facts form and indisputable and indispensable part.[70]

Brown passed on to a litany of 'Hitlerist' crimes in the Highlands: Culloden and Butcher Cumberland, the Disarming Act, the Clearances, Skye's contribution to the tears, toil and sweat of empire building, and the heartless dictatorship blighting fishing and seafaring. Brown concluded:

> Now the Highlands have been declared a 'protected area' by the Government against which they require protection. Similarly, in Germany, the Gestapo takes its victims into protective custody (even the vocabulary does not vary!) Can the Highlands survive the economic and social hardships imposed by these actions of the London Government? Yes. But only if we secure the establishment of a Scottish Government which will restore the land to its rightful owners and develop the hitherto neglected resources of this great area.[71]

The author of this legally published polemic granted that there was considerable freedom of speech in Scotland, but this freedom was 'every day diminishing. The imprisonment by the English Government of Arthur Donaldson and Matthew Hamilton without charge or trial shows the danger of rousing the resentment of our London rulers ... Scotland, under the domination of a permanent English majority in the House of Commons, has no more freedom of action than Norway under Nazi occupation'.[72]

Indeed, the authorities had begun to move against a suspected Nationalist 'fifth column', beginning with Matthew Hamilton.[73] Hamilton had been born in Glasgow on 1 April 1901. After some time in Ireland, he returned to Scotland in 1922 and with his brother opened a roadside garage near Lamancha, in Peeblesshire. He first came to the attention of the police in August 1933 when, at a DSSO meeting with Wendy Wood at the Mound, he exclaimed: 'I am one who suffered and made sacrifices for England. We will have no more of it. The next sacrifice we will make will be for our own country.' In 1937, when an excise officer called upon him and his brother to see if they had a licence to sell the cigarettes they were selling at the garage, 'Hamilton ordered him off the premises quoting old Scots Law and saying that he did not require a licence or recognise English Law.'

Hamilton's nationalism led him to support a position of neutrality in a future war with Germany. Indeed, this stance had a racist rather than purely pacifist underpinning, for on 24 May 1939, he wrote to Rolf Hoffmann, the Nazi propaganda chief in Munich:

Your 'News from Germany' is dispelling the lies against Germany propagated by the English Press in Scotland (which is controlled by Jewish freemasonry). There is a strong opposition against an English conscription in Scotland. There has already been anti-conscription disturbance in Glasgow and Cowdenbeath – recruiting offices windows smashed in, and PO van overturned – these disturbances are being carefully censored in the Press. Also police have been armed with 'concealed' revolvers. The Celtic peoples of Scotland, Ireland and Wales (who are becoming united) desire no further participation in continental wars on behalf of Jewish-controlled England. I would be pleased to have a call from any Germans who happen to be in this vicinity, as there are many things hidden politically, and removal of Jewish, English and Ulster Orange influences (under aegis of Jewish Foreign Freemasonry) would result in a Scots-Celtic-Germano-Social and Commercial Alliance. Enclosed find historical and legal propaganda circulating in Scotland and elsewhere, which will give you an idea of the real position of Scottish Rights. We fly a string of Welsh, Irish and Scottish flags, and would like a small swastika flag

to fly alongside to show our good feeling. Wishing you every success
for German Liberty and World Peace.

Yours sincerely,

For Scottish and German Rights

Hamilton was also involved in what Special Branch described
as the 'highly seditious and dangerous Scots Order'. Fellow con-
spirators were Douglas Stewart Forbes, psychotherapist; Douglas
Emslie Stewart, journalist; and William Bryce (18), an apprentice
lithographic printer who intended to join the Irish Free State Air
Force and was understood to have 'threatened to shoot his mother if
she divulges anything'. The Scots Order met every Sunday evening
at the Melbourne Boxing Club, and its activities included sticking
leaflets on Edinburgh post boxes.

On 14 January 1940, again at the Mound, Hamilton described the
application of the Military Service Act to Scotland as high treason,
publicly burned two calling-up papers, and advised his listeners to
treat all calling-up papers in this fashion. He was also suspected of
getting youths liable for conscription out to the Free State. Hamilton
and his comrades were also present at the Scottish Peace Conven-
tion, held in Glasgow on 6 and 7 April 1940, where 509 delegates
from 298 organisations condemned the present war as a war between
rival imperialist powers. According to Special Branch, 'he decries
the Royal Family and objects to members of the Royal Family being
evacuated to Scotland during the war'. He was 'obviously mentally
unstable and utterly irresponsible . . . but is not certifiably insane'.

In these febrile times, Hamilton had nevertheless done enough to
merit internment under Defence Regulation 18B on 3 June 1940. He
had 'incited and endeavoured to incite persons liable to be called up for
military service to evade the duties which they had become or might
become liable to perform . . . [and] engaged in propaganda subversive
to the State'. He was sent to Peveril Camp, Peel, Isle of Man.

It was there, on 24 July 1941, that Hamilton appealed to history
to protest this internment:

I claim my Rights to the Protection of Scots Limitations and Security Acts, 1701-4-7, and the Treaty of Union, Provisions 1707. Also
all Provisions and . . . for the rest of my life, and from any further Acts
on my Scottish Liberty and Privileges, which have been won by the

Sacrificial Blood of my Scottish Forefathers on many a Sacrificial Field, and in the full strength of these aforesaid Acts, Sue for and Hereby Claim my Liberty.

He was unsuccessful. On 30 October 1941, Detective Superintendent Cormack reported negatively on a man who had been 'extremely active in spreading anti-British propaganda':

> Since Hamilton's arrest, the organisation known as 'Scots Order' ceased to exist and no trouble has been experienced from the former supporters. Several of these supporters, however, are still at large and the Police are quite confident that should Hamilton be released, he would immediately contact them and continue his former activities in a more hidden and dangerous way.

Major Perfect concurred with this assessment: 'The dividing line between this man's obvious eccentricity or probable madness is, I should imagine, extremely slight, and I think that he still is a fanatic who might cause the Police a great deal of trouble, if he were to be released.'

On 30 January 1942, it was reported that Hamilton had left camp to work at Balaquane Internment Hospital. He was 'quiet and well-conducted', 'an active and healthy man who takes great delight in physical exercise'. Yet his views remained more or less intact:

> He is obviously an ardent, if not fanatical Scottish Nationalist . . . He evaded any questions involving his attitude, as a Scot Nat, towards England in war-time . . . [and] it seems fairly clear that he would not join the fighting forces. He has great conceit of himself as an engineering genius and asserts that he 'could have designed an aeroplane which would have been far beyond anything yet known and might have helped win the war'.

On 20 May 1942, Superintendent Ogden, camp commandant, reported on this inmate:

> His general behaviour in Camp shows no indication of an unbalanced state, but he has a definite kink: he answers questions with that cunning evasiveness which seems peculiar to insane persons; in times

of stress he has the appearance of an insane person . . . My impression
is that his brain is deteriorating and the probability is that he will
eventually end his career in a mental hospital.

Hamilton's Scottish nationalist views were 'as strong as ever and
there is no doubt that this subject will always be his mania'. But he
had stated that 'he has changed his views relating to the war since he
has been detained; he realised that it is too late to keep Scotland out
of the war; if his ideal of Home Rule for Scotland is to materialise the
war must first be won'. What's more, he 'has no German sympathies,
dislikes Germans and is very much against Scotland being ruled
by a Royal family of Hanoverian descent; his attitude to the war, if
released, would be one of disinterested aloofness'. Ogden concluded:

> He is not a clever man; he has a slow brain, which, it would appear, is
> fast becoming slower. He is not a potential fifth columnist; he states
> that if any other country invaded Scotland he would fight in defence
> of this country. He has not the personality to enable him to influ-
> ence others to any extent. Most people would rightly regard him as a
> crank. I do not think that his release would involve such an interfer-
> ence with the war effort as to render his further detention necessary.

In July 1942, Matthew Hamilton was released on the proviso that
he kept police informed of his place of residence and notified them
of his movements monthly in person.

Hamilton was the only Nationalist interned under Defence Reg-
ultaion 18B in 1940, but police repression continued by other means.
On 3 May 1941 the police carried out raids on the houses and premises of Nationalists opposed to the war effort: ten in Glasgow, four
in Edinburgh, one in Aberdeen and one in Argyll.[71] Various items
of interest were found. It was reported that 'the censor, who seems
to be keeping an eye on C.M. Grieve's correspondence, may have
held up the "Brief Survey of Scottish Politics" which runs to 20,000
words. You may be wise to glance through the file'. One Nationalist
target was Harry Miller, who had taken an active role in the 'Scottish
Defence Corps', defunct since 1936. In April 1940, he had moved
from the SNP to the Scottish Socialist Party and taken part in the
anti-conscription Nationalist Mutual Aid Committee. His police
interrogator was particularly interested in possible links with Nazi
intelligence:

I further questioned Wheeler [Miller] regarding the SNP and their association with common enemy, when he admitted that it was his knowledge that immediately prior to the outbreak of war, the Party HQ were visited by a German agent who purported to be interested in the Scottish Nationalist Movement and was desirous of obtaining information regarding the Party for publication in Germany. Wheeler admitted the opinion that the agent entered Great Britain and contacted the Nationalist Party for propaganda purposes and expresses the firm belief that his visit had ulterior motives behind it. He could not state definitely that his agent contacted the man Arthur Donaldson but expressed the belief that contact between Donaldson and the agent had taken place. Wheeler stresses the point that he is not in sympathy with Nazi Germany or dictatorship of any kind and intimated that he would be in direct opposition to any individual using the Nationalist Party for spreading Fascist propaganda.

The police reported that they had seized a pamphlet ('Halt Conscription'), a poster ('No National Service until Scotland gets Home Rule'), and advice against national registration, as well as Fascist propaganda leaflets and correspondence.

The raid on R.E. Muirhead seemed particularly fruitful:

In the course of the search we took possession of a number of papers and documents bearing on extreme Scottish Nationalism. We also took possession of a quantity of gunpowder and a small pistol and some fireworks. No importance was attached to the gunpowder, pistol or fireworks as they did not seem to be of recent issue and appeared to have been kept in a place for some considerable time . . . Also taken possession of was a copy of a letter which Mr Muirhead had sent prior to the war to Dr von Teffenar [sic], Berlin, a known Nazi agent who visited this country on two occasions before the outbreak of hostilities in an endeavour to enlist the support of Scottish Nationalists.

In Aberdeen, Douglas Young told the police: 'I certainly am a Scottish Nationalist and do not recognise the Westminster government, but there is nothing subversive to be found here that would injure the war effort'. The poet George Campbell Hay, on the run from the military, was in hiding in Argyllshire. At his home was found a letter from Iain Haig which said: 'I wish more than ever now that Germany would win the war and create a hell of a change in this bloody country'. That said, the investigators could find 'nothing of a seditious or pro-German nature . . . in the correspondence'.[75]

These raids, and the detention of Arthur Donaldson, were met with indignation. On 13 May 1941, James Maxton raised questions in the Commons, denouncing the 'melodramatic nonsense and rubbish' used by the authorities to justify their actions. On 15 May 1941, Miller wrote tellingly to Tom Johnston, Labour's Secretary of State for Scotland: 'In your recent broadcast, you emphasised that there were no Quislings in Scotland. We agree entirely and would point out that we were fighting Fascism and Nazism when people in high places were supporting them in every possible way.' On 18 May, Miller wrote to Grieve: 'Questions have been asked about stories of Scotland being ready to make a separate peace with Germany. "Haw Haw" [William Joyce] has also made references to the position in Scotland. Needless to say there is not a chance for that outfit doing a deal with Nationalists and Republicans in Scotland. Funny that Hess should fly to see a member of the ruling class, the only bunch who are likely to do a deal with Hitler, and who probably will.'[76]

On 25 May 1941, it was the turn of Grieve/MacDiarmid to write to 'Dear Comrade' Tom Johnston.[77] Apropos the seizure of his typescript, 'it is a historical survey and analysis, was written before the War, and does not deal with the War in any way'. The Scots Renaissance poet went on:

Neither I nor any of the Scots Republicans who have been raided have had any subsidisation from our dealings with the German Nazis – nor any subsidisation from any other foreign source. The whole thing is a base English Imperialist manoeuvre to throttle and libel the now rapidly growing Scottish Socialist Republican Movement – and to divert public attention from the pro-Nazi Fifth Column traitors who are not to be found in our ranks but in the ranks of our aristocracy, plutocracy, and the 'internment' movement itself, where there are plenty who will sell us out to Hitler if they get a chance – though they are posing meanwhile as the most active and vocal of 'patriots'. English imperialism (the interrogations of those raided show) is especially anxious about, and eager to hook or, more likely, crack to destroy the affiliations many of my associates have with the Breton, Cymric, Irish and Indian movements.

He protested the raids on *Scottish Socialist, Free Man, Scottish News* and *Comment*, the internment of Arthur Donaldson, and the treatment of Douglas Young, who had been 'raided, questioned and grossly victimised by the English Gestapo'. What's more, the police had seized Gaelic manuscripts by great eighteenth-century Scottish poets 'simply because they are in Gaelic and ipso facto objects of suspicion to our ignorant English and Anglo-Scot CID people'. MacDiarmid concluded his letter by 'entering my most emphatic protest against your Government's illegal detention without trial and removal furth of Scotland, of Matthew Hamilton, the Scots law student, who has done invaluable work in exposing the way in which the English Government has illegally subverted the Scottish Law'.

The authorities did make a distinction between those Nationalists who were loyal and those who were not. On 24 May 1941, it was noted that 'John MacCormack [*sic*] is a loyal British subject and does not countenance the United Scottish Movement sponsored by Arthur Donaldson. On more than one occasion, Mr MacCormack has assisted the Police in connection with enquiries regarding extreme Scottish Nationalists.'

Radical anti-war Nationalists would create the Donaldson Defence Committee, denouncing the 'arbitrary and tyrannical treatment' of this dangerous dissident. According to the security services, Donaldson was 'an extremist Scottish Nationalist who has been engaged in the formation of an organisation called United Scotland which is more extremist than the SNP from which Donaldson has been expelled'.[78] He had 'made statements indicating that in his view England would be completely crushed by the early spring of this year, that the Government would leave the country and that the movement in Scotland must then be able to show the German Government that it is organised and has a clear cut policy, that it is not with England in the war and that when fire and confusion is at its height in England the movement can start in earnest'. He had also suggested the introduction of a whispering campaign which would spread rumours regarding, for example, shipping losses.

Moreover, Donaldson was the organiser of 'a body called the National Aid Society which has branches in Edinburgh, Glasgow,

Aberdeen and Stirling and which assists conscientious objectors on Scottish Nationalist grounds to go into hiding'. Special Branch concluded that 'it seems apparent from his activities and the above references that he is building up an organisation with a view to his assuming the function of Scottish Quisling when invasion takes place'.

Donaldson had first come to the notice of Ayrshire police in April 1939 in connection with the distribution of leaflets for the Scottish Neutrality League and United Scotland. Born in Dundee in 1894, he had emigrated to the USA in 1922 and returned in 1936 to set up as a poultry farmer in Lugton. According to a police report, he was 'described as being very dogmatic and inconsistent in these matters and is regarded as eccentric'. Expelled from the SNP in June 1940, Donaldson formed United Scotland, 'a nucleus of extreme Nationalists who would be prepared to take advantage of an opportunity for furthering Scottish Independence by violence if necessary'. He was also suspected of contact with the enemy. When *The Scots Independent* denounced Gerhard von Tevenar, Donaldson was reported as having told one of his associates, Mary Ramsay: 'We have yet to meet a Nationalist of repute, particularly of the so-called "extreme" category, who ever met or knew of him'. The police report remarked that it was 'to say the least, peculiar that Donaldson should go out of his way to ridicule this story ... [when] there is a strong possibility that he himself knew Von Teffenar [*sic*], though we have no definite evidence to support this view'.

Donaldson's seditious activities were confirmed later that year with his involvement in the National Aid Society: 'At least six Nationalist Conscientious Objectors are known to have gone into hiding in Inverness-shire. While "on the run", provision is made for them to use Youth Hostels, Caves, etc as hide-outs'. In addition to R.E. Muirhead, 'who was a contact of Hoffmann of the German Press Bureau', Mary Ramsay, 'soap-box agitator', and Harry Miller, 'an agitator whose activities range from window-smashing to slogan-painting', his associates included Oliver Brown and Wendy Wood for 'theft of explosives'.

He also had contacts abroad, being 'known to have been interested in Celtic Nationalism as a whole, and contributed to Breton Nationalist papers'. There were reports from internees of an agent named Donaldson working for Germans in Edinburgh. Werner Walti, a

German agent, was captured in Edinburgh on 30 September 1940. Donaldson was 'known to have been in Edinburgh on that day, and was extremely perturbed when told he had been seen there'. There was, however, no proof that he contacted Walti.

Donaldson was reported to have 'pro-Nazi and subversive views'. On 5 January 1941, he gave great praise to Germany:

> The Government would leave the country and England's position would be absolutely hopeless, as poverty and famine would be their only reward for declaring war on Germany. Scotland on the other hand had great possibilities. We must, he declared, be able to show the German Government that we are organised and that we have a clear-cut policy for the betterment of Scotland; that we have tried our best to persuade the English Government that we want Scottish Independence, and that we are not in with them in this war. If we can do that you can be sure that Germany will give us every possible assistance in our early struggle. The time is not yet ripe for us to start a virile campaign against England, but when fire and confusion is at its height in England, we can start in earnest. He then went on to tell them that he had an idea in his mind for fixing up a wireless transmitting set in a thickly populated district in Glasgow or Edinburgh, in order to give broadcasts to the public.

Donaldson's propaganda work involved intensive slogan painting during the 'moonless period' along all bus and tram routes, including the declarations:

> Scotland's peace aim – independence
> Scottish workers – beware of English 'Pétains'
> To Hell with England!

On 13 February 1942, the police informant, who had by then been in close contact with Nationalist circles for nearly nine months, 'was asked his opinion of Donaldson, and stated that he considered him 100% pro-German. His wife shares his views. Donaldson sees himself as a Scottish Quisling, who will come forward when invasion takes place with a complete "New Order for Scotland" which he will present to Hitler, and which he believes will be acceptable. When invasion comes, Donaldson's aim is to use his party for spreading confusion by false reports and minor acts of sabotage such as the cutting of telegraph wires'.

It was therefore concluded that 'Donaldson has a mind which works along National Socialist lines; he is building up an organisation which includes political extremists of all shades whose common quality is a fervent nationalism; he is influencing young men against taking part in the War effort; and he firmly believes that a German conquest of England would be to his own and Scotland's advantage'.

However, despite Donaldson's subversive views, there was no substantive proof of potential Quisling activity. It was instead concluded that Donaldson 'caused and may still cause a certain amount of Parliamentary trouble'. The audience and influence of Donaldson and his associates were negligible: 'The political side only started when Maxton began asking questions in the House of Commons.' Therefore, on 12 June 1941, Tom Johnston came to the conclusion that 'his indefinite detention in Barlinnie Prison is not necessary'.

The clemency of the authorities notwithstanding, raids and arrests would encourage in Scottish Nationalist ranks a drift away from fortifying the Cheviots against Nazi invasion and toward fortifying them against the Auld Enemy. Already in January 1941, the *Scots Independent* had led on Westminster's mistreatment of Scottish hill farmers and the threat from English workers coming north. The headline in May was 'Go south or starve!', as Nationalists protested the 'forced drafting of Scots girls to England'.[79] In June 1941, the arrival of Rudolf Hess gave rise to accusations of another 'Fifth Column' in their midst. 'Sennachie' reported:

The astonishing escapade of Party-comrade Rudolf Hess set no serious problem to one Cockney hair-dresser who, to a London Scot, explained: 'He came over to get in touch with the Scottish Nationalists. Compton Mackenzie is behind the whole thing.' This was only one among many richly inaccurate interpretations of the episode. For example, one chain of American newspapers flashed from ocean to ocean the story that Hess's arrival in Scotland was a 'Buchanite coup'. And, no doubt, the Cockney hairdresser's suspicions were deepened when he read in his newspaper that Hess, in hospital asked for books on Scottish history (no bad idea if some Anglo-Scottish politicians did likewise). But the fact is that, when Deputy Führer Hess came to

Scotland he asked to see, no wicked Nationalist, but the eminently respectable premier duke of Scotland, his Grace of Hamilton. And all Hamilton ever had to do with Scottish Nationalism was to oppose its candidates in elections.

Elsewhere in that issue, the Nationalists asked: 'Is there a Gestapo in Scotland?' The raids on radical Nationalists, including the interrogation of a young lady, Mary Ramsay, were deplored. At the same time, *The Scots Independent* still distanced itself, albeit disingenuously, from this fringe:

> It has always been the aim of our organisation to develop Scottish Nationalism along liberal lines and to avoid any doctrine of hate or the stirring-up of any kind of racial animosity as between England and Scotland . . . The total membership of these organisations, however, would scarcely constitute the equivalent of one branch of the SNP and their influence in Scotland amounts to nothing at all.[80]

However, by the following year, the radicals would be in the ascendancy in the SNP itself. The pro-war, moderate leadership of John McCormick would be replaced by hardliners opposed to conscription and prepared to contest elections.

The 'martyrs' for the cause would soon resume their radical activities and attract the attention of the authorities.[81] In April 1942, Special Branch reported on a public demonstration in Glasgow organised by the Scottish Secretariat Study School – including Arthur Donaldson, Oliver Brown and R.E. Muirhead – to commemorate the 622nd anniversary of the Declaration of Arbroath. It was attended by 100 people, and was opened by the Clan MacKenzie Pipe Band, playing the platform party on to a lorry.

A series of Nationalist orators followed. Harry Miller said the meeting had been called 'to commemorate an event greater than the Gettysburg speech of Abraham Lincoln, which was looked upon as the acme of democracy, and it was certainly greater than the Atlantic Charter'. Arthur Donaldson then declared that he had been put in prison because 'he was a Scotsman trying to obtain the freedom, politically, socially and economically of his country'. Grieve/MacDiarmid outdid him in patriotic zeal:

The Declaration of Independence of their country, which they had met together to commemorate, was a great statement, far in advance of anything else at that time and also far in advance of any ideas which the English had on the subject at the present. Grieve said that he hated Fascism wherever he found it, were it in Germany, Italy, Spain or England. We are told we are fighting against Fascism but all the time English Fascism is shackling itself on us. The treatment of the *Daily Mirror*, the sacking of the Special Commissioner, the Conscription Acts, Regulation 18b, the dragging of Scottish girls to England to work, were all incidents in the progress of English Fascism. The Scots people, he declared, had better be careful lest, while they were being beguiled into taking a leading role in fighting for imperialism, with the thought that they were fighting against Fascism, they found themselves in the grip of Fascism at home. German Fascism, he said, was bad but it was nothing to English Fascism. Scotland is a working-class country and can best help the working class of England and the world by asserting her rights under the Declaration of Independence and by taking control of her own country to attain a decent standard of life and security for all within it ... Grieve went on to say that he had written a special poem for the commemoration, expressing Scotland's love of freedom and hatred of Fascism, and he hoped that the audience would not mind his reading it in memory of the Scotsmen who had established freedom in this country against the English Barons in 1320. He then read a tirade against what he termed English Imperialism, but most of it was inaudible.

Alexander Sloan MP continued to concentrate fire on English imperialism rather than that of others: 'The same minds who indulged in these oppressions were the minds which had by their treatment of the Malayans allowed Japan to walk into Malaya.' The Labour Home Secretary Herbert Morrison was 'a twopence-halfpenny dictator'. The places in which Scots girls were put in England for work 'made the houses in the Gorbals seem like palaces'. Not to be outdone, Oliver Brown called those who did not support his demand for self-government of Scotland 'Quislings'. Indeed, they were in cahoots with a power that outdid in evil the Third Reich: 'The Germans had removed all the vital factories to inaccessible areas, so that they could not be bombed but the English had placed their factories in vulnerable areas and were now forcing Scottish girls to go to work in them, while English persons were sent up here for safety'. Britain had 'a sham Parliament, a sham democracy, a sham religion and a sham army'. Before dispersing, the demonstrators sang *Scots Wha'Hae*.

These radical positions were echoed in the *Scots Independent*. The issue of April 1942 condemned the 'forced labour' in England by 'Scots girl conscripts'. In July, Douglas Young contributed 'Quislings in Scotland. Review of the Fifth Column'. His evidence was a 'Statement to give expression to public opinion in Scotland in opposition to agitation for a Scottish National Parliament', published in Glasgow in 1933. The list of signatories showed 'solid vested interests', a 'roll of infamy' that included dukes, earls and Unionist chief whips. Young concluded:

> Now, if it is a sin and a crime to be a quisling in Norway, if it is a sin and a crime for Laval and Co in France to collaborate with the foreign intruders, then it must be a sin and a crime for anyone in Scotland to be opposed to the freedom of the Scottish nation through democratic self-government.[82]

In August 1942, when Colin Walkinshaw wrote of 'Freedom or Fascism', he meant 'this planning racket' that would be 'death to Scotland' and open the road 'towards fascism'. At the end of his assault on the 'slave state', he declared: 'This is just fascism, though fascism in a peculiarly English dress with the Old School ties taking the place of the brown or black shirt.' The fascistic nature of the British state was confirmed by the jailing of Douglas Young for refusing conscription. In August 1942, *The Scots Independent* wrote of the treatment of this patriot: 'It is significant that the English have always avoided a discussion of the Act of Union – and any resolute attempt to get to the root of the subject is invariably met with the mailed fist.' Young was 'not a pacifist nor is he Anti-War ... He wants a genuine Scottish war effort for genuine war aims and for that he insists that the Scottish people must be free'. Young was replacing another martyr detained at his majesty's pleasure:

> Matthew Pollock Hamilton, the first Nationalist to be incarcerated under the notorious 18B regulation, has been released, his health impaired but his spirit undaunted. Hamilton was flung into Saughton jail in June 1940, subsequently transported to English prisoner-of-

war camps and finally to a concentration camp on the Isle of Man. No charge has been brought against him or reasons given for his arrest. He was among the first to take a stand on Scottish constitutional law against Military Conscription and Defence Regulations as applied by the Westminster Government, the same stand that has been since taken by other Nationalists, including the Chairman of the National party, who are now in British prisons. His compatriots welcome his release and pay tribute to his courage and sacrifice in the cause of individual freedom and Scottish independence.[83]

In September 1942, it was announced that England was 'bleeding Scotland white'. It was 'The Clearances all over again': 'Under threat of starvation or imprisonment, girls are shipped off in droves to foreign surroundings, their ties with family, social life, religious organisations broken and themselves exposed to the dangers which war strain imposes on social behaviour.'[84]

The authorities continued to keep an eye on the anti-war but 'anti-fascist' Nationalists.[82] On 24 November 1942, they considered the danger posed by the *Scottish Socialist*: 'This publication comes out every two months and its circulation is believed to be about 400 to 500 per issue ... I cannot see that "serious mischief" would result from a continuance of this foolish and unmannerly paper with its negligible circulation'. On 17 March 1943, the head of the Fife Coal Company wrote to Home Secretary Morrison expressing concern about the threat posed by the sale of the *Militant Scottish Miner*:

I have also discussed it with Mr Abe Moffat, Chairman of the Scottish Mineworkers Association. He, like myself, believes it should be suppressed ... It contains untruths and statements which are likely to reduce production and is definitely anti-war. I believe its backers to be persons who prior to Russia entering the war were adherents of the Communist Party and who today do not follow its leadership because their party does not provide a sufficient platform for their imaginary grievances.

Again, the idea that such a dissident publication posed a real threat was dismissed. What is more noteworthy is that the Communist Party, which dominated the 'Little Moscows' of West Fife, had shifted from denouncing an 'imperialist war' to collaborating with management in fighting Scottish Nationalist militants who undermined coal production.

Under the leadership of Douglas Young, the SNP was half-hearted at most about the struggle against Fascism. In September 1942, the *Scots Independent* claimed that the freedom of Scotland's youth was put in peril by being corralled into 'the British *Jugend*'.[83] On 25 August 1943, the Home Office reported on a leaflet beginning '1314 Bannockburn 1943', which stated it was 'high time for another Bannockburn' and for the clearing out of Scotland of her worst enemy 'the London imperialist Boss Class and the English would-be *Herrenvolk*'.[84] In October 1944, as the Allies advanced on all fronts, Young complained of 'peace, *imperfect* peace', and protested at the 'conscript police'.[85] As the Third Reich teetered on the verge of total collapse, the readers were exhorted to 'go into battle' for the 'reconquest of Scotland'. In June 1945, Robert McIntyre, briefly MP for Motherwell and Wishaw, declared that 'the future of Scotland is not in the hands of bogus peace conferences and foreign ambassadors and agitated prime ministers. The future of Scotland is in the hands of her own people'. McIntyre's success at Motherwell, as well as Douglas Young's strong showing in a previous by-election in Kirkcaldy, proved that there was an audience for Scottish Nationalism. But the dismal results of the July general elections (where returning soldiers played a decisive role) showed the SNP to be badly out of touch with a geopolitical dynamic which saw the Labour landslide, an overwhelming identification with 'Britishness', and, in Europe, the high water mark of anti-Fascism and Communism. At least for the time being.

Last Steps of a Footslogger

Despite such marginality, and the discredit that accrued from a lack of commitment to the war effort, the SNP kept the stubborn sympathy of Hugh MacDiarmid and the novelist and poet Naomi Mitchison. The movement was joined by another major Scottish writer, Graham Seton Hutchison. As we have seen, this once rabid supporter of national socialism had, like A.K. Chesterton – Mosleyite and future founder of the National Front – been disillusioned by the aggressive (i.e., anti-British) expansionism of the Third Reich. In his last novel, *The Red Colonel*, published in 1946, year of his death, Seton Hutchison seems to settle scores with his Nazi past.

Colonel Duncan Grant is parachuted into Germany during the final days of the war. He is to foment an anti-Nazi insurrection, 'Red Plan', and make contact with an old friend and dissident scientist, Heinrich Messer, who is working on a secret weapon, the 'Fire Wall', which Hitler hopes will miraculously turn the tide against the Allies. In one of the many speeches in this novel, Heinrich seems to express Seton Hutchison's own political disappointment:

> All my life I've fought for the people. You'll remember that I was their champion in 1918, how I led the revolution, first in my father's works then in the Rhineland. The people I have never forgotten. I supported Hitler in the beginning because I believed in his programme and the leadership, but when the classless comradeship which seemed to be the spirit of National Socialism was diverted to military ends and the Party vaunted itself in the suppression of border peoples and racial minorities in our midst, I realized that Hitler was betraying the trust of the German people. . . . Once he'd unified the German people, Hitler placed them in chains.[89]

The 'Red Colonel' dons the clothes of another scientist and accompanies Heinrich to Hitler's bunker in Berlin. It is there that the hero meets not only the Führer but an old flame: 'The strength of Eva's passion for Duncan Grant had been revealed in Marienbad.'[90] 'Why did you come here?' demands Hitler, to which he answers slowly: 'To save Germany's soul.'[91] For Grant, the Nazi regime had turned out to embody the triumph of Hate. It could never last a thousand years:

> The Parthenon is architecturally superb, but not without the blue skies of Athens. The vanishing points of its lines pierce the Heavens; its arcs would embrace the Universe. The Parthenon was, and still remains, a symbol of Athenian democracy. The Third Reich was perhaps a good model, but it never realised a world background. You did not build as the Athenians built. The Third Reich is like a sky-scraper built amid the mediaeval beauties of Rothenburg. It is incongruous, a monstrosity. Your Reich can never fit into world politics . . . [92]

In a dramatic denouement, when it seems for a moment that Grant and Heinrich will be shot, the latter manages to plunge a poisoned syringe into Eva's naked thigh and break a phial of cyanide on Hitler's teeth. The Red Colonel leaves the bunker and is accompanied through the apocalyptic ruins of Berlin by a mongrel, to which he declares: 'This is the end of the war, of all wars. Science knows too much ... Science has mastered man. ... I wonder when man will discover that Love is the only power which can save the world ...?'[93]

The Red Colonel therefore disowns Nazi affiliations. It is also striking for its assertion of a Scottish, rather than British, identity. In conversation with James Watson, his editor at *The Meteor*, Grant declares:

> What is Britain? A composite monster made up of vested interests, big business, speculators, what are called 'sportsmen', and an army of bureaucrats. Geographically, Britain indicates these islands; nothing more. As a political expression, Britain means London, although Manchester thinks it has some influence. Britain is a soulless monster.[91]

A sense of difference is asserted when contact is established with the German underground:

> Father and son were overwhelming Grant with their greetings. 'My good old friend, the English Colonel.'
> 'Scottish,' corrected Grant in bantering tone.
> '*Ja*. I remember. You always used to tell me the Scottish are different. It was your king, Wilhelm Wallach, who fought for liberty. The great democrat! To think that *Oberst* Grant should come to my house in this hour to fight shoulder to shoulder with us for Rhineland liberty!'[92]

Nationalist sentiments are expressed in Seton Hutchison's last essay, *The Highland Division can Save Scotland*, published by the SNP in 1945.

> The Highland Division must stand for something new and revolutionary in Scotland's life ... Through the spirit of the Fifty-First, there will either be a free Scotland, a regenerated people, a progressive prosperity, a quickening of life, a renaissance of our culture; or, alternatively, with grim finality all Scotland is doomed to repeat what evicted Highlanders once before murmured as they left their glens – 'Lochaber no more'.[96]

Seton Hutchison was 'profoundly conscious of the fact that a Scot is different from an Englishman. And I have always flatly declined to describe myself as "British" '.[97]

Since 1915, the Highland Division of the British Army had managed to unify: 'by [a] mysterious alchemy a Scotland once artificially divided between Highland and Lowland sentiment has been fused into one nation'.[98] But surveying the political and economic situation, the author remarked that 'Scots are not free men but slaves':

> There is only one possible way by which Scotland can regain her freedom and have a culture which again and again has served civilisation, and that is by the unanimous demand of her soldiers, her sailors and her airmen, of all her people, that a war fought for the Freedom of mankind shall mean also the Freedom of Scotland ... There is only one organisation with an understanding of this high mission, only one into which all Scots, no matter what their political or religious alignment can come without losing their identity. It is the Scottish National Party.[99]

If fascism had been rejected, Seton Hutchison's perspective was still not far from the world-view he expressed in the early thirties: 'The race of Scots is different from any other. That is due to the facts of biology, to climatic conditions, to Scotland's topographical features, and not least, to the Clan system.'[100] The clan system, with its vertical rather than horizontal divisions, which echoes Italian corporatism, seemed to anticipate the ideal of a classless society:

> The affinities between the naturally-produced Scottish leaders and the masses of the Clansmen are very real ... Love is a great leveller. True democracy rests perhaps more firmly than anywhere else on a sentiment which easily passes the bounds of Class and Caste, and unites in closest affection those belonging apparently to the most estranged ranks of society.[101]

Communist theory of class warfare was therefore also rejected, though Seton Hutchison acknowledged Karl Marx's trenchant analysis of the profit motive: 'with it he condemned Judaism, which equated Western Commercial Civilisation and American Dollar Imperialism'.[102]

The 'comradeship of the Clan' could therefore show the way. After all, 'the Fifty-First Division led the grand and fearful onslaught
across the Rhine on 24th March, 1945'.[103] Scotsmen, he concluded,
'have always been great lovers and great haters';[104] and so, 'swiftly in
the wake of Hate must Love come with its creative power, a revivify-
ing, constructive, regenerative force'.[105] But this visionary warrior,
Scots Nazi turned Scots Nationalist, would soon be at eternal rest.

5

Tartan Treachery

In 1938, Tintin and his faithful companion Snowy landed on the Black Island off Kiltoch. There they discovered two terrifying secrets: a deadly gorilla called Ranko and a counterfeiting operation master-minded by the sinister Dr Müller, who would be Tintin's nemesis in future adventures. The inspiration for this story had come in February 1934, when Hergé read an article in the sensationalist newspaper *Le Crapouillot*. It revealed the activities of one Dr Georg Bell, a Scot settled in Germany, who had worked with the Nazis to flood the Soviet economy with fake roubles. According to the newspaper, Bell had been liquidated by the Nazis when it seemed that he was going to tell all. In *The Black Island*, the political aims of the activi-ties of Müller and his accomplices – which extend across Europe, as the notebook discovered by Tintin shows – are not made explicit. However, it is not insignificant that the doctor's chauffeur is called Ivan or that the leader of the gang is called Wronzoff. If the ape is an allusion to *King Kong*, Tintin's adventure also carries the influence of Alfred Hitchcock's 1935 adaptation of John Buchan's *The Thirty-Nine Steps* (1915), in which Richard Hannay is pursued across the Highlands by Nazi spies. In the imagination of Hergé and others, Scotland therefore seemed rife with tartan treachery on behalf of Nazi Germany. That said, if, as we have already seen, the 'Nazi Laird' had some basis in reality, Scots of different walks of life, and differ-ing motives, were prepared to turn, or appear to turn, traitor for the Fascist cause.

Hitler's Hairdresser

On 16 May 1938 at Edinburgh Sheriff Court, Jessie Wallace Jor-dan, 'Hairdresser, Masseuse and Beauty Specialist' of 1 Kinloch

Street, Dundee, was sentenced to four years' penal servitude for espionage. Jordan had pleaded guilty to a modified indictment, according to which she had been in communication with foreign agents between 1 June 1937 and 2 March 1938 'for purposes prejudicial to the safety and interests of the State'. 'At a place in Fife, being a prohibited place', she 'did make a sketch thereof . . . calculated to be directly or indirectly useful to an enemy'. She had obtained information concerning coast guard stations and coastal defence 'at various places on the East Coast of Scotland between Montrose and Kirkcaldy . . . or elsewhere in Scotland to the prosecutor unknown . . . and to have recorded part of this information on a map'. *The Scotsman* reported:

> A woman of 51 years of age, and of below average height, turning grey, maintained a calm demeanour throughout the proceedings, which were of brief duration. She wore a black coat with grey fur collar, and a green suede hat having a small fur plume. She heard the sentence unmoved. As she left the dock accompanied by two policemen and a policewoman, her daughter, who had been seated at the back of the courtroom, burst into tears.[1]

It was soon revealed that the Dundee hairdresser was part of a spy network which extended as far as Havana and Prague. Her case would briefly generate a media frenzy in which she herself took part. The guilty woman had been born illegitimate on 23 December 1887 to Elizabeth Wallace, a domestic servant from near Coatbridge. At the age of 16 she ran away from home and obtained employment in domestic service herself. In 1907 she met a young German 'in distress' and accompanied him back to Hamburg, where they married. According to the defence counsel, that was 'the only comfortable and happy period of her life'. Her husband fought on the German side in the war, and died of injuries and disease contracted during service. In 'My Amazing Life', serialised in the *Sunday Mail* in June 1938, Jordan recounted how, after the death of her 'unfaithful' first husband, she had soon built up 'one of the finest beautifying businesses in Hamburg'. That said, because of her origins, it was 'suspected I might be a British spy'.[2] In 1920, she married her husband's cousin, who soon began an affair with her young assistant in the salon. They would divorce in 1936.

According to Jordan's version of events, her difficulties in Hamburg increased when the Nazis seized power. Many of her clients were Jewish women, and her insecurity was increased by the Jewish sound of her married name. This racial taint thwarted the ambitions of her pretty blonde daughter, Marga, an aspiring soprano. She could have no stage career because of her 'Jewish blood', at least so long as her mother was unable to prove the nationality and creed of her grandfather James Ferguson, who had fled to America after the scandal of her mother's birth.

It was therefore a desire to prove the Aryan blood of her daughter that made her leave Hamburg for Leith in February 1937. While staying with a brother in Perth, she acquired a hairdressing salon on Kinloch Street, Dundee, 'with a fine view of Firth of Tay and Tay Rail Bridge'. She did, however, have a secret mission. On her way to catch the boat to Leith, she had, the story went, run into a German friend whose husband was an official in the Gestapo. She received instructions from the secret service organisation at Hamburg to the effect that she was to expect letters from the USA. Jordan had known a woman named Dora and had been in partnership with her in Hamburg in a hairdressing salon. Dora left for the USA, from where she would forward letters to Dundee that would in turn be taken to 'Otto Moser' in Hamburg. Jordan was also asked to make sketches and provide other information on coastal defences.

She told the *Sunday Mail*: 'I only did it to oblige friends in Germany, and because I felt it would afford some excitement . . . Nationality meant nothing to me. My eyes were open all through, and I simply took what was coming to me.'[3] On 19 March 1938, in a letter to the Governor of Perth Prison asking for permission to 'write my life', she had declared: 'I may say that my life has had nothing what ever to do with Politicks although I lived thirty years in Germany, and my position is as such today.'[4] On 30 April 1938 it was judged that 'the narration of Mrs Jordan's nefarious activities for the German Secret Services could easily disclose information prejudicial to the State'. But such reservations were nothing in the face of press curiosity and Jordan's own desire for fame and fortune.

On her arrival from Hamburg, she turned out to be a much better hairdresser than spy. Frederick Fraser, who worked for her, said she was 'a woman of moods', but that, although the business did not bring her large profits, 'she managed to make it pay its way. She was a good hairdresser and particularly quick'. She made, however, no particular effort to conceal her mail, and she often left maps of different parts of Scotland lying about the shop.

Concerning her role as post box for German espionage, Jordan claimed to the *Sunday Mail* that she 'thought they were love letters'. She was more honest about her trips down the coast: 'With my map in hand, I might have been a tourist. But once I was in a quiet spot, my innocent map turned into something to be hidden and kept secret. On it I had marked what I saw during my walk.'[5] In the *Argus*, C.C. Nielens recounted how this 'plump pleasant-looking German Scot', who had already carved herself a local reputation for her special 'Viennese wave', would leave her shop in charge of assistants and, 'dressed in old clothes, went off to mark positions of defence stations, on ordnance maps she had bought'.[6]

This hairdressing salon in a poor quarter of Dundee aroused suspicions. The previous owner, Mrs Curran, later claimed to have seen Mrs Jordan's handbag lying on a table in the back of the shop. It contained an AA map marked in black lead with Montrose Barracks, Auchmithie, Carnoustie, Broughty Ferry, St Andrews, Fife Ness, Crail, Anstruther and Kirkcaldy, among other sensitive coastal positions. Mrs Curran and her husband also claimed that, from the beginning, Jordan had 'appeared unusually keen to buy the shop'. She then had it redecorated and the latest hairdressing appliances installed. When asked about the opulence of her equipment, she told Mrs Curran that she got the latest pomades from Germany, and when asked how she was able to get them past the customs officials remarked that things 'were easily done if one had a head'. The Currans had also found a piece of paper bearing the word 'Zeppelin', which they took to be a rude word. In November 1937, the Currans alerted Tayside police, and one Inspector Carstairs sent a policewoman to Kinloch Street to get a 'perm'. Jordan's regular trips back to Germany had also aroused the suspicions of a shipping manager at Camperdown docks, who noticed that – though poorly dressed – she went eight times from Dundee to Hamburg in eight months, travelling in small cargo steamers carrying few passengers.

In fact, British intelligence had become aware of Jessie Jordan's activities as far back as July 1937. The mail she received from the

USA was being intercepted, and her trips to Hamburg shadowed. It was finally on 2 March 1938, as recounted by the *Daily Express*, that Colonel Hinchley Cook of MI5 paid a visit to her salon.

'I'm sorry but I am afraid you'll have to come with us.'

'What for?' asked Mrs Jordan, smiling at him.

'Espionage', he replied. 'You are being arrested on a charge of spying for Germany.'

Mrs Jordan laughed incredulously but began to put on her coat and hat.

'I really don't know what you are talking about,' she said.

But she knew alright.

And so was arrested 'no Greta Garbo, but a charwoman complete with cracked boots, rough hands, and straggled hair!'[7] Jordan would plead guilty to the lesser charge of entering a prohibited area of Fife, while intelligence cracked a rather hapless espionage network which included one Gustav Rumrich, student at Prague University, recruited by Johanna Hoffmann, a beautiful red-headed hairdresser on board the ss *Europa*. At Jordan's trial, defence counsel A.P. Duffes's appeals for leniency for the 'unwanted woman' were rejected, but the British authorities refused an American request to interrogate her: 'If Mrs Jordan is deported on expiry of her sentence her position in Germany will be very difficult if she has given evidence against her American associates.'[8]

The triumph of British intelligence was little appreciated by the Currans of Dundee. The couple demanded that Tayside Constabulary reimburse them for phone calls, bus and tram fares, and unpaid wages. They also sold their story to the *Daily Record*. On 21 May 1937, Mrs Curran told how they had unmasked a spy. 'I want to get my name cleared. People are saying I was a German spy because I was friendly with Mrs Jordan. They don't know I found her out. They never suspected it.'[9] Such claims were dismissed by the police. On 1 December 1938, the chief constable wrote to Hinchley Cook: 'All along they seem to have been out for notoriety and money.'[10] In fact, it was known that Mrs Curran had, as cleaning lady at the local cinema, pinched items from coats and bags.

Jessie Jordan was visited in Saughton Prison by her daughter Marga, who soon after arriving in Scotland had married one Thomas

Reid. This union appears to have been as unhappy as those of her mother. Already on 21 October 1938, Sir Vernon Kell had written to J. Fulton of the Prisons Department:

> One cannot help feeling very sorry for Mrs Jordan's unfortunate daughter, although I anticipated from the very beginning that her second marriage to T. Reid (who was actually unemployed when the marriage took place) would turn out a failure. In my opinion it was never more than a marriage of convenience, so as to enable her to acquire British nationality and prevent deportation at the time of Mrs Jordan's arrest.[11]

The *Bulletin* of 14 November 1938 reported the departure of the ss *Gothland* from Leith, carrying Marga Reid. Although a British subject by her marriage early that year, she was travelling as a German subject with a German passport. She gave no answer to the immigration officer when asked why she did not travel with a British passport. The *Bulletin* remarked that her cabin – No. 1 – was the same one used by her mother on her various journeys between Germany and Scotland. Mrs Reid had bought two single tickets, for her and her daughter. She told journalists: 'The reason for my return to Germany is that I feel the need of a holiday after the strain of recent events. After that my husband and I may return to Germany together. I shall not go back to the stage as I intended at first.' Standing on the quayside, 'Mr Reid was able to talk to his German wife, who leaned against the handrail. She chatted freely, smiling now and then, but obviously moved at the prospect of leaving her husband and Scotland.'[12]

In 'My Amazing Life', Jessie Jordan had told the *Sunday Mail*: 'I can say that one good thing did come out of our stay in Scotland. As a result of our persistent inquiries, we were able to gather some facts about Marga's grandfather and she hopes that the German authorities will now allow her to go on the stage there.'[13] But in fact, there was no future for Marga, who died on 20 January 1939 in Hamburg. On 8 February 1939, Thomas Reid wrote to 'Mutti':

> I will always look upon you as my mother and if [Marga's daughter] Jessie comes home it will be my endeavour to work hard so that when you come out it will be to a home of your own where your grand-

daughter will be a comfort to you. *Even if it is true* about my dear Marga, I forgive her for in our short life together she proved herself a wife even under the handicap of my foolishness.

The ending of his letter was utterly bleak: 'The friends I think are good friends are *not what they seem* and . . . as soon as the Police releases Marga's luggage they will all be fighting over it'. On 14 March 1939, Kell was himself moved to write: 'One cannot help feeling sorry for the convict in her additional predicament.'[14]

There was little peace for this 'unwanted woman'. The *Daily Mail* of 1 August 1938 headlined: 'Woman spy enjoying life in Saughton Prison'. Mrs Jordan had shown herself to be an 'expert needlewoman'.[15] But that month she underwent a hysterectomy. She was then transferred to Perth, then Aberdeen prisons. On 15 December 1939, she requested to have 'the *Bulletin* in her cell, Brabazon work in her cell and also a strong light in her cell'. On 23 December 1939, she pleaded to the authorities:

> I beg of you to send me back to Edinburgh as my health won't stand this prison. I have been here ten days, and the whole place has never been without wet clothes, from top to bottom outside clothes men's heavy moleskins heavy sheets *und so weiter*. When we Prisoners go to bed it is damp and cold that we can't sleep for pains, I asked if the men's place was also hung with clothes. The answer was no, why we women?? Please let me go back.

She was shown little sympathy. On 9 January 1940, the governor of Aberdeen prison described her as 'a discontented person, and has been so, since her arrival here'. She was, however, 'quite a good worker'. A request for naturalisation was refused. On 11 December 1940, the governor wrote: 'I will be glad when orders come for her to be removed from here, as she gets depressed at times seeing she is checkmated about getting free, and might (she is of such a dour and determined disposition) try to do herself in when the devil takes her.' He was also concerned about her developing relationship with one Miss Harrison of a charity looking after women convicts: 'She is a person that would lead Miss Harrison unwittingly to act as a tool for her. The Huns make full use of their kindness or friendship for their own ends.'[16]

Suspicions about her subversive potential remained. On her release from prison on 14 January 1941, Jessie Jordan was immediately detained under the royal prerogative and imprisoned at Royal Holloway, alongside interned female Blackshirts. She was repatriated to Germany at the end of July 1945. The last letter in her file is dated 14 January 1952. From her home at 7 Limmer Street, Hanover-Linden, in the British Zone, she asked: 'would you be so kind and give me an official statement that I was operated on. This statement the Health-Insurance authorities want from me before they allow me my pension'.[17] So ended a spy story predicated on blood and identity.

Dundee Spy Fever

The press sensation caused by the affair of Jessie Jordan probably explains the spy fever that briefly gripped Dundee as the phoney war came to an end and France fell. Dundonians denounced by fellow Dundonians figured on the list of aliens detained in Barlinnie Prison on 10 June 1940.[18]

First of all, there was hotelier Louis Meotti, a Swiss Italian born in 1900 and naturalised in 1925. It was alleged that, in June 1938, he had attended an exhibition of Italian films at the local cinema. On 6 May 1940, one Cathie Ruxton gave Tayside Constabulary more frightening information:

> He even sayd Hitler is a great man ... To me he is too comfortably near our docks someway I've a strange presentment that his Pine Grove hotel has been built by the Nazis and may be their quarters for a puppet government if they ever get here. He is supposed to be Swiss, but many say he is a German ... Please destroy this as I'm putting my full name and address. If the Gestapo were to walk in Bell St and find this filed I would lose my head.

As a post-scriptum, she added: 'You see I was in the Holloway Prison staff 13 years.'

Another internee was Mrs Elly Robertson (née Joosten), aged 39, formerly of Dutch nationality and who became British by marriage. Her husband was a wireless operator who had been in Calcutta for the last two or three years. In April 1939, CID had noted: 'the woman lives very expensively and during the past winter she has acquired three very expensive fur coats'. According to an informer, 'it is a usual course to see men of different ages leaving her house at all hours of the day and night'. Suspicions were increased when, in early 1939, she received a visit from her mother, who lived in Germany. What's more, 'a bus conductor on whose bus Mrs Robertson frequently travels says she is very talkative, and that one day she pointed out a building and asked what it was. When I told her it was the Orphanage, she said "Yes, it was an orphanage, but it is not that now, are there not soldiers in it?" '

Robertson and Meotti were joined in Barlinnie by Charles Frenz, a linotype operator at the *Courier*. Born in Edinburgh in 1903, son of a German pork butcher, he aroused suspicions among those who came into contact with him. John Crabb, manager of a shoe shop, told the police that 'while in conversation with Mr Crabb he appeared very confident that Hitler would be victorious and stated that the British people would get all they deserved'. John Johnston, a garage proprietor who had sold an Austin car to the suspect, reported:

At the time Frenz was looking very tanned and I remarked that he was looking fit. He said, 'Oh yes, I have just returned from Germany where I have spent a nice holiday.' He then showed me a photo of himself dressed as a Storm Trooper. I did not know the uniform was German and I asked him where he got it. He told me that he had borrowed it from a friend in Germany while on holiday.

Indeed, there was some incriminating evidence. The *People's Journal* of 29 June 1935 had run an article entitled 'Dundee Man's Holiday in Germany. Lived Quite Near to Hitler'. In this lengthy feature, Charles Frenz told the readers of the difference between life on Tayside and in the Third Reich. 'We say "Good morning" or "How do you do" ... but young Germans greet you with "Heil, Hitler", [and] salute in the Nazi fashion at the same time'. Since 1933, 'The Hitler regime ha[d] not lost in popularity'. Instead, Frenz said,

Most young Germans to whom I spoke were anxious to learn how we over here regarded the state of modern Germany. When I said that the general opinion was that Hitler was interfering too much with individual freedom they strenuously denied that such was the case. As one young storm-trooper put it, 'today we have hope. Before the rise of Herr Hitler we had none'.

Evidence of the leader's popularity, he claimed,

is got everywhere. The news spreads rapidly when he is about, and crowds collect and wait hours in the hope of seeing him. One of my uncles, with whom I stayed in Berchtesgaden, near which is Hitler's summer residence, has spoken to him, and was greatly impressed. I myself just missed seeing him by a matter of minutes when on a hike near his residence. I saw General Goering, however, and heard him speak.

Frenz revealed that one of his cousins was a storm-trooper: 'this is entirely a voluntary organisation, for which no payment of any kind is received'.

It was therefore a quite idyllic image of Germany that Frenz conveyed to his Dundonian readers, contrasting painfully with the Depression back home:

During my stay in Germany I saw no beggars or hawkers, and I was told there were none. A few disabled men, however, hold special permits to do door-to-door trading. One of my cousin's pals is in a labour camp. He earns threepence per day, but seemed quite happy with his lot. The men all live together in barrack-like buildings, and a guard is kept by a member bearing a spade in place of a rifle.

Frenz spent eight days in Bavaria, visited Cologne Cathedral, saw Ulm steeple – the 'highest in the world' – and Munich *Munster*. In Munich, too, he saw 'the Hitler cell, where the leader once served a term of imprisonment. This cell is now a sort of national monument, and is never occupied by prisoners'. At Friedrichshaven he surveyed a gigantic new zeppelin. Throughout this trip he was struck by the schoolchildren devoting their energies to hard work and hiking. Every village had a football pitch.

This feature helps explain why since 1939 Frenz had been under surveillance. But the garage owner had also said: 'While in his company I have never heard him say anything against this country.' As for Meotti, he may have figured on the contribution list from the Italian colony of Dundee District, but on 13 September 1940 it was reported that 'a Home Office Warrant has failed to reveal anything of interest other than the fact that Meotti was very heavily in debt and that his son, James Meotti, is in the habit of betting'. As for the theory of espionage surrounding the third internee, 'it is quite clear that there is another explanation of Mrs Robertson's comparative affluence since the departure of her husband to India'. On 31 October 1940, the detention orders were revoked.

An Officer in the Tower and on the Airwaves

Norman Baillie-Stewart had a career in treachery far longer than that of Jessie Jordan and her fellow Dundonians. Born Norman Baillie on 15 January 1909 in Willesden, to an illustrious line of Highland warriors, he left Sandhurst aged 18 for the Seaforth Highlanders. He changed his name by deed poll to Baillie-Stewart, to continue his mother's family name of Stewart, which had died with his uncle. His military talents impressed his commanding officers. He was rapidly promoted to captain, but, in August 1932, fatefully contacted Reichswehr HQ in Berlin, offering to sell classified technical information.

The material Baillie-Stewart offered could easily have been gathered from British military journals, while his impromptu approach merely aroused the suspicions of his pre-Nazi German contacts, who tipped off the British authorities. Nevertheless, Baillie-Stewart was allowed to pursue contacts with representatives of the German army in Holland, all of them monitored by the British War Office. The renegade was arrested in January 1933, held in the Tower of London and, in March, court-martialled under the Official Secrets Act. He was sentenced to five years' penal servitude. Considered naïve and ludicrous by the press, MI5 deemed him 'tactless, rather obstinate, self-confident, tends to resent advice and correction. This attitude is put down to conceit and excessive self-valuation'.[19]

On his release from prison, the 'Officer in the Tower' gave an exclusive to the *Daily Express*, recounting and explaining his espionage adventure. His motivations were not strictly selfish. On 6 September 1937, he told the paper that 'the map of dismembered Germany after the Treaty of Versailles was anathema to me'. Details of all British aircraft, tanks, and armoured cars were familiar to him, and would become useful in the negotiations to come. A catalyst was an encounter with a beautiful blonde German girl on a steamship to South Africa: 'from her I learned love and sympathy for the German race. My exchange of ideas with her and her compatriots made me want to be one of that race'.

Under the influence of this Marlene Dietrich figure, he drifted inexorably into espionage. In August 1932, he left for Berlin, 'furthering my self-annihilating scheme'. Again, his motivations were not simply narcissistic: 'Germany was defenceless in the centre of Europe, and could only rebuild her strength by copying the methods of surrounding Powers.'

Things started well: 'I lied to perfection, wasn't caught once'. He gave information on British tanks to one Herr Obst in Holland. But his downfall came very soon after. And yet, he still strutted his difference: 'My court-martial opened at the Duke of York's HQ, Chelsea, on March 20 1933, with a flourish. Grand was the military panoply. Brass hats, field boots, spurs and swords abounded everywhere. My solitary kilt was in queer contrast to it all.' Once consigned to the dreaded Tower, 'I could have escaped any night I liked. I exercised on Raleigh's Walk between the Bloody Tower and the governor's lodgings.' Like the doomed Lady Jane Grey, he left a mark on his door. He was regaled with stories of how spies were shot in the Tower, but was not afraid.[20]

On his release in 1937, Baillie-Stewart settled in Vienna, where he came under the wing of a Nazi agent, a woman calling herself Edith Shackleton and claiming to be a sister of the explorer. In February 1938, Baillie-Stewart was interrogated for five hours by the still-independent Austrian police and accused of engaging in Nazi activities. He received no sympathy from the British consular service. He would return to Vienna in March 1938, immediately after the *Anschluss*, and in September applied for German citizenship, gaining it in July 1940. Six months later, Baillie-Stewart contacted the Vienna branch of the Nazi Ministry of Propaganda, criticising the poor quality of Berlin's English-language broadcasts. He was invited for a voice test and, in August 1939, was asked to Berlin for a three-week trial as an announcer.

The former Seaforth Highlander was viewed with suspicion. He adopted the name 'Manfred von Krause', apparently that of a German forebear. But his relationship with the German Broadcasting

Corporation did not last: during September 1939, William Joyce gradually usurped the position of Germany's number one English-language mouthpiece.

In Joyce, Baillie-Stewart seems to have found his Celtic nemesis. On 21 September 1934, an informant had offered this appreciation of the future Lord Haw-Haw:

> As an Irishman he is naturally a person of very definite opinions and these opinions always tend towards extremes. He is, for instance, a rabid anti-Catholic, and a fanatical anti-Semite. He has decided tendencies towards absolute monarchy, absolute sovereignty, dictatorship, etc, and underlying it all is that romantic streak common to all Celts which makes them doubly effective and doubly dangerous.
>
> Good: Boundless physical and moral courage; considerable brain power; tremendous energy and application; well read politically and historically; very loyal to his friends; a sense of humour; patriotic.
>
> Bad: Little stability due to over-developed intellect and Celtic temperament; very violent temper at times, at others extremely quiet and calculating; a tendency towards theatricality; marked conspiratorial complex. Celtic prejudices very deeply rooted; not to be swayed by arguments where his inherent instincts are touched.[21]

In December 1939, after incautious remarks about the scuttling of the German pocket battleship *Graf Spee* off Montevideo, Baillie-Stewart was temporarily replaced as newsreader by a 16-year-old, Jim Clark. In an article for the *Sunday Chronicle* on 31 July 1940, 'I meet Lord Haw-Haw', the American journalist William Shirer elaborated on this peculiarly dangerous and fractious expat community:

> There is another British traitor to note here in Berlin. He is Baillie-Stewart, a former s/o of the Seaforth Highlanders, who a few years ago was sentenced to imprisonment in the Tower for betraying military secrets to a foreign power ... The girl who led him to this was a German siren and after his release he followed her here ... He did some broadcasts at first, but his Scottish nature was too unbending for the Nazi officials of the Propaganda Ministry and the German Broadcasting Corporation. He is now off the air and working as a translator in the Foreign Office.[22]

In the face of such career frustration, Baillie-Stewart indicated that he wished to return to Vienna, but the Foreign Ministry offered him a place in its own English-language broadcasting team. He would produce and present radio programmes as well as giving lectures at Berlin University and writing for *The Camp*, a German-sponsored tabloid distributed to British POWs. From February 1942, he began his own broadcasts to Britain, under the name 'Lancer'.

On 31 July 1942, in the *Sunday Pictorial*, nine traitors were 'unmasked', with Anthony Hern tearing 'the veil from the faces of the rats of radio'. Traitor number three was Baillie-Stewart, who promised that 'utter defeat is in store for the British and defeat combined with the Red Plague of Communism is a ghastly combination indeed'. Hern poured vitriol on someone who had passed from being an unsuccessful actor to an unsuccessful spy, who was once 'the Officer in the Tower' and was now '*the Scotsman* of Unter den Linden':

> Baillie-Stewart, an officer in a famous Regiment, was cashiered from the Army and sent to gaol for five years for selling military secrets to a foreign power. Baillie-Stewart was supposed to have betrayed his country because he was infatuated with a German dancer. Only since the war has the truth come out. He didn't betray his country in a moment of infatuation. He betrayed his country deliberately and of malice aforethought – because he preferred the Nazi system of government to the British. Until he was released from Maidstone Gaol a year or so before the war – he spent most of his spare time writing bad poetry – he went almost at once to Germany. The servant went crawling to his masters. He began in the early days of the war to broadcast anti-English fake Scottish Nationalist stuff. But Goebbels didn't think much of this Scottish braggart. He was taken off the regular strength of the German quisling broadcasters. Now he does translations in the Wilhelmstrasse (the Berlin Whitehall). But occasionally his voice comes over the air on the 'Caledonia' programme to remind his handful of listeners that this young ex-officer has not changed his ugly spots.[23]

Between February 1942 and November 1944, 'Lancer' gave three talks a week. Titles included 'Calais Magazine', 'After Five Years', 'Allied Methods' and 'Russian Rule'.[24] Initially, Baillie-Stewart had alternated in reading news announcements with William Joyce. There followed humorous soldier stories; a broadcast on the 'Battle of Berlin', in which he accused Britain of 'attacking women and children, just as you did in the last war'; the Japanese war and wishful thinking – 'Your boys will *never* return'; and attacks on Jews' military service, and English ignorance of Europe. Across the airwaves, Baillie-Stewart warned that 'Italy is between the devil (Bolshevist-Russia) and the deep blue sea (Anglo-America)'. He also attacked racial discrimination against Negroes and Mexicans in the USA, and sang the praises of the train service in Germany. During this time, he managed to try his hand as a librettist, adapting German hits for the singer Lale Anderson. In May or June 1944 he was transferred to Vienna, where he was to produce propaganda programmes for the local *Reichssender*. As the war situation worsened, he was called up for the *Volksturm* – Nazism's 'Dad's Army' – and it is at this point that he seems to have made an escape.

In May 1944, Baillie-Stewart's doctor had diagnosed incipient cirrhosis of the liver, gastritis and a duodenal ulcer: 'We recommend a KARLSBAD CURE. A LENGTHY STAY AT MEDIUM ALTITUDE IN FOREST region necessary, where a diet rich in carbo-hydrates will be possible.'[25] Baillie-Stewart followed this advice and rushed southwards, along with others aware that the ship was sinking.

On 21 May 1945, Norman Clark, correspondent for the *News Chronicle*, announced that Baillie-Stewart had been captured at Alt Aussee, a lake-side Austrian village:

> In Tyrolean chamois leather shorts, heavily embroidered braces, forester's jacket of green with finely sculptured deer's teeth on each lapel, and thick white woollen stockings, Norman Baillie-Stewart – the 'officer in the Tower' of 1932 – languishes tonight in the gaol here. He might have been at liberty, mixing among the Austrian aristocracy that now overcrowds this Alpine village of musical comedy, ignoring the tragedy in its midst.

Baillie-Stewart had posed as a member of the Free Austrian Movement, and even acted as interpreter to the military governor. But he had been trapped mistranslating the statement of a suspected Dutch Nazi. His identity had been confirmed by a friend, Countess Platen von Hindenburg, cousin of the field-marshal. The renegade told the paper:

> I am completely disillusioned about everything, and don't care what happens to me. But I want it understood that at no time was I ever a member of the Nazi Party or the Labour Front. But despite that I shouldn't be surprised if some sort of case can be trumped up to place me once again behind bars, as the British secret service which ruined my life long ago will always try to do something.

He then laid in to William Joyce, 'a thug of the first order. Gradually he took over my job. He was a great friend of Goebbels, wore a uniform and carried a gun'. He went on to criticise German propaganda and recounted how he had been threatened with being sent to a concentration camp. But he had not rallied to the Union Jack: 'I do not want to return to England; I want to become an Austrian.'[26]

He was taken into military custody in Brussels, but there remained the thorny question of his German citizenship. On 6 June 1945, he told his interrogator, Captain Spooner:

> I am not the same Baillie-Stewart of the period 1933 to 1937, whose object was to seek sensation in return for the sensation thrust upon him under circumstances which could have been avoided. I have become a German by force of circumstances, and will not disown Germany.[27]

On 1 October 1945, MI5 also took a statement by Countess Platen, whose daughter Baillie-Stewart had met at the Foreign Office in Berlin:

> The Countess's first reaction was to think that here was a traitor to his country, but then she decided that he was the type of Scot who was 'a considerable egoist, a material optimist and a believer in some fantastic ideal' and she felt a certain pity for him as even then he realised that Nazism was not so full of ideals as he had thought.

She also thought that he 'was wasting his abilities' and 'always drank too much'.[28]

Baillie-Stewart was put on trial in the Central Criminal Court at the Old Bailey. The capital charge of treason was dropped on condition that he plead guilty to having 'aided the enemy' under the Emergency Defence Regulations of 1939. In comparison with William Joyce and John Amery, he was considered to be politically harmless and to have done little real damage. In his defence, he gave his affection for a German woman as the deeper cause for his actions. The judge declared that 'the sooner this man is got away from this country the better'. When the attorney-general pointed out that the Allied Control Commission was legally bound to penalise Nazi collaborators, Baillie-Stewart was sentenced, on 10 January 1946, to five years' imprisonment. The judge recorded that he was 'one of the worst citizens that any country has ever produced'.

After a short time in prison in Brixton, Baillie-Stewart was transferred to Wakefield in Yorkshire and, after an escape bid, removed to the high security centre at Pankhurst, on the Isle of Wight. On his release he was still barred from Germany, and lived in Quaker guest houses under the name 'James Scott'. In October 1949, he entered Ireland, on false papers provided by the Quakers, and settled in Dublin. In November 1950, he married a Dublin shop assistant. He died on 7 June 1966.

Radio Caledonia

Baillie-Stewart was joined on Hitler's airwaves by another Scottish renegade, Donald 'Derrick' Grant, the voice of 'Radio Caledonia'. Grant was born in 1907 at Alness in the Black Isle, where his father was a grocer. He was educated at Alness Public School and Dingwall Academy. On leaving school, he enjoyed mixed success as a commercial traveller in England and Ireland. Following that, he went to Bradford, where he had an uncle, for a short holiday. He then proceeded to London and worked for the radio multiple firm of Lloyd Radio and also for the Hoover Cleaning Company.

A man who briefly knew Grant in Alness is Farquhar Ewen, who helps run the heritage centre of the village. Ewen remembers Grant as 'a loner, who became fascinated with dangerous ideas', ideas which would lead to his father banning him from the family home. Both Ewen's and Grant's mothers did cleaning work at the Gledfield estate owned by the Bainbridges of Ardgay, who regularly held fascist seminars during the thirties. Ewen remembers his own encounter with William Joyce – 'a very courteous and smartly-dressed man' – who gave him a brand new 1938 penny coin for his birthday. It may be surmised that contact with the glamorous world of thirties fascism in Easter Ross could have seduced the young Grant.[29]

However, Grant did not mention this to his interrogators. According to his October 1946 account, it was while in England in 1934 that he moved towards Fascism.

> I had taken the average interest in politics and was particularly interested in social welfare. I had the desire to see England a still better place for her people to live in and, being not entirely satisfied with the achievements of the political parties at that time, I became attracted to the Fascist movement. About July 1938, I became an ordinary subscribing member of the South Kensington branch of the Mosley Party. I undertook no activities in that Party apart from taking an interest in and giving some assistance to the Film Unit. I was interested in film technique and had studied this subject to some extent. I was thoroughly disappointed with the general conditions prevailing in the party and also with the majority of the type of people who were in it. Certain leaflets on agricultural and financial matters issued by the Imperial Fascist League attracted my attention and led me to become a member of this organisation about the month of September 1938. I undertook the work of trying to form a small group in the Earls Court district. We did not have more than about six members.[30]

Grant also began to receive propaganda literature from Nazi Germany. In 1938, he wrote to Rolf Hoffmann of the Propaganda Department in Munich:

> An instructress of the 'Women's League of Health and Beauty' has asked me about the physical training of women in the new Germany. Any literature on this subject will be much appreciated and passed on. By the way I should like to correspond with either a member of the Party, the Hitler Youth or BDM. I am Scotch, 31 years of age and a member of the Imperial Fascist League (which has no connection with the British Union of Oswald Mosley) . . . I would like to go to Germany for the first time to see the miracles which Fascism has accomplished there. Best wishes from a British Fascist.

Hoffmann replied: 'I am delighted to hear that the literature you received was of interest; *News from Germany* will be sent to you regularly.'[31] In March 1939, and now referring to himself as 'Derrick F. Grant', he received literature in Earls Court, including the pamphlets, *Who wants war? By Dr Goebbels*; *Adolf Hitler offers France 25 years of Peace*; and *Jewry and Penal Punishment*. Under this influence, Grant's connection with the Third Reich deepened:

> As, in the interests of world peace, I was in favour of promoting an Anglo-German understanding, I joined the Anglo-German Link, probably in spring of 1938. I did not occupy any position in this organisation other than that of a subscribing member. As a result of my desire for world peace and an understanding between the nations, I became a member of the '*Weltklub Union*', probably sometime at the beginning of 1938. This club had centres in various countries in the world. The meeting place in London was at the Linguists Club in Holborn . . . Through the medium of this club, I got into contact with the daughter of a German family in Magdeburg. I forget the actual address but the name of the family was Dietrich and they owned a small champagne factory. The daughter desired to come to England for a few weeks to improve her knowledge of English and we agreed on a holiday exchange. She came to London a week or two after the Munich affair in 1938 and I paid the cost of some four weeks' stay. Under the usual conditions of such a holiday exchange it was agreed that I should go to Magdeburg the following year and stay for four weeks with her family. I was glad to do this, having heard conflicting accounts about the conditions prevailing in Germany I was interested to see for myself. In the Spring of 1939 my parents begged me to go home and help them with their business. I agreed to do this after I had had my part of the holiday exchange. I secured a British passport and left for Germany on July 7 1939. For some time I had been receiving literature about Germany from an office in Hannover. Informing these people of my intended visit to Magdeburg, they asked me to break the journey in Hannover for a couple of days. This office turned out to be the Nordische Gesellschaft [a Nazi propaganda outfit aimed at Scandinavia] which had its rooms in the building of the Gauleitung in Hanover. After two days' stay in Hannover I proceeded to Magdeburg and stayed there for the agreed period.[32]

This was quite a time for a British subject to holiday in the Third Reich. MI5 were sceptical about his motives. He was 'alleged to be a member of the Imperial Fascist League and ADC to its leader Arnold Leese . . . in charge of incriminating documents belonging to the IFL which were subsequently destroyed. Source said that Grant was believed to have been on some Fascist-Nazi mission just before the war, have been engaged in activities on behalf of the Germans'.[33]

Anyway, Grant could later claim:

> Despite the threats of war, the actual declaration came as a surprise to me and I could hardly credit that we had gone to war over the question of Danzig and the Polish Corridor especially in view of the fact that prominent Allied men had declared the existence of the Corridor to be a menace to World Peace. I held the fairly common view that the whole thing would just fizzle out. As the German authorities did not take any immediate steps against me and as I had money enough for a further 10 days' stay I decided to wait for that period. Five days after the outbreak of war it was announced that no foreigner was to leave the town where he lived.[34]

On 11 September 1939, he was arrested and imprisoned. On release, he was sent to work on the construction of a sports ground near Hanover. Later he did the messy job of colouring typewriter ribbons. Helena Jirka, secretary of the local Nazi party Gauleiter, recommended Grant as a lodger to one Frau Beyer. In 1945, Grant's landlady recalled that 'he came to her in August 1939 and stayed with her for about six months. He started on the outbreak of war to work at cleaning the streets and later worked in a carbon paper factory, from which he used to return with his head and hands bright blue. She objected to this, but otherwise found him a pleasant and well-behaved lodger'.[35] In June 1940, Grant received a letter from the Rundfunk radio service in Berlin, inviting him to interview with one Dr Erich Hetzler, head of the English section. According to Norman Baillie-Stewart, Hetzler was 'a fanatical Nazi who . . . strutted around the station not merely in his impressive uniform but wearing his sword as well'.[36] Grant recalled:

> The interview took place on the day that Marshall Pétain declared that France must lay down arms. It was explained to me in Berlin

by Dr Erich Hetzler that the work concerned the effort to secure a mutual peace between Britain and Germany and the promotion of an understanding between the two countries. I declared frankly that I was always prepared to help in the work of stopping any war and promoting understanding between my own country and any other and particularly Germany because I believed that understanding between that country and my own was absolutely essential to world peace.

On taking on this work, he surrendered his British passport, in return for which he received a *Fremden*/Freedom Pass under another name, that of Donald Palmer.

[Hetzler] suggested that we should start a small short wave radio transmitter to be addressed to Scotland with the aim of advocating a peace and development of understanding between the two people. I agreed for the following reasons: 1) I sincerely wanted to see the Scottish people at peace and devoting their energy to their future welfare. 2) Taking a purely objective view as a Scot, I could not see that the war really concerned Scotland. Firstly, no threat was involved to Scottish interests and secondly, because of the cause of the declaration of war, namely Danzig and the Polish Corridor. I was further influenced by the fact that France was heavily defeated and I feared for the fate of my country. I declare frankly that I went into this business with open eyes but without the idea of working for the interests of Germany or securing any personal gain.[37]

Since the fall of France, Britain had become Germany's main target. Preparations for a landing in the British Isles were accompanied by the stepping up of clandestine broadcasts in English. The Büro Concordia set up a series of secret stations which gave the impression of broadcasting from within the enemy country. On 5 July 1940, Rudolf Stache, head of Radio Intelligence, presented Goebbels with a survey of all existing and projected secret stations directed against Britain: 'Concordia North West is now operating as Caledonia, which is ostensibly an amateur station dedicated to the ideal of Scottish independence.'[38]

It was on 27 June 1940 that the transmitter 'Radio Caledonia – The Voice of Scotland' went on the air for half an hour daily. Its programmes were aimed at the dockyards on Clydeside, appealing largely to Scottish nationalist sentiment. Although Foreign Ministry officials were dubious about the likely receptivity of the Scots, they approved of the Propaganda Ministry's plan. Grant later told his interrogators:

> My own idea of the line this station should adopt will be clear from my previous statements. This course however, could not be definitive because of the interference of the German authorities and particularly Dr Erich Hetzler, chief of our department. On those occasions when I was given a free hand to write and talk, I chiefly devoted talks to the economic betterment of Scotland and a better future for her people.

The exact content of these broadcasts, which Grant initially wrote with a Scottish POW, Sergeant Macdonald, remains elusive. There are no surviving recordings or transcriptions, nor are there recollections by Scottish listeners. In October 1945, Herbert Krumbiegel, an electrical engineer, tantalisingly told interrogators:

> One of the English speakers with whom I came into contact in the normal course of work was a civilian internee named Palmer, who came to Büro Concordia in the summer or autumn of 1940 and remained there until the Büro closed down at Helmstedt. I believe Palmer came to the Büro from the Hanover district, where he had been in business before the war. I think he originally came from Scotland. Büro Concordia was the name of the section dealing with propaganda broadcasts from secret stations; for instance in the case of English broadcasts the pretence was that the broadcasts originated from secret transmitters situated in England. It is obvious that Palmer would know of this pretence. Palmer's programme was the 'New Caledonia' programme, which closed down in about the autumn of 1942. During the time he was employed on the 'New Caledonia' programme I and my colleagues used to record his talks daily. I have myself recorded more than 200 of these talks. Recordings were done between 1600 and 1800 hours and the broadcast took place – so far as I can now remember – at about 2000 hours, British time. Whilst Palmer was speaking I could see him in his cubicle and could also hear his voice, as I had a loudspeaker fitted in my room for that purpose. I understood very little English at that time and therefore

cannot say what he was speaking about. He was always a willing worker. I think he was paid 605 marks a month. I also think he wrote his own scripts. Palmer always enjoyed complete freedom and lived privately in Berlin. He was always dressed in civilian clothes.[39]

As the engineer said, Radio Caledonia lasted two years. Grant described thus his subsequent wartime activities:

In August 1942, having been long of the opinion that the station was serving no useful purpose I begged Dr Hetzler that it be discontinued. This was agreed and the last transmission was made a few days later. In the period that followed up to the beginning of April 1945, I remained at the same department and mainly devoted myself to Archive work. This consisted of reading the British papers when received and filing any articles contained in them of interest for the other two stations, the NBBS [New British Broadcasting Service] and Workers' Challenge. I was occasionally asked to write news items for the NBBS and Workers' Challenge. Not being in agreement with the line adopted by these stations I did this work most unwillingly and frequently managed to avoid [it] on the excuse that I had too many English language newspapers to read.

In April 1945, after a period of convalescence for bronchitis, he managed to 'make good my escape. I undertook this work willingly and without any form of coercion. I was paid for this work by the German Government. I had free movement in Berlin and free movement in Germany on the receipt of a pass from my office. In addition to my pay I received Red Cross parcels which had been acquired for me from a nearby Stalag'.[40]

It was by intercepting mail from the Red Cross that the British authorities began to take an interest in Grant. Major Perfect informed Ross and Cromarty police that on 16 August 1941 a letter had been sent by Grant from Hanover to his mother: 'Keeping very well. Have everything I need. Still Golfing? Would enjoy a game.' A PC Macdonald of the Ross and Cromarty Constabulary, who was asked to make enquiries about Grant in his home village, called on the local doctor, Farquhar Macrae. Grant's mother, it transpired, had told the doctor that 'Derrick was very avid on the German Nazis'.[41] But nothing further was learnt of his activities in Germany until

September 1944, when one Corporal Paton, a British POW who had recently escaped from Germany, made a statement concerning a number of British renegades whom he had met there between September 1943 and February 1944, and alongside whom he had worked for the NBBS. In October 1944 another British POW, Lance-Corporal Roy Courlander, who had visited Paris on behalf of the enemy in January 1944 and subsequently escaped, was shown a photograph of Grant. He stated that he recognised it as that of a man who in January 1944 was working in a branch of the German Foreign Office in Paris.

After the fall of the Third Reich, with Grant still in hiding, MI5 gathered statements concerning him and other renegade broadcasters. POWs forced to collaborate on these programmes were particularly useful. On 15 May 1945, Pilot Officer Freeman, a Nazi sympathiser recruited for 'Germany Calling' but who had nevertheless been at constant loggerheads with the German Foreign Ministry, declared:

> This NBBS had the finest collection of poor type Englishmen one could wish to meet, but in passing I should like to record that one, Palmer, was a sincere man. He was deluded and knew it, but had the courage not to say it, he was sincere in his basic beliefs and managed to avoid becoming a hireling in the sense the other men [were.][42]

Two days later, it was the turn of a German employee, Margarete Eberhard:

> [Palmer] worked at Concordia writing and broadcasting talks for Caledonia until it closed down. He stayed on doing nothing except read the newspapers and produce the occasional idea until he was sent on leave with bronchitis in Feb 1945. I do not know where to. He was an honest fellow, very Scottish, anti-Jewish, but not anti-British. He tried to leave, but Hetzler would not release him.

William Griffiths, a POW from the Welsh Guards who was recruited for Welsh National Radio, had this to say about Palmer:

> At first he had a station of his own solely for Scotch listeners. He ran the station himself, but I do not know the name of it. He wrote and broadcast his own work. Afterwards, in the summer of 1942, when

the station closed down, he was employed on reading newspapers, and cutting out pieces for reference and propaganda. He was very anti-Jewish.[43]

A female renegade, Susan Hilton, alias Ann Tower, who also worked for the department's Irish station, told interrogators:

> I proceeded to write talks for the Scottish sender until January 1942. I wrote three to six talks a week. These were of a varying character, touching upon industry, economics, farming, and every subject to do with Scotland. To assist me I was given by Hetzler extracts from BBC broadcasts and from newspapers, magazines, etc, and the theme of my script was to react against the British point of view as expressed in their propaganda. The idea was to lead the British people to the German point of view . . . I was assisted in my work by a young Scotsman named Donald Palmer. He hated having to do this work . . . His job in Concordia was exactly the same as mine, except that he did the speaking as well, owing to his Scottish accent.[44]

In October 1945, MI5 received an interrogation report concerning Vivian Stranders, Sturmbannführer in the SS. British by birth, but naturalised as a German in 1932, Stranders was behind the abortive British Free Corps, and served also as a radio commentator called 'Mediator':

> Apart from university work Stranders was fairly busy and worked for Concordia. Palmer struck Stranders as an idealist who wanted to work for an Anglo-German friendship and they met occasionally. Towards the end of the war Stranders told Spaarmann that the Goebbels propaganda was wrong and he wanted to have his own sender called the 'Nordic Front' (based on the friendship idea) and, if it had been allowed, he would have had Palmer in charge of it . . . Originally Palmer had wanted to go and fight the Russians but Stranders persuaded him not to do this.[45]

On 26 November 1945, MI5 investigators tracked down Helena Jirka. Her home in Hanover was standing in an almost completely bombed-out street. The name of her recently deceased architect father was still outside the door. She was not very co-operative: 'She failed to identify the photograph of Donald Grant. It was soon clear that she was lying.' She finally stated that Donald Grant 'went to Magdeburg in 1939 to stay with a girl who had visited him in England in 1938. These visits were made under an exchange scheme operated by the Anglo-German Link. She gave no clear account of how she first met Grant, but she herself was secretary to the Gauleiter of the NSDAP'. She said that in 1940 Grant left Frau Beyer and went to Berlin to work for the Rundfunk. During the war, she received a number of Red Cross letters from Grant's mother, the last in about January or February 1945, which she forwarded to Grant under the name of Palmer. She had burnt all the letters and postcards received from him.

During this conversation, Jirka's mother appeared. She 'strongly disapproved of Grant and his treacherous activities and of her daughter's allowing him to use their address as a post-box'. She accused her daughter of being *mitleidig*: 'soft-hearted'. The MI5 officer was unconvinced: 'A tougher and less pleasant specimen of Nazi humanity could hardly be conceived than Helena Jirka ... She was clearly keen to protect Grant, probably from mixed political and emotional motives, although she professed to regard him as a traitor to his country.'

Frau Beyer seems to have been much more helpful:

She was away when he left for Berlin, some time in 1940. Shortly afterwards, he wrote her a postcard from Berchtesgaden, without giving any address, but the card was lost in the bombing of Wiesenstrasse. He visited her in the new year, probably of 1941, just to greet her and see how she was, but he never stayed again with her. She did not know what he was doing in Berlin, but Jirka told her that he was working for the radio. It is clear from Beyer's information that Jirka was lying on one or two points; clearly it was Jirka who got Grant his job at the Rundfunk, through her party connections, when Grant found his employment as a crossing sweeper and in the paper factory intolerable. Equally clearly, Grant must have re-visited Jirka when he revisited Hanover in the new year of 1941.[46]

Donald Grant managed to avoid capture for more than a year despite being number 22 on a 'Civilian Renegades Warning List'. Because of an 'irresistible' homesickness he eventually surrendered himself to a British liaison officer in Baden Baden, in the French occupied zone, on 31 October 1946. He was carrying the pass of a 'displaced person', under the name of Michael Ryan, travellers' guide, born in Cork in June 1905. One Major Davies ensured he was given a packet of cigarettes and a meal. In return, the badly disillusioned Scot told all. In his report to MI5, Major-General Lochhead, chief of the intelligence division, concluded that Grant was 'a pathetic figure now reaping the fruits of misguided and illegal actions'.[47] This assessment may explain the lightness of his sentence, especially in comparison with that given to William Joyce/Lord Haw Haw, hanged on 3 January 1946. On 6 February 1947, under the title 'Aiding the Enemy', *The Times* reported the end of Grant's trial:

> He pleaded guilty at the Central Criminal Court yesterday to doing acts likely to assist the enemy during the past war by broadcasting, preparing propaganda, and acting as archivist in the German Propaganda Service, and he was sentenced to six months' imprisonment.
>
> Mr Edward Clarke, pleading in mitigation, urged that Grant's offence was a small one compared with that of people like Joyce. The Judge then said there was no evidence of what Grant actually broadcast for 'Radio Caledonia', and suggested that the jury might possibly have found that he did so with intent to help, not Germany, but Scotland. The absence of evidence as to the nature of Grant's broadcasts was due to:
>
> 1. The fact that it had always hitherto been successfully argued in these cases, that anyone who broadcast for the German broadcasting service in wartime, must know that such broadcasts were intended by the enemy to help Germany, and therefore that he must himself have intended to help the enemy.
> 2. The difficulty, if not impossibility, of linking a monitor report of an anonymous broadcast with any particular broadcaster.
>
> In Grant's case, this difficulty was not insuperable, as Grant was apparently the only broadcaster for Radio Caledonia, which broadcast appeals to Scotland to dissociate herself from England's war.

On his release from prison, Grant returned to his mother's grocer's shop at Pretoria House in the high street of Alness. When news got around, an angry crowd descended on the shop and stoned their disgraced son out of the village. Donald Grant emigrated to apartheid South Africa, then returned to London, where he is believed to have died in the mid-1980s.

'We have always lived dangerously and there is nothing like it'

In early 1940, the Home Office received a report calling Raven Thomson 'one of the most extreme members of the party, and probably one of the more dangerous members'.[48] Thomson was both editor of *Action* and director of Sanctuary Press. His wife Lisbeth, of German citizenship, ran the Anglo-German Agency, which organised the domestic employment of young German and Austrian women and the sale of air raid protection equipment of all kinds. Up until July 1939, New Era Tours were conducted by Thomson's step-daughter Helga.

Raven Thomson was considered to be 'one of the most ardent pro-Germans'. He had made five visits to Nazi Germany, firstly to Nuremberg, where he was received by Hitler, then to Breslau for the annual Nazi Youth Rally and to meet Goebbels, with whom he agreed a subsidy for the BUF. He also attended the Berlin Olympics in 1936. As the phoney war drew to its end, British intelligence noted that 'the existence of a particularly subversive and revolutionary section of the BU was reported recently, and it was said that this section, known as the Suicide Squad, was probably not known to Mosley, but was known to Francis-Hawkins and Raven Thomson'. What's more, Thomson had reportedly told his wife: 'After all, it's great fun, even if it is a little dangerous. We're going to win whatever happens, and the bigger the fight, the greater the satisfaction. We have always lived dangerously, and there is nothing like it.' Prior to his detention, he 'was addressing meetings at which he indicated violent anti-Government and pro-Fascist views'.[49]

It was therefore no surprise that Thomson was arrested on 4 April 1940. In his personal effects were found fourteen sheets of paper containing routes between large towns in Great Britain, for example the A2 London–Dover. 'This may have a sinister significance', it was noted. However, Thomson protested his patriotic credentials:

> I remember a meeting I held at Dumfries many years ago to which some Reds came from Glasgow. They put the question to me directly:

'If we were at war with a Fascist country would you fight for Britain?' I said 'Certainly, we defend our country from any attack by a Fascist country.' This Red said 'You are no good. If there was a war with Russia I should not fight for Britain, I should fight for Russia.' It was a typical internationalist mind.[50]

Thomson's only son was a sergeant in the RAF (and would go missing in August 1941).

According to Thomson's biographer, Peter Pugh, 'the reasons for detention were insufficient to form a prosecution under conventional law'.[51] Nevertheless, he was incarcerated in Brixton Prison, alongside other suspected traitors. This period of imprisonment inflicted considerable psychological damage on Mosley's former Director of Policy. On 27 November 1942, Thomson requested in vain to visit his mistress, Olive Burdett, the BUF's chief women's organiser, at Royal Holloway. He wrote obsequiously to Home Secretary Morrison:

> I deliberately chose South Hackney as the seat I would contend for British Union, because I held you to be an opponent worthy of my steel. I shall be sorry if we permitted political opposition and the conditions of this detention to become the cause of permanent personal embitterment, when we have both this much in common – our love and respect for the magnificent people of East and North London who have already suffered so severely in this unfortunate war.[52]

On 2 September 1943, he complained that 'my health and nervous condition are suffering in consequence of the prolonged confinement and inability to find sufficient means of active occasions'. On 22 September 1943, the senior medical officer at the prison reported: 'he says he occupies most of his time here writing but on occasions plays cricket or rounders. He now says he wants physical occupation eg farm work. He tells me he is very worried over private domestic matters – a love affair, of which the authorities are fully aware, and this is affecting his sleep'. He was suffering from 'mild nervous and physical debilitations'.[53]

On 2 December 1943, Thomson was finally transferred to Peel Camp on the Isle of Man. This does not seem to have done him any good. On 15 January 1944, he pleaded again with the authorities:

I must ask you to send me back to Brixton, as I find the prevailing Anti-British sentiment in the camp, which is now largely composed of Anglo-Germans and Anglo-Italians, quite intolerable! ... As I joined British Union as a patriotic British subject, however critical I may have been of the government of this country, I cannot tolerate the continual attacks I hear on the British people and this country, which are having a most adverse effect on my already shaken nerves.[54]

On 23 May 1944, a psychiatric report on the Scottish Blackshirt found that he

had great difficulty in distinguishing the borderline between actual happening and these fantasies (as he calls them). He refused to do any farm work and brooded over his condition. Early this month I had a definite reply from the lady in question which stated that she did not wish to correspond with him any further. After I had discussed this with him his condition became worse and he now denies all insight into his system. In fact he professes never to have had such insight ... His general behaviour has not changed, in his habits he contrives to be dirty and he has not been able to do any real work of any kind. He associates with other people and is quite talkative – mostly on abstract philosophical problems ... He is very logical in all his conversations with me if they are not concerned with his delusions and in fact at times he is rather cunning. He himself mentions the paranoiac schizophrenia as a possible diagnosis and he wishes to have his memory restored either by hypnosis, narcoanalysis or some other active treatment [*sic*]. He is in touch with his family and has even asked them to send him money ... Raven Thomson himself was rather against being sent to a mental home on the grounds that it might create a bad impression.[55]

The malaise afflicting the author of *Civilization as Superman* seemed, in fact, to be rather banal. On 25 May 1944, another psychiatrist wrote: 'His real trouble appears to be, that for years he has been living with an unmarried wife by whom he has had three children, and another woman has now appeared on the scene.' On 13 June 1944, 'he was found to be suffering from obsession in connection with his past life, and his neighbours ... He suffers severely from insomnia, and finds that life here is unbearable'.[56]

In September 1944, as the end of the Third Reich began to come clearly into view, Raven Thomson and other British Fascists were released. He certainly did not put the past behind him. By the beginning of 1946 he had rejoined Mosley's inner circle and was busy organising book clubs, addressing private meetings, and managing the affairs of Mosley Publications Ltd.

Hitler's Harvester

A smaller fish in this dark little pond was Alexander Proctor, of Blairgowrie, the man behind Tripod Harvesters Ltd.[57] Son of a flax spinner, he became a captain in the Black Watch and travelled and worked extensively in Tsarist Russia. He served as a Special Service Officer in Russia from 1914 to 1920, directing the transit of British war materiel. As British Military Representative at Archangel, he was – he later claimed – the first British officer delegated to negotiate with a Bolshevik minister of state. As with the Earl of Glasgow, Proctor was turned by the October Revolution and its aftermath into a rabid enemy of Communism and the 'Jewish conspiracy' associated with it.

On 17 November 1936, Proctor wrote to Joachim von Ribbentrop to 'welcome' him as new Nazi ambassador to London. Proctor claimed to have been 'the first Nazi in Britain since 1922', before turning to current affairs. 'Today we see Spain ravished and almost destroyed by the Red Dragon of Bolshevism and Anti-Christ!' Fortunately, there was an archangel to take on this scourge:

> The Glorious Leader of the White Nations – Germany's Führer Adolph Hitler, who with your Great Nation is the Spearhead of resistance to the onslaught of the JEW-controlled BOLSHEVISM all the World over, has appealed to all Nations to unite in over-throwing their barbaric attack on Civilisation.

The harvester from Blairgowrie could be of help in this titanic struggle between good and evil:

> Having probably had the widest experience of any living Englishman amongst Russia's Peasantry in Pre-War days, and also having held the greatest administrative post of any British Officer in Russia during

the War and Revolution, I think my services might be of considerable value in the coming conflict to free martyred and enslaved Russia from its ghastly bondage, and the World from the terrific menace of Jew-run Bolshevism. Therefore, I hereby solemnly offer my faithful service to the World's saviour, A. Hitler and to Germany at any time when required to fight or work with your Great New Army in the swiftly approaching conflict with the vile forces of World Revolution.

There was also more earthy business to attend to:

Another object of this letter is also to place the use of my Tripod All-Weather Harvesting System and its Equipment at the disposal of the German Ministry of Agriculture, together with the benefit of my experience as a specialist in the perfect harvesting of all cut crops by Natural Air-Drying, which has triumphed so notably this past wet summer in England.

At 50, he was 'still athletic and physically fit' and concluded thus: 'I wish to state that it is my keen desire to fight for the White Crusade against Jew-controlled Satanic Soviet Russia and all the foul villainy it stands for, whether Britain is involved or not in the coming Struggle'.

Such correspondence alerted the authorities. Intelligence reported of Proctor:

Uses a good car in which he travels extensively and is apparently able to procure an unlimited supply of petrol. He frequently visits farms in Lincolnshire and Norfolk, ostensibly for the purpose of selling his harvester. He does not, however, make any serious attempt to effect sales but treats his visits to farmers as a convenient opportunity for indulging in Fascist propaganda.

He was also a member of the Nordic League:

Proctor is violently pro-Nazi in sympathy. He has now, and has had for some years, a great admiration for Hitler, and the Nazi regime. After the Munich crisis he was heard to say 'I wish to God I was in Germany now.' 'I hope Hitler will win if we go to war.' He has written to Hitler and is in possession of a letter signed by Hitler.

Proctor is perpetually saying that Hitler is his leader. He has also said that when Hitler takes control in England he, Proctor, will have a good position.

Through the Nordic League, Proctor was in touch with Captain Archibald Maule Ramsay MP during the months immediately preceding the latter's detention. Conversations intercepted in March and May 1940 referred to their mutual friend, the Duke of Buccleuch, not simply on the use of tripod harvesting, but also a letter from the duke which Proctor 'would like to show to' Ramsay. In the light of this intelligence, Proctor was detained under Defence Regulation 18B and sent to the Isle of Man.

On 6 October 1940, Proctor appealed to the Advisory Committee on internment, stressing his patriotic credentials. A brother had been killed at Gallipoli, while another had served in India and South Africa before being 'blown to bits on the western front'. In the present war, he had a son in the RAF and one on the flagship of the Mediterranean Fleet. He asked: 'With this big contingent of my own Kith and Kin in the forefront of the present Conflict, is it not LUDICROUS to suppose that I would play the part of a Traitor to them, as well as to my King and Country?' He offered his services to the Auxiliary Fire Service of Central London, or pleaded for at least 'a transfer to a Concentration Camp somewhere in England'. His assessors at Peel Camp were unswayed: 'We are firmly convinced that Proctor would regard the victory of this country as a victory for international Jewry ... we feel very uneasy about him and hope that the Committee may feel justified in ordering his continued detention.'

But as the years passed, it was reported that whatever threat he posed had diminished. On 15 July 1943, an officer at Peel Camp reported:

I think the real truth is that Proctor is a crank and that before his detention he allowed himself to be carried away by his hatred of Russia and all things Russian. He is, however, in many ways an intelligent man and he has been a little over three years in detention so that he will have learnt his lesson ... Although he made disloyal utterances over three years ago I do not believe that he would do anything actively subversive or be disloyal to this country if released.

He has throughout maintained that he is anxious to do what he can to assist; he is now over 60 years of age and is said to be an expert on the subject of growing flax so that he should have no difficulty in finding employment[.]

Five days later, it was reported:

It seems clear that Proctor is still strongly anti-Russian, and has not really lost his admiration of Hitler, but he apparently purports to have reached the stage where, mentally exhausted, he can no longer afford to allow himself to worry over ideologies. Whether he can keep quiet for long may be open to doubt but the public expression of his views seems more likely to cause damage to himself than to the war effort.

He was therefore free to return to Blairgowrie. In the meantime, however, Tripod Harvesters Ltd had been deemed so inefficient that the Ministry of Supply had taken it over.

The Gauleiter of Peebles

Alexander Proctor was a very minor 'traitor' in comparison with his fellow Nordic Leaguer, Captain Archibald Maule Ramsay MP, the only member of the House of Commons to be detained during the Second World War. Born in 1894 to a distinguished Scottish aristocratic family, Ramsay had attended Eton and Sandhurst before serving in the Coldstream Guards and being seriously wounded in France in 1916. He would be made a member of His Majesty's Bodyguard for Scotland. In 1931, he was elected Conservative MP for South Midlothian and Peeblesshire. As a member of the Potato Marketing Board, Ramsay seemed to be pursuing a solid and undistinguished parliamentary career well suited to his rural constituency.

However, while a member of the Committee for Subversive Activities, he took on a much more dangerous hue. 'Severe vibrations' hit Peebles at five minutes to midnight on 21 March 1938, and people in their homes all over the town experienced what proved to be a slight earthquake. Another severe disturbance in the locality was when the local MP began to make virulently anti-Semitic statements. It was around this time that Ramsay came to believe that Bolshevism was Jewish. Ramsay would recall how he decided to 'oppose and expose the activities of Organized Jewry, in the light of the evidence which came into my possession in 1938 ... Our hope was to avert war, which we considered to be mainly the work of Jewish intrigue centred in New York'.[58] He set his sights on fighting the 'internal enemy' that had made of Britain, in the words of his own notorious ditty, a 'Land of Dope and Jewry'. At the same time in the House of Commons, writes Richard Griffiths, 'he stressed his patriotism, and attempted to convince people of the distinction between anti-Semitism and pro-Nazism, fearing that the Home Secretary would be stampeded into "identifying the two things by a ramp in our Jew-ridden Press"'.[59] One notable success in Ramsay's campaign to maintain a Christian society against the attacks of the 'godless' was in June 1938, when his Aliens Restriction (Blasphemy) Bill was passed on its first reading by 165 votes to 134.

It was at the beginning of 1939 that Ramsay's utterances, and their consequences, ratcheted up. On 13 January 1939, the *Peeblesshire Advertiser* reported that Ramsay's wife, Ismay Ramsay, had told the Arbroath Business Club: 'There was not the smallest doubt that there was an international group of Jews who were behind world revolution in every single country at the present time.' This provoked an outraged response from Dr Salis Daiches, Chief Rabbi of Edinburgh. 'There is not the slightest foundation for this allegation ... I challenge her to name the International group to which she refers.'[60] The Presbytery of Peebles also protested against this anti-Semitic outburst.

Ramsay leapt to his wife's support. On 20 January he explained to the local paper the peril represented by the Third Communist International. Quoting Reverend Denis Fahey's booklet *The Rulers of Russia*, he pointed out that of the 59 members of the Central Committee of the Soviet Communist Party in 1935, 56 were Jews and that the remaining three, including Stalin, were married to Jewesses (Ramsay omitted to mention that this very same Central Committee had just been decimated during the Great Terror). Ramsay repeated this point on 13 February, in a speech to the Nordic League deploring the 'onslaught from a Rabbi with whom the churches had joined issue against him, and from sections of the Jewish-controlled Scottish Press'. His wife, speaking on his behalf at Arbroath, 'had dared to tell the truth about Red Spain. She also had been maliciously assailed from the same quarter'.[61]

There were limits to the outrage caused by such remarks. The

Arbroath Herald had even felt flattered by the attention residents of nearby Kellie Castle attracted. Richard Griffiths remarks on the 'naivety of the local community in Arbroath, prepared to take much of what it was told, provided it came from a member of the aristocracy'.[62] Indeed, also in January 1939, the *Montrose Standard* had praised a lecture given to the local Workers Educational Association by Dr Kenneth Hayens, Reader in German at University College Dundee, in which he had praised the Nazi regime for 'carrying out, for the benefit of the people, the things which people wanted'.[63]

Back in Peebles, the local newspaper noted on 10 February 1939 that Unionists were 'uneasy' and gave the defeated Duchess of Atholl as an example of how an MP's dabblings in international politics could lose him or her constituency support: 'Captain Maule Ramsay will have to learn that the constituent whom he represents, like the customer, is always right . . . He can do much for himself by listening a bit more to the woes of the sheep farmers of the Moorfoots and Peeblesshire hills, and showing he is ready to help them.'[64]

Nevertheless, on the eve of Ramsay's speech to the Nordic League, the Peebles Conservative Association expressed its 'solidarity and unanimity'. The paper noted that, in the Association's statement, there was 'no mention of Captain Ramsay's anti-Jewish pronouncements, and thus, in the omission, would seem to condone them'. Indeed, in mid-March, at a well-attended meeting in the Parish Church Hall, the captain received an enthusiastic welcome. He stood by his previous statements on the Jews: 'He was placed in a curious position. He was faced with withdrawing a statement which he believed to be true . . . He did what he believed everyone else in the same position would have done (cheers).' The MP then moved on to other things, notably his activity on the committee for agriculture, which had led to his nickname 'Spud'. He was 'a humble member of National Government', concerned about the future of the tweed industry and old-age pensions. And as a proof of loyalty, he expressed his 'hundred per cent support for Neville Chamberlain's attempts to avert war (applause)'. Nevertheless, some in the audience pressed him on his links with the shady Militant Christian Patriots, and his sympathies for continental Fascism:

Is it a fact that along with another 60 MPs you sent a letter of congratulation to Mussolini on the success of Fascism? – I am not a

Fascist and have no intention of becoming one, and my signature never appeared in any letter of congratulation. – Then someone must have forged it? (Laughter)[65]

Ramsay had supporters abroad. On 24 March 1939, the *Advertiser* reported that the Nazi central organ, *Völkischer Beobachter*, had given its front page to the attacks on Ramsay for 'telling the truth about the Jews'. In its editorial, the *Advertiser* remained concerned about their MP's anti-Semitic stance:

> We ourselves, contrary to the belief in certain quarters, have no po-litical opinion on the Jewish controversy; our interest is ethical, and like the bulk of the electors who feel that Captain Ramsay in view of his position on the Committee of Subversive Activities, must have strong reasons for his attitude, we would like him to explain his rea-son, and so satisfy our British sense of fair play.[66]

Captain Ramsay did nothing of the sort, and as his public anti-Semitic and anti-war activities were reaching their height, he created the conspiratorial Right Club in May 1939. This secret organisation, made up of Wardens, Stewards, Yeomen, Keepers and Freemen, was devoted to fighting the Judeo-Bolshevik menace. The membership was kept in the 'Red Book', a private ledger secured by brass fasten-ers and fitted with an automatic lock. This clandestine creation by a member of the Committee of Subversive Activities was at the limit of legality.

Fifty years after the end of the Second World War, the contents of the 'Red Book' were divulged to Richard Griffiths. The member-ship list includes William Joyce and A.K. Chesterton, significant figures of the far right of the time. It also contains a large number of Scots. Firstly, there are aristocrats: Lord Ronald Graham, second son of the Duke of Montrose; the Earl of Galloway; and Lord Colum Crichton-Stewart, younger brother of the fourth Marquess of Bute and Unionist MP for Norwich. There are other MPs: John MacKie, Conservative member for Galloway; Provost Hunter, member for Perth; and Samuel Chapman, member for South Edinburgh. There are military figures, for example, H.W. Luttmann-Johnson, and the businessman Sir Alexander Walker, former chairman of Johnnie Walker's. The membership also included a neighbour of Captain

Ramsay's, Lord Carnegie, and Peebles constituents including Alec Cowan.[67]

Was the Right Club organising a 'fifth column'? Around this time, it was reported to MI5 that Mosley had offered Ramsay a future role as Scottish Gauleiter:

> According to Captain Ramsay, Mosley had promised Scotland as the area for which he would be responsible, but Captain Ramsay had refused the offer. Captain Ramsay's words were: 'Mosley said, "We have nothing in Scotland. I wish you would take it over". I said "I do not approve of Fascism or I would join you".'[68]

However, Ramsay allegedly promised to Mosley that, in the case of a Communist uprising, he and his associates would be the first in the front line.

Throughout 1939, the captain pursued his campaign against the Anti-Christ in all its forms. After an attempt on the life of Chamberlain by the IRA, which Ramsay typically characterised as a Communist-controlled bombing financed by Jewish gold, he offered his help to the prime minister. His offer was declined. On 8 June 1939, MI5 reported Ramsay's speech to the Carlton Club, where he elaborated on the 'gigantic conspiracy' as laid out in the *Protocols of the Elders of Zion*. The IRA, he notably claimed, was directed by the Grand Orient in Dublin. A week later, he addressed a meeting of the Link at the Crofton Hotel. It was 'a very successful meeting. Ramsay talked all night', outlining the aims of the Link: 'the main idea and object of the Groups is to abolish all Jews in England and then get England to become friendly with Germany'. They should 'hire fleets of small vans with loud-speakers and men who could speak well'. For the captain, Anthony Eden and Philip Sassoon were 'thugs and bandits', and Hitler 'that splendid fellow'. On 21 June 1939, after attending a meeting of the Nordic League, the MI5 agent remarked:

> All our observers agree that this man is either a completely honest fanatic or a most dangerous mixture of fanatic and crank. At the meeting which he addressed on behalf of the Nordic League his speeches display[ed] a lack of control beside which the speeches of William Gallacher of the Communist Party appear to be mild. It is certain that if any member of the CP made speeches like many of the

speeches recently made by Captain Ramsay . . . he would certainly lay himself open to a charge of incitement to violence.

It was reported that a mass rally in the Albert Hall was planned for December 1939, and that, in the case of war, there would be 'underground activity'.[69]

Among the Right Club's membership were Tyler Kent, a cipher clerk at the US embassy in London, and Anna Wolkoff, daughter of a former Tsarist naval attaché. For Wolkoff, 'Hitler is a god . . . He is of this century and it would be wonderful if he could govern England.'[70] Kent, a man of isolationist sympathies, had access to highly sensitive communications between US ambassador Joseph Kennedy, President Franklin Roosevelt and Winston Churchill concerning military co-operation. This information was to be passed on treasonably to Ramsay, who could have used it on the floor of the House of Commons, but also to the Germans. Thanks to an MI5 operation, Wolkoff and Kent were arrested in May 1940. The affair was a catalyst for the authorities to strengthen the Defence of the Realm Act and imprison a far right 'fifth column' including the founder of the Right Club. Suspicions inevitably fell on Ramsay – although in 1941, from prison, he would successfully sue the *New York Times* for libel.

When the phoney war came crashing to an end, Captain Ramsay was detained for 'actions prejudicial to the public safety or the defence of the realm'. On 23 May 1940, the editorial of the *Peeblesshire Advertiser* opined: 'It would be correct to say the news horrified most, but it did not come in the nature of intense surprise'. A stigma 'could have been averted', but the 'failure to face facts' had ended in the 'inevitable'. Only a matter of three weeks before, the *Advertiser* had written that it 'detected propaganda of a certain vile type'. The paper looked back at the political earthquake which commenced in early 1938, with Ramsay's letter attacking the co-operative movement as a Communist conspiracy. Then, in August 1938, there had been his signature on a group of MPs' letter of congratulation to Il Duce. That had been sickeningly followed by the Jewish controversies and pro-Nazi statements of 1939. The editorial concluded: 'This stain on the constituency should have been and ought to have been averted by Peebles Unionists. In this hour of national trial, we ought to have been saved from such direful calamity.'[71]

The detainee saw things slightly differently. On 30 May 1940, MI5 reported:

> He said he was the founder of the Right Club which was an organisation to combat Jewish and Communist influence in this country, and he went into a tirade against the British government alleging that it was Jew-ridden and controlled, that the press was in the hands of the Jews and that the war had been engineered by Jews. On 73 occasions, he said, he had risen in his place in the House of Commons to speak on the subject of Jews and Communists and failed to catch the Speaker's eye. Captain Ramsay said he was the only Member who dared attack the Government on their policy and he was being removed to prison as a menace to that policy.[72]

At the end of June a search of Kellie Castle was ordered. There was found a letter from William Joyce (a Warden of the Right Club), and a German Nazi badge. The investigators admitted they were 'rather disappointed with the search, but feel that it would have been very remiss of us not to have taken the choice'.[73]

Ramsay pointed out to his captors that two of his sons were serving in the war, and that one had been wounded in fighting at Narvik. But this did not sway the Advisory Committee, who were particularly interested in Mosley's offer of the Gauleitership of Scotland. On 18 July 1940, it noted:

> It would appear that this conversation took place some considerable time before the outbreak of war, but indicated that in certain circumstances of public disorder Mosley was suggesting to Ramsay that he should take part in the Government of Scotland, as one of Mosley's lieutenants. However ridiculous and fanciful this may sound, it indicates that Captain Ramsay was prepared to consider taking action which was quite outside the ordinary work of anti-Jewish propaganda.[74]

So Ramsay remained in Brixton Prison, alongside Raven Thomson and other 'renegades'. On 9 September 1940, the MP protested to the attorney-general that he was currently subjected to 22.5 hours per day of solitary confinement. By what right, he asked, 'do MI5 carry out the methods of the Gestapo on British civilians whom Parliament has authorised the Home Secretary only to detain?'

These constraints would eventually be loosened. In his memoirs, Admiral Sir Barry Domvile offers this description of life in prison with Ramsay and others:

> We had many a jolly game of cricket and rounders . . . Captain Ramsay, one of these Etonians, temporarily absolved from attendance at Westminster, coached eager disciples from Soho and Shepherd's Market, and greatly raised the Brixton standard of cricket. It was a treat to see Captain Gordon Canning, another Etonian, lift a half-volley over Lenin's tomb (the Recreation ground lavatories) into the Fire tank – quite as good as one over the Pavilion at Lord's. The ball often sailed over the prison wall, and I should like to pay a tribute to the decency of the people who returned it, in these days of shortage.[75]

It was a strange fall from grace. The *Daily Herald* examined the fate of this 'tall, handsome, eagle-looking man . . . Scion of one of the oldest families in Scotland'. Lest we forget, the author of 'Land of Dope and Jewry' had been elected in 1935 under the slogans 'Fair Play for all Classes' and 'No Dictators Wanted Here'. The *Herald* reached an astonishing conclusion: 'No fewer than 13,671 hard-working Scots, men and women of Midlothian and Peebles, believed this and voted for Ramsay! Only 12,209 thought it was the bunk! And we are still paying Captain Ramsay MP £600 a year!'[76]

In the eyes of the authorities, their detainee was incorrigible: 'This man, though he sincerely regards himself as the most loyal and patriotic of British subjects, is led by his morbid obsession with Jewry and international finance to adopt views which in effect are both traitorous and dangerous. He should remain in detention.'[77] The character of Ramsay's correspondents confirmed this view. Lady Maxwell-Scott was 'a woman of French extraction born in Ohio. She has been described as a hysterical woman, very anti-Russian, and anti-Semitic, pro-Pétain'. Her husband was 'an elderly and rather sick man. He was connected with the Home Guard in the war and had a distinguished career in the last war, he is thought to share to a lesser extent his wife's views . . . It was reported that he had been at the same military college in France with Franco. Both he and his wife held Fascist sympathies and indulged in defeatist and anti-British talk'.[78]

On 1 October 1943, MI5 remarked that it was 'quite hopeless to expect any change of heart from Ramsay'. On release, he was likely to form another secret conspiracy, while intelligence personnel worried about the 'possible effect of Ramsay's release upon our relations with the Soviet Union'. Indeed it was reported that the captain had told his wife: 'I would welcome civil war with shots in the streets.' As for Mrs Ramsay, her first reaction had been to plot her husband's escape from Brixton:

> She hoped that advantage might be taken of the disorganisation re-sulting from air raids, revolution or invasion, to force the gates of the prison with bombs. She hoped for the help of Fascist sympathisers, and the Army and added: 'Both Bob and I have taken note of every detail on the way to Jock's room and of everything we can see on our visits. We shall not fail, and I long to see the Home Office people swinging and hanging from lamp posts.'

It was also reported that, on 17 October 1942, Mrs Ramsay had said that 'she did not think we could possibly win the war, in fact, she did not think that we should be able to last out for more than a year. There would be a frightful crisis after which her husband and his friends would come into their own and take over the reconstruction of the country'.[79]

On 1 September 1943, intelligence officer Mary Robertson reported that Ramsay had said 'how the Jews must be laughing at the idiotic goyim', but also: 'One good feature that I see is that U boats do not seem to have sunk much of our shipping lately. I wonder whether we have mastered them at last. It would be nice not to starve, I must say.' Robertson justly remarked: 'So far from there being any foundation in fact for Ramsay's belief that he is the victim of Jewish persecution he would appear to be fortunate indeed in being held as political detainee in Brixton Prison, rather than as a convict sentenced to a long term of penal servitude.'[80] But Ramsay was not immune to the tragedy of war. On 23 August 1943 it was announced that his eldest son, an officer in the Scots Guards, had died in a military hospital in Johannesburg.

Herbert Morrison ordered the unconditional release of Captain Ramsay on 26 September 1944. He could retake his seat in the House of Commons. The *Peeblesshire Advertiser* expressed its sadness:

We had come near to the point of forgetting Captain A.M. Ramsay, when on Tuesday, the atmosphere was stirred; the news came over the wireless that he had been released from detention ... Many moves were made to relieve the constituency of the unfortunate position; very many moves, including a petition signed by all sections of the community, and also the request from the Unionist Association that he resign his seat. Nothing was effective; every move was checkmated ... It seems we must await a General Election before Captain Ramsay, as an unwanted candidate, as he evidently is, can be deprived of his post as Member of Parliament for Peebles and South Midlothian.

The announcement of Ramsay's return also caused outrage elsewhere, with the Communist MP for West Fife at the forefront:

Willie Gallacher: 'Are you aware that this man is a rabid anti-Semitic?'
'Out of order.'
'Anti-Semitism is an incitement to murder. Are the mothers of this country, whose lads are being sacrificed, to be informed that this sacrifice has enabled the Home Secretary to release this unspeakable blackguard?'
'Order ... withdraw.'

Gallacher was ordered to leave the House. Morrison justified the release of Ramsay and other detainees on the grounds of 'the success of the arms of the United Nations and the certainty that the forces of evil arrayed against us are doomed to complete overthrow'.[81]

Mary Robertson noted that the news 'came as a complete surprise' to Ramsay: 'He reached home that evening about nine o'clock and the following morning went straight down to the House of Commons where he appears to have met with a more favourable reception than he had anticipated.'[82] Indeed, according to the *Peeblesshire Advertiser*, 'as several MPs walked into the Chamber they crossed to Captain Ramsay and shook his hand. Captain Ramsay had a smile for them all ... He sat for a few minutes chatting with Admiral Beamish (Unionist, Lewis) and, as the Admiral rose to take his place on the opposite side of the House, turned to his left and carried on a short conversation with Mr Duckworth (Unionist, Moss-side)'. Ramsay told reporters that his release had been unexpected, that he intended to devote himself to obtaining the release of other detainees, and that he had made no plans for the future.

According to Robertson, Ramsay 'lost no time in contacting his Fascist friends', notably A.K. Chesterton. He was also looking for a political future outside Peeblesshire: 'Ramsay, presumably dented by the general hostility of his own constituency, was thinking of fighting the next election in a London Dock area – possibly Bermondsey, where he had been testing reaction in the local public houses with his son Bob.' Ramsay had certainly not changed his views on the Jewish conspiracy, although sometimes his motivations were unclear. Robertson noted:

> It will be remembered that Ramsay's original interest in the Hidden Hand is believed to have been encouraged by his wife in an effort to compete with the rival attractions of his secretary, Ruth Erskine. It has been clear, however, that since his release Ramsay has been paying less and less attention to Mrs Ramsay and more to the secretary.

Ramsay believed himself 'in danger of assassination by the Jews'. To defend himself, he was collecting 'a mass of information on private lives and activities of members of the Government'. He found a very sympathetic interlocutor in the founder of the Imperial Fascist League:

> We learnt in June that Ramsay had recently visited Arnold Leese, with whom he carries on a prolific correspondence about Jews and alleged Jews, and had put forward definite proposals for future underground activity. Leese disagreed with Ramsay's insane views about an ultimate resort to violence, but agreed to co-operate freely with him in other respects.[83]

The MP for South Midlothian and Peeblesshire's last hurrah came in June 1945, when he moved – unsuccessfully – the re-enactment of the Statute of Jewry. Ramsay told the House: 'The repeal of the Act (in 1846) released the very evils which Magna Carta and the Statute of Jewry recognised and against which there were specially directed Jewish extortion, exploitation and violence.'

Ratcliffe's War

Another sympathetic ear for Captain Ramsay's anti-Semitic elucubrations was the Reverend Alexander Ratcliffe who, on the MP's release, had planned to put out a substantial pamphlet called *The Vindication of Captain A.H. Maule Ramsay, MP*. This erstwhile enemy of 'Papist' fascism and 'Franco the Baby-Killer' had, with an implacable logic of sorts, converted to pro-Nazi anti-Semitism.

Already, in the *Vanguard* of June 1939, he had written: 'Our correspondent points out that Hitler is killing Catholic Action in Germany and disbanding all Roman Catholic youth organisations. And so, as the Pope cannot fight Hitler, he's getting Chamberlain to do the fighting for him ... Britain is preparing for war; war against Germany. And it will not be Britain that will benefit, *but the Pope*.' The leader of the Scottish Protestant League's new attachment to Hitler was confirmed by a visit to Nazi Germany in July and August 1939. In an article of 30 September 1939, on religion in Hitler's Germany, he told his readers he was 'agreeably surprised' during his visit. He noticed on his journey how England had taken in what Germany had thrown out. In London, he had witnessed an 'actress with her legs pretty well exposed. My readers will pardon me inserting that account of stage immorality and vice in London, but I do so in order to inform them that that is the sort of thing which the Germans threw out of Germany on Hitler procuring control'. There could be no doubting the religious rectitude of the Führer from Linz: 'Hitler, having been born a Roman Catholic, knows the Roman Catholics, and thus the Romanist priests are specially watched.'[84]

In October 1939, the *Vanguard* asked: 'Is Hitler the Man 666?' Hitler, it was explained, 'was not the first personality who has been picked out as the Beast 666. During the last War it was the Kaiser. Previously it was Napoleon. Before that Nero'. The Beast was in fact 'the Latin Man, the Pope', leader of the 'Jesuits' war drive'. Over the 2,000 miles Ratcliffe had travelled in Germany, he had found the German people 'happy and contented'.

The *Vanguard* therefore opposed the distribution in the streets of Glasgow of a pamphlet entitled *The Berlin Liar*: 'our simple Scots folks will fall from the net of these Jewish moneybaggers whose sole purpose during this War, as in all Wars, is to "make hay while the sun shines" '. The same issue attacked 'Rome's verminous evacuees!'[85]

On 25 November 1939, under the banner 'Protestant Unity Now!', Ratcliffe answered the question of whether he was a pro-German:

What I am concerned about is not whether Hitlerism should be crushed or not. That does not concern me. It does not concern a single true Protestant in this country. What I am concerned about is the Protestants of Europe, and especially the Protestants of Britain; more especially my own country, Scotland. If I believed that this country going to war against Germany were in the interests of Protestant Christianity (for there is no other kind of Christianity) then I might have something to say about it. But emphatically I believe that this War is being run, as all Wars are run, in the interests of Jewish Moneybaggers and the Pope of Rome. I believe that Britain is being used for an ulterior purpose, and that our pact with Poland was a Popish and Jewish plot to get this Protestant country embroiled in War with Protestant Germany. [86]

On 6 January 1940 Ratcliffe's readers were offered 'unique articles' on 'The Truth About the Jews', 'The Palestine Ramp', and 'Why Germans put out the Jews'. The issue of 20 January vilified the 'pro-Jew menace': the *Jewish Echo* was published in 'Jew-land', the Gorbals; the press of the country was controlled and influenced by the Jews; the Jews were not God's chosen people; Jews were the enemies of the Christian faith; Jesus had repudiated Judaism and Jews were responsible for the crucifixion of Christ. On 2 March 1940, Ratcliffe quoted Martin Luther saying Jews were 'veritable liars and vampires'. Even Finnish resistance to Stalin was denounced as a 'war ramp': General Carl Gustav Mannerheim's daughter was a 'Papist'.[87] In May, the *Vanguard* denounced 'the pernicious little dictator! No, not Hitler, just Mussolini!' In June, the paper opined: 'We are very kind to the Roman Catholics in Scotland, of course, the reason being, seemingly, that we have no Hitler in our midst to eject popery!'[88]

This anti-Catholic logic meant there was no sympathy for fallen France. In July 1940 'The Treacherous French!' were attacked. Britain had committed the cardinal error of an alliance with Catholic countries like Poland and Belgium. As for the French, 'a more treacherous people are not to be found. Papist and atheistic, that country has been the enemy of Protestantism for centuries'.[89] The wounds of St Bartholemew's Day remained fresh: 'It is not 368 years since that terrible crime took place and the treachery of the French of those days is on a par with the treachery of the French of today.' A month later, Ratcliffe declared: 'Let us sever all connections with Papist countries!'[90]

Attention then turned from Papists to Jews. The issue of September 1940 looked approvingly at Hitler's 'prophecy' of 30 January 1939 on the annihilation of the Jewish race in Europe:

> An ominous prophecy! And so far as the Continent of Europe is concerned, especially that part of the Continent now over-run by the Germans, the prophecy seems about to be fulfilled! Amazing and strange are the times in which we live. But let no-one be downhearted, for God moves in mysterious ways, His wonders to perform! [91]

In October 1940, readers learned that 'The Jews are of the Devil!'[92] The November issue decried 'The Jews' nude shows!', and the December one the sins of 'God's Chosen people!' 'Our next issue,' it was announced, 'will startle you!'[93]

Over the course of the war, incendiary pamphlets were churned out by Ratcliffe's press in Bearsden. In January 1941, Commonsense War Pamphlet 1 asked *Are you fighting for democracy? Or the Great Illusion!*: 'Let not the simple souls of British Democracy be surprised or shocked if the day comes when they will be told that, after all, we all make mistakes, and that, after all, Hitlerism is not just what we thought it was!'[94] Mr Churchill had to be put on trial. The day was coming when propaganda smoke-screens would be 'cleared away by the words of Truth'. Invoking the old saying, 'Whatsoever a man soweth, that shall he also reap', Ratcliffe wrote: 'The present war is a mere fulfilment of the laws of God and teaching of Jesus Christ . . . France has been the first to reap what she sowed!'[95] The Poles and the Czechs had been incapable of governing themselves. The 'treachery' of 1918–1919 'cried out to high heaven for retribution'.[96] Germany was robbed of Danzig and the Corridor and over two million of her people handed over to the 'Papist Poles', while Transylvanian Protestants had been handed over to 'Catholic' Romania. Hitlerism, claimed Ratcliffe, was 'the illegitimate child of the whorings of Britain and France'.[97]

Ratcliffe caused the most public outrage, and soul-searching by the authorities, with his pamphlet, *The Truth about the Jews!*, published in early 1943. In this work, the Protestant leader claimed that 'there is not a single authentic case of a single Jew having been massacred or unlawfully put to death under Hitler's regime'.[98] Instead, Ratcliffe trained his fire on the nefarious activities of Jewish traders in Glasgow: they overcharged on cosmetics, overcharged for linoleum and illegally transferred ration coupons. There was a 'Jewish Monopoly': 'If every Jew shop in Argyle Street, from Glasgow Cross to Hope St, and in Jamaica St, Union St and Renfield St, were to be closed, there would hardly be an open shop left!' The Jews practically owned Glasgow.[99] What's more, they put on 'obscene and immoral shows': 'The "Strip Tease" turns are Jewish; the almost nude women who immediately show their flesh (as much as the Law allows) are mostly Jews.'[100] They owned 'Bawdy Book Shops and shops where "Birth Control" goods are sold'.[101] The Left Book Club was totally Jewish, while such 'vermin' preferred boxing, dog-racing and horse-racing to 'clean sport'. They were even worse than Ratcliffe's usual adversary: 'The crimes for which Roman Catholics are guilty are the common offences of pilfering, drunkenness, breach of the peace, etc. But the Jews go in for crime on the wholesale system.'[102] The minister concluded rather ambiguously: 'To say that the Germans, with Hitler at their head, are out to exterminate the Jews, to massacre them, is both foolish and absurd. For if every Jew were exterminated, the world would still go on with its evil and crimes.'[103]

Were such anti-Semitic outpourings publishable at the height of the war against Nazism? On 8 March 1943, the Home Office reported to the Lord Advocate on a proof of *The Truth about the Jews!*:

> While he claims not to be anti-Semitic, Ratcliffe brings out the stock complaints of anti-Semites against the Jews. He states that they monopolize trade, finance, industry and entertainment, control large sections of the press, and that as a result they have a position of influence and privilege out of proportion to their numbers . . . The pamphlet is a pernicious document . . . We cannot stop its publication however.[104]

The Lord Advocate concurred with this tolerant view: 'It appears from this that the publication of anti-Semitic material, however virulent, is not a crime in Scotland . . . Did they desire to incite the people to violence, to create disorders and disturbances, and generally to offend against public order? NO.' On 13 March 1943, Herbert Morrison wrote to the Lord Advocate: 'It is a deplorable document, but I cannot, of course, prevent its publication.'

This judgment was not shared by everyone. On 9 April 1943, the

Metropolitan Police wrote that 'the contents of the booklet are so violently anti-Semitic that it may be considered that the publication is one likely to cause hatred and strife between Jews and non-Jews'. The *Jewish Chronicle* declared on the same day: 'This is about the vilest anti-Semitic pamphlet yet produced in Britain, and it is pure – or rather impure – [Julius] Streicher from beginning to end'.[105] Three days later, the *Daily Worker* denounced an 'outrageously anti-Semitic pamphlet'.[106]

On 28 April 1943 it was reported that 2,000 copies of the pamphlet had been printed and were being sold in England by Edward Godfrey of the British National Party. Ratcliffe was still holding well-attended meetings every Sunday in Central Halls, Bath Street, Glasgow, and the *Vanguard* was selling 2,000 copies monthly. On 29 May, Special Branch reported on Ratcliffe to the Scottish Home Department:

> Prior to the outbreak of war he visited Germany and on his return acquired a great admiration for the German nation and its method of Government. Despite this outlook, however, one could not say he was anti-British. His sojourn in Germany only lasted a fortnight and in all probability his tour would have been a conducted one. It appears that from then on he became anti-Semitic and up to the moment, my Special Branch who have been giving him considerable attention are unable to determine whether this attitude is real or assumed for financial purposes.

Special Branch concluded that '100,000 copies could easily have been printed and sold. It is obvious that the pamphlet was well read and that there is a decided wave of anti-Semitism spreading throughout the country'.

A second edition of *The Truth about the Jews!* was printed by the Right Review, based at Half-Moon Cottage, Bookham, Surrey, and owned by Count Potocki, pretender to the throne of Poland. Again, the authorities were unable to prove seditious intentions and public mischief. Ratcliffe's pamphlet therefore escaped the fate suffered by some of Arnold Leese's anti-Semitic publications before the war.

In May 1944, the *Vanguard* was denouncing 'Jewish massacres in Palestine'. In October, it attacked Papacy and Churchill's visit to the Vatican. Circulation was reported to have risen to 2,500, up 500 on

1942. Nevertheless, the authorities decided that the *Vanguard* was still entitled to a certain proportion of paper.

On 17 March 1945, it was noted that 'the objectionable nature of the articles to which MI5 draw attention is due to pro-German sentiment rather than anti-Semitism. They are the product of Ratcliffe's peculiar mental attitude'. In the view of the SPL founder, National Socialism was 'the nearest approach to New Testament Christian Communism that the world will ever see'. He now obsessed about the 'Bolshevik world drive ... Our people are being filled with a hatred for Protestant Germany engendered by that Godless limb of Satan, Marshal Stalin. Unless a stop is put to it, Bolshevism will spread to our shores, and Hitler is our only hope.' But the report concluded again that such opinions were 'not seditious libel'. The *Vanguard* would be 'allowed to remain as a memorial to the latitude of opinion which may safely be tolerated in this country in wartime'.

Ratcliffe continued to the end of the war in this same vein. In February 1945, he declared that 'Britain's only hope lies in Hitler'. In March 1945, the preacher appealed to the Houses of Parliament:

> The Hounds of Hell are now let loose upon the earth, and the spirit of vengeance and hate becomes more and more bitter as the war-gods demand the sacrifice of more and more human flesh ... Is it not high time to cease the unnatural whoredom with a Nation that is steeped in the spiritual and moral plague of an atheistical Bolshevism? Gentlemen: heed the words of the Prophet of old![107]

Atrocities were 'not German!', exclaimed the April issue, which also announced the creation of the Friends of Protestant Germany League. In May 1945, the *Vanguard* called for 'equality of sacrifice, homes for heroes, freedom from want'. At the same time it denounced the Pope, 'Protestant Namby-Pambyism' and 'Presbyterian Poltroonery', while deploring the fact that the Spanish Gospel Mission had been 'wiped out by Franco the Fascist'.[108]

It was recognised in June that an appeal for funds had been responded to by less than 3% of members of the Scottish Protestant League. But Ratcliffe kept the faith. The *Vanguard* of July 1945 gave 'The truth about the German atrocities!' Concentration camp inmates had been 'starved to death', victims of the Allied blockade. In August 1945, Ratcliffe mourned 'The Passing of

Hitler': 'To-day, with a "Victory" that is a stench in the nostrils of every Protestant Christian man and woman, where Bolshevism has not been enthroned in Europe, Romanism has stepped up back to its place of honour.' It was a triumph for 'Moscow mendacity and Vatican venality'. Gone with Hitler were 'the blessings which Hitler rule brought to the German people, and this the German people never will forget. May Almighty God bless the country and people of Martin Luther!'[109]

In October 1945, the *Vanguard* denounced the use of German POWs' 'slave labour' to prepare Glasgow housing sites. In November it attacked 'Allied Bestiality!': 'What an aftermath! Protestant Germany destroyed, and this in the direct interest of the twin-anti-Christs, Jewry and Papacy!' There were 'shameful conditions in prisons in Germany!'[110] In February 1946, the cover of the *Vanguard* was emblazoned with Hitler's coin commemorating Martin Luther. In October 1946, Ratcliffe returned to 'the futility of Fascism'. Mussolini had courted the Papacy and received its blessing. In this, Il Duce contrasted with the Führer: 'It is true that Hitler was born a Roman Catholic: and so were Knox, Luther, Wickliffe and Calvin. And Hitler battled against the Papacy, as did Hitler's Nazism, as stubbornly as did the Reformers, and sometimes more so.' Italian Fascism had lacked 'divine spirituality'. It was 'solely material in aims and objectives'.[111]

Despite failing health and finances, Ratcliffe did not relent. At the height of the disturbances in British-controlled Palestine, the *Vanguard* of June–July 1946 warned of 'the menace of Zionism'. His press also produced his 'Banned speech at Caxton Hall', where he was to tell his audience: 'You can no more satisfy the Jews than you could satisfy the blizzard or the tidal wave.'[112] In January 1947, the *Vanguard* declared:

> The crime of Nuremberg was vile because it was a violation of Divine Teaching; vile because its purpose was fundamentally an act of envy, spite and vindictiveness, and it was vile because its chief perpetrators were the enemies of God and His Christ ... Let Popery and Jewry perish, the twin savages of the Civilised World!

But it was admitted that '*The Vanguard* is much smaller', and that the Scottish Protestant League had suffered much financially in the editor's absence through illness.[113] That very month, Ratcliffe met his Maker.

Slighting the Sassenach

This tableau of tartan treachery is not complete without a renegade who discovered his Scottishness in the course of internment. Born in 1906 of Kiwi parents, Angus 'Juan' MacNab studied classics at Oxford. In 1934 he joined the BUF and became a paid employee in its press department, but accompanied William Joyce when he left in 1937 to found the National Socialist League. He was Joyce's second in command. MacNab was with Joyce in Germany shortly before the outbreak of war, returning to England 15 days before the declaration of hostilities. Along with Joyce's brother, he was detained from May 1940 to September 1944 under Defence Regulation 18B, at Peveril Camp, Peel, on the Isle of Man.[114]

A devout Roman Catholic, MacNab also seems to have rediscovered his Scottish roots. In 1943, appealing against his detention, he notably declared to the Advisory Committee examining his case:

I am not an Anglo-Saxon, I have no English blood in me at all.
Q: You are a Scotsman.
A: Yes, I am a Celt and the English have always been a puzzle to me really.
Q: I expect you have some English blood in you.
A: Not a drop.
Q: Some of us have, we cannot help it.
A: A Sassenach is always a Sassenach, but joking apart I have always found the English methods of thought extremely difficult to follow. I am much more at home among Latins. I live in an Italian house in the Camp. I find I can understand them much more than the English, they seem so much more logical.
Q: What an extraordinary thing, your people were born in New Zealand.
A: Yes.
Q: Was your mother Scottish?
A: She came from near John o'Groats.
Q: So you are a Celt.

The committee concluded: 'MacNab is a traitorous man with every advantage in the way of education. He desires the victory of Germany. He should remain in detention.' Nothing had changed by October 1943:

> Throughout his detention MacNab has shown from his letters that he is that rare species of humanity – a true renegade ... In repose MacNab's face is not unpleasing, but in conversation the expression becomes somehow distorted or twisted, and one has the feeling afterwards that there is some lack of moral sense or fibre in the man ... I mentioned MacNab's enthusiasm for the Latin races. As he said before, Spain is the country of his choice; Franco the man who best typifies his ideal of political leadership now that Mussolini has gone. And to Spain MacNab will go after the war, all being well, where he says he will be quite happy living on very little – because he will feel at home ... MacNab now wishes to obtain Spanish nationality and become a member of the Falange.

MacNab escaped the fate of his best friend Joyce. In May 1946, after release from detention, he smuggled himself to Eire via the Isle of Man and settled in Toledo, Spain. He found work broadcasting English lessons on Radio Nacional, while translating the complete works of proto-Fascist dictator Primo de Rivera. According to a report sent to Kim Philby, MacNab was 'a stubborn and unrepentant national socialist ... [who] intends to devote his energies to anti-British activities'. British intelligence kept tabs on this renegade. In August 1946, their source 'made contact with MacNab for his first English lesson, but as he had not money on him to pay, MacNab, true to his Scottish blood, refused to proceed with it'. Later, the source reported that 'his third lesson was brief as MacNab had visitors. MacNab's incidental remarks were confined to a few virulent anti-British observations. He stated his parents were New Zealanders and of Celtic blood and that he had no time whatsoever for the English'. Around this time, intelligence personnel intercepted a poem by MacNab in homage to the late war criminal Hermann Göring:

> By the same death Benito went before,
> And he of all men whom I loved the best,
> By equal shame in equal glory dressed.

There they await you through the open door:
Fight on, Kshatriya Herman, evermore
Vertical, like the angels, without rest!

In 1948, it was reported to Philby that MacNab 'is disliked by his colleagues, who describe him as conceited and prone to give himself the air of being the only genuine fascist in the world'. MacNab would never return to these shores. Instead, true to his love for Spanish and Moorish history and culture, he wrote the highly-regarded *Spain Under the Crescent Moon*.

6

The Third Reich No More?

Adolf Hitler never found the consolation he sought in his bunker bedtime book, Thomas Carlyle's *Frederick the Great*. It was on 11 March 1945 that Goebbels had presented the Führer with an abridged German translation of Carlyle's 1858 biography. Visibly pleased, Hitler recalled Carlyle's theory of 'exceptional personalities', individuals who not only left their mark on history but also provided inspiration for future leaders. One such example was the 'miraculous' Frederick the Great (1712–86), who appealed to both Carlyle's great leader theory and his hatred of representative government. According to Timothy Ryback, 'Carlyle's lyrical blend of brutality and sentimentality spoke to Hitler's own toxic emotional constitution'.[1] Carlyle's works had occupied shelf space in Hitler's first ever bookcase, in Linz. Now, in the the twilight of the thousand-year Reich, Carlyle's biography held out a glimmer of hope: as Frederick's empire was on the verge of ruin at the end of 1761, with the great forces of continental Europe assembled against him, news came from St Petersburg that his sworn enemy, the Tsarina Elizabeth, had died. On 12 April 1945, jubilation therefore swept the bunker when it was learned that President Roosevelt had succumbed to a massive brain embolism. And yet, within a month, the Führer, his mistress and his propaganda chief had taken their own lives, and the Third Reich was no more.

Untergang for the Übermensch

Few were spared by this cataclysm. Rudolf Hess's friend Albrecht Haushofer had joined the anti-Nazi resistance and was associated with the failed attempt on Hitler's life by Claus von Stauffenberg in July 1944. Imprisoned in the Gestapo headquarters in Berlin,

236

Haushofer was eventually taken out and shot on 23 April 1945. His father, too, had been briefly imprisoned in Dachau concentration camp. After the war, Karl Haushofer's American interrogators brought him before Rudolf Hess in his Nuremberg gaol. Hess insisted he could not recognise his former professor of geopolitics. On 11 March 1946, the elder Haushofer and his wife committed suicide. As for Hess, he would be sentenced to life imprisonment in Spandau prison, only terminated by suicide in 1987 at the age of 93.

On the day Britain declared war on Nazi Germany, Unity Valkyrie Mitford, confidante and rumoured lover of the Führer, had taken her pearl-handled revolver and shot herself in the head. She failed to reach Valhalla. Instead, she was repatriated to the family home on Inch Kenneth off the Isle of Mull, where in 1948 she died of meningitis. On a window pane is scratched a swastika, testament to her undying faith.

It was also hard for female Fascists in the fictional world: Muriel Spark's Miss Jean Brodie, who had preached the virile virtues of Il Duce to *la crème de la crème* of her Edinburgh private school, only survives for one year after the Second World War, unaware that she had been denounced as a fascist by her very own protégée, Miss Sandy Stranger.

In 1945, British Fascists, who had always been a sickly growth, were now cast beyond the pale. Richard Thurlow remarks: 'Anti-Fascism was no longer dominated by Communists and their allies but now was now a deeply engrained part of British character and the national culture'.[2] Fascists would now be 'neo', their passion rarely daring to speak its name.

However, the triumph over Fascism and the trial of its criminal leaders did not extinguish anti-Semitism. Scotland was affected by the August 1947 riots that shook Britain. According to Tony Kushner, 'during the Second World War the image of Jews in Britain as black marketeers gaining from the war but not contributing to the military effort was a powerful one. The end of the war did not stop such negative images and the continuation of rationing and shortages of goods created a sense of strain and gloom'.[3] The Zionist campaign against the British military presence in Palestine would provide an outlet for such lingering hatred. On 30 July 1947, two kidnapped British sergeants were brutally murdered and the area around their bodies booby-trapped by members of the Irgun, the military wing of the extreme Revisionist movement. On Friday, 1 August, the *Daily Express* published a massive front-page photograph of the hanging sergeants in a picture 'that will shock the world'. Drink-fuelled holiday boisterousness turned into violence, notably in urban areas particularly touched by austerity and unemployment. Jewish shops were attacked in the Gorbals early in the day. There followed in Glasgow, as in English cities including Manchester and Liverpool, a week of anti-Semitic disturbances ranging from the breaking of a few windows to mob violence.

This flare-up of anti-Semitic feeling did not benefit electorally the familiar pedlars of far right ideology. But they carried on regardless. Captain Ramsay expounded his conspiracy theories in *The Nameless War*, which he dedicated to 'the memory of those Patriots who in 1215 at Runnymede signed Magna Carta and those who in 1320 at Arbroath signed the Declaration of Independence'. From his fastness in Kellie Castle, the former MP for Peebles recounted the nefarious interventions of the Jew in British history. The Reformation was inspired by a man whose name, Cohen, was thinly disguised as Calvin. During the Civil War, Oliver Cromwell carried out orders from a synagogue. The Treaty of Union in 1707 represented the 'Triumph of the Moneylenders':

> The political and economic union of England and Scotland was shortly afterwards forced upon Scotland with wholesale corruption and in defiance of formal protests from every county and borough. The main objects of the Union were to suppress the Royal Mint in Scotland, and to force upon her, too, responsibility for the National Debt. The grip of the moneylender was now complete throughout Britain.[4]

The French Revolution was also the product of Jewish financial interests, as Sir Walter Scott had demonstrated in his *Life of Napoleon*. Typically, however, 'this important work by Sir Walter Scott in nine volumes, revealing so much of the real truth, is practically unknown, is never reprinted with his other works, and is almost unobtainable'.[5]

Looking at the twentieth century, Ramsay called the Russian Revolution the beginning of the 'vital inter-relation between Jews and the USSR'.[6] This was confirmed during the Spanish Civil War, on the very uniforms of the International Brigades: 'This star [of

David] and the Seal of Solomon were upon the signet rings of NCOs and Officers in this Communist horde of ill-disciplined ruffians'.[7]

When Nazi Germany emerged to 'bell the cat', Jewry had declared war, with disastrous consequences. In his conclusion, Ramsay was adamant: 'the "Jew-wise" know that we have in Britain a Jewish *Imperium in Imperio* which, in spite of all protestations and camouflage, is Jewish first and foremost, and in complete unison with the remainder of World Jewry'. It was of paramount importance to 'inform people of good will as to the truth of the matter, particularly in regard to the real anatomy, aims, and methods of the Marxist enemy. It is to this end that I humbly offer the contents of this book to all, who are determined to fight Communism'.[8]

Captain Ramsay died three years later. On 18 March 1955, the *Peeblesshire Advertiser* recalled its attempts to make the then MP come clean on fascism. However, given the conspiratorial nature of the Right Club founder, the paper came to the rather disingenuous conclusion that 'Ramsay was frank and open, he did not seek to hide anything'.[9]

Scotland in Europe

What remained of the fascist tradition in Britain was concentrated in the south of England, and looked even further south. The new slogan of Mosley's Union Movement (UM) was 'Europe a Nation': 'Britain should now join with the other peoples of Europe, just as we English previously joined with the Scottish, Welsh and Irish to make our previous civilisation'. And this Europe would join up with an Africa divided between white and black. Mosley and his followers were for 'the extension of patriotism', under the guiding light of 'the Idea of Kinship'.[10] Reviewing the recent carnage on the continent and elsewhere, the Leader wrote in the *Mosley Newsletter* of January–February 1947: 'The tragedy was that the revulsion produced too narrow a Nationalism. When you are told that you must kiss Harry the Hottentot on both cheeks as a condition of taking a walk down the street you are apt to confine yourself to the close circle of your own family!'

Mosley expounded this new vision in his book *The Alternative*. The union of Europe and the development of Africa went alongside the union of European and American policies in relation to the world

menace of Russian Communism. Mosley aimed for a 'higher synthe-
sis', a 'union of mind and will in a higher type'. And this higher type
constantly met the obstacle of 'the great negation'. Such had been,
up until now, the 'fate of the Great Englishmen'. The embodiment
of the 'negative mind in life and death' had been 'the Jew, Disraeli',[11]
responsible for a conspiracy against Peel. Obviously embittered by
his political isolation, Mosley claimed that the ruling class preferred
a natural sycophant to a vital leader. They hated the 'father figure' of
the man of action, such as Lloyd George and Churchill. In the face
of this 'triumph of spite', Mosley, the providential man for these
dangerous times, made an 'Appeal to the British':

> Again and again I have been brought down in the service of high
> things by the triumph of the small, the mean and the false; but each
> time, the experience has made me stronger. All that matters is to rise
> always from the dust, with will and character even stronger from the
> test – that you may serve yet greater ends until relentless striving
> brings final victory. Such has been the character of the Englishman in
> their sunlit, creative periods, and that nature still lives in the real Eng-
> land. The great river still flows in deep and calm, if latent, purpose;
> but the scum on the top is thick. Beneath are still the great qualities
> of the English; your kindness, your toleration, your open-minded
> sanity, your practical sense, your adaptability in plan, your power to
> endure, your final realism, even your ultimate dynamism; all the great
> qualities are still there, which took you out of the Northern Mists to
> see with the Hellenic vision of the Elizabethan bright lands which
> you held and moulded with firm, Roman hands. Will you rise and
> use your genius in time?[12]

This appeal for an Elizabethan revival did find at least one sympathetic reader north of the border. On 13 December 1947, the inventor Douglas S. Spens Stuart wrote to Mosley congratulating him on
his fifty-first birthday and *The Alternative*: 'In this book you have
undisputably demonstrated that you are as profound and perspica-
cious in thought as you are decisive and indomitable in action – in
a word, the ideal Thought-Deed man, for lack of whom the world's
civilisation is now crumbling.' Stuart had shared Mosley's pacifism:
'When Britain had attacked Germany, I did all I could against the
war.' There was no doubt in his mind of who had been the victim in

this conflict. 'Recently I made the acquaintance of a German POW formerly an officer in Hitler's body-guard who upon my expressing the opinion that Hitler lost his chance of winning the war because he tried to wage it humanely, declared that he himself had come to the same conclusion.' Spens Stuart was therefore an enthusiastic volunteer for the Movement:

> Referring to your new Union, I should like to help as far as possible, perhaps by attempting to start a branch in Perth, and interesting some friends of mine in Edinburgh, particularly Mr John F. Stewart, Chairman of the Scottish League for European Freedom, in which he and Lord Mansfield are doing much good work, and are strongly anti-communist, as you will see from the enclosed pamphlet, *Elections in Poland*, which makes pretty ghastly reading.

It remained urgent to combat 'international finance and the Jews'.[13]

The connections boasted by the inventor show how the onset of the Cold War was providing safe havens for people who had committed atrocities for the Fascist cause. The Scottish League for European Freedom, led by John F. Stewart and strongly supported by the Duchess of Atholl, effectively championed former SS men from the Ukraine, Poland and the Baltic States. Some of those transferred to Scotland were placed in former POW camps, notably at Haddington, while others, recognised as assets by MI6, were sent to the secret language school at the former RAF base in Crail. In the name of freedom, former perpetrators of the Holocaust would be parachuted back into their homelands to reinforce large-scale insurgencies against Stalin. Thanks to the master spy Kim Philby, they fell invariably to their deaths. Those who remained in Britain survived longer. Vladislav Dering, a dapper Polish doctor who arrived in Scotland in 1946, and was immediately embraced by Stewart and the Duchess of Atholl, would two decades later be brought to justice for sadistic sterilisation experiments carried out on Jewish camp inmates. He vanished into obscurity. Only in 1992 did a Scottish Television programme expose the role of Anton Gecas, a former Lithuanian police battalion commander, in the mass murder of thousands of men, women and children. Gecas had settled near Edinburgh in the late forties as a mining engineer, and, as an MI6 informant, provided intelligence for Baltic operations. The British state continually obstructed Soviet attempts to extradite him.[14]

But if fascism was to be resurrected in Britain after 1945, urban England, and especially the East End of London, remained the most promising terrain. A focus for the Mosleyite UM's outdoor activities was Ridley ('Yidley') Road in Dalston, where weekly speeches by Jeffrey Hamm attempted to foment the popular anti-Semitism generated by the situation in Palestine. These meetings became the target for violence by the Jewish 43 Group, as in March 1949, when 5,000 people gathered to oppose 150 UM members at Ridley Road. The main haunts of the UM were East End pubs: the Railway Arms in Dalston, the Jolly Butcher in Brick Row, and the Blade Bone in Bethnal Green. There was also a network of nearly 50 book clubs, organised by Raven Thomson, which, like the Chelsea Modern Thought Club and Discussion Group, were mainly concentrated in the London area. However, such activities met with little popular success. At the May 1949 London Municipal Elections, the UM came bottom of the poll in all eight boroughs: 16 candidates got 1,993 votes out of 4,097,841. Their highest scores were for candidates standing in the proximity of Jewish settlements. In Shoreditch, the Movement's three candidates, including Thomson, got 14% of the vote. But this was a far cry from the thirties, and, in the years that followed, the out-migration of socially mobile Jews from these areas put paid to this particular Fascist hunting-ground, at least until the arrival of new 'aliens'.

It was also difficult to unite a fractious and fissiparous neo-fascist diaspora. In March 1949, Mosley despatched Thomson to Madrid. The trip appears to have been a disaster, with Thomson first alienating his Falangist hosts, then renewing festering feuds with expatriate Fascists like 'Juan' MacNab. In February 1951, Mosley made a farewell speech at Kensington Town Hall, denouncing Britain as an 'island prison'. He then exiled himself to his beloved Ireland for three years. Martin Walker writes: 'Once again, as in the 1930s, his rationalization for failure was that the expected slump had failed to come, that the economic and political crisis which he need to succeed had unaccountably failed to happen.'[15]

But not all hope had evaporated. In March 1953, *Union* drew inspiration from the Stuart dynasty's move from Holyrood to St James in 1603, which had not led to a loss in national 'stature':

Let us have the courage of the Stuarts, so that it shall not 'come with a lass and go with a lass'. Let us make that bold leap into an unknown future – into a Union not only of the Kingdoms but of the peoples of Europe – which the spirit of our times demands of us. What if we do take the risk that it may lead to our next king Charles dying on the scaffold, or fleeing from another bloody Culloden. It is our duty to live dangerously – if, indeed, we would live at all. THE BRITISH EMPIRE IS DEAD: LONG LIVE THE EUROPEAN EMPIRE.[16]

In January 1955, *Union* reported that donations from Scotland to the support fund were up by 20%.[17]

But despite the Leader's return from exile, Mosley and his follow-ers seem to have retreated to mainly intellectual activity, most no-tably in the form of *The European*, an 'analytical review' and 'journal of opposition'. Edited by Diana Mosley, this eclectic and elegantly reactionary publication managed to combine essays on Céline and Proust with ones on apartheid and the churches. It was also on the lookout for new trends in contemporary literature. For example, in April 1954, *The European* wrote: 'since 1950 it has been faintly dis-cernible that the younger poets, scared by the frigidities which so frequently marked the new romanticism, have been casting about for a subtler and more profound orientation to what we might call "oth-erness"'.[18] As illustrations of this trend, the review included 'Cosmos' by Denis Goacher, and future Makar Edwin Morgan's translation of 'The Seafarer' from the Anglo-Saxon. Morgan seemed to capture the travails of the 'Thought-Deed Man':

> This verse is my voice, it is no fable,
> I tell of my travelling, how in hardship
> I have often suffered laborious days,
> Endured in my breast the bitterest cares,
> Explored on shipboard sorrow's abodes,
> The welter and terror of the waves.[19]

There were, of course, more explicitly political matters. In that same issue, Mosley addressed 'The African Problem and England's Future', arguing for 'Euro-Africa'. In July 1954, Geoffrey Vernon denounced 'The Ulster Police State', while other articles decried a 'Putrid wave of Soviet sycophancy' and mourned 'The Death of Dresden'.

Failing health did not prevent Raven Thomson from remaining Mosley's most loyal lieutenant. In 'Russia and the West', published in the issue of February 1955, Thomson called for a European vision of the future that was 'neither Marx nor Spengler':

> Let Europe have confidence in her own destiny, and look neither to America nor to Russia for her future deliverance from internecine strife. Once united, she can look forward to a resumption of her rightful place in the forefront of world affairs, pointing the way to the more backward cultural systems with whom she can proudly accept co-existence as *primus inter pares*.[20]

Despite his attachment to the European idea, and his long-term residence in the East End, Thomson also remained attached to his Scottish roots, and therefore became involved in a lively discussion on the issue of Scottish identity. In May 1955, Scottish schoolteacher Alastair Harper contributed a provocative essay, 'The Scot, Race and Nation'. Harper began:

> To seek to investigate the ethnic constitution of a nation is to court the charge of racism, and thus to disconnect oneself from that current of sympathy which today animates the thinking mass of the West. Nevertheless there is a need for a proper appreciation of the racial components of the Scottish nation, so that the extreme nationalism which dominates the minds of many Scots may be transmitted into the ampler enthusiasm for European kinship.[21]

The Scots were a nation, he argued, 'but although the nation has a markedly singular ethnic basis in the Nordic race it is by no means pure as a breeding group, and embodies two distinct racial types, Nordic and Mediterranean'.[22] In fact it was 'the cosmopolitan influence of this century' which prevented Scotland from 'coming to a high level of racial homogeneity'. Harper was not implacably hostile to all mixing. He did not oppose the large Italian presence: 'As a breeding group they are reserved, and constitute a worthy addition to the community.'[23] He also welcomed East European soldiers and displaced persons, which reinforced the 'Alpine' component.

The community of Scottish Jews, 'a twentieth century innovation', was 'of no consequence genetically, since that people is given on principle to inbreeding'.[24] And happily in Scotland 'we are not yet in a position to see the dangers inherent in the introduction of negroes, which can be observed in the cities of Liverpool and London'. Thus the 'ethnic picture' of Scotland revealed 'an eastern and northern preponderance of Nordic types, and a Western disposition which almost amounts to a majority of Mediterranean types'.[25] Nevertheless, at the end of his racial analysis, Harper raised the alarm:

> In common with the other countries of Western Europe, the population of Scotland is doing no more than maintain itself. However glibly we may justify this as the mark of a high civilisation, we cannot fail to see the danger to the national existence in this curbing of the population, and lament that those most blameworthy belong to the higher social and intellectual classes. Bearing in mind the entropic tendency of our Western society, that political faith should be judged good which urges on the Scots, amongst whatever political considerations, the socially hygienic virtue of a high birth rate, especially in social classes I, II and III [the higher end of the UK Census's five-class structure], and the vigorous preservation of the folk structure from further racially alien adulteration.[26]

In the following issue of *The European*, Raven Thomson published a robust riposte which merits being quoted at length:

> In my opinion this sort of investigation of the racial origin of the Scot, or of any other European people, is somewhat beside the point. Sir Oswald Mosley once pointed out that it is not, after all, of paramount importance from which herd of primeval buffalo our present domestic cattle are descended – provided they supply us with a sufficient yield of milk. What matters is not the racial origins of a people, but its present capacity to advance the culture of the world, and in this respect the Scots have done extremely well owing to their great respect for education, the excellent quality of which in Scotland gives the emigrant Scot a quite unfair advantage over his southern prototype.
>
> What Mr Harper seems to have ignored is the division of the peoples north of the Tweed by the Highland Line into Celts and

Lowlanders, which is generally misunderstood by Southerners, who have come to regard the Scots as a homogeneous people, all [...] descended from one clan or another. Actually, as every Scots schoolboy knows, Scotland was two hundred years ago divided into a peace-loving, dour but loveable people in the Lowlands, continually menaced by outlandishly dressed savages in kilts, who from time to time raided their lands, stealing their cattle and looting their cities.

It is a tribute to the propaganda of Sir Walter Scott that he was able at the end of the eighteenth century to persuade the pot-bellied Regent to adopt the kilt and other Highland regalia in a masquerade to Edinburgh Castle, and Holyrood Palace, after which the leading Lowland families came to cherish their Highland ancestry – most of which remains completely mythical. If this has had the result of making the Scots regard themselves as a united people with strong characteristics of their own, then so much to the good. After all, it is the business of propagandists to present the facts of the past in such a light that they will advance the prestige of the people of the future, and in this sense Sir Walter Scott was perfectly successful.

It remains dubious, however, whether it is the business of *The European* to further such propaganda at the present time, when it is the aim of the journal to emphasise the similarity of the European peoples rather than their differences, and in this respect it would be better for the Lowland Scot to remember that he belongs to the most Germanic of all the races in these islands, as his dialect of broad Scots, especially if he comes from Inverness-shire, can speak a very much clearer and better English than the English themselves.

The fact remains that the Scots are the best educated people of these islands, and, on account of their frugal tradition, are capable of advancing themselves to places of power and responsibility in the actions of the UK. They are the most conceited of all the British, with their slogan of 'Wha's like us', but they can point to much justification for this conceit in contemporary achievement. I am not particularly interested in their racial origin, which is as diverse as that of most of the European peoples. What matters is whether they will continue to exercise leadership in British affairs as for many generations in the past.[27]

Such fundamentally anti-racist arguments – at least as far as European peoples were concerned – would not dissuade Alastair Harper from co-founding, in 1958, the Northern League, which combined pan-Nordicism, anti-Semitism and determinist racism, and adopting as its emblem the swastika-like 'tryfoss' rune.

Thomson therefore emphasised a policy of 'Scotland in Europe'. On 25 July 1955, Mosley wrote to him asking to give at the UM's annual conference 'the following definition of European society':

> European society is the development by a fully united Europe of European resources in our own continent, in white Africa, and in South America, for the benefit of all the people of Europe, and of these other European lands, by every energy and incentive that the active leadership of European government can give to private enterprise, workers' ownership, or any other method of progress which science and a dynamic system of government finds most effective for the enrichment of all our people and the lifting of European civilisation to ever higher forms of life.[28]

In his last article for *The European*, published in October 1955, Thomson continued his theoretical reflections, this time on 'Automation and Egalitarianism'. Rejecting 'the nemesis of levelling down', Thomson concluded: 'it is by the joint development of Europe and Africa with European technical skill and African unskilled labour that the solution can be found'.[29]

Thomson was also preparing a 'world-history' manuscript, theorising *homo socialis*. Civilisation, he claimed, was diseased: *homo socialis* would direct society and replace failing instinctive service with the perpetuating force of rational socialism. In fact, the Blackshirt thinker was riddled with cancer. On 5 November, *Union* announced on its front page the death of Raven Thomson, his name in Gothic script. Mosley's homage to his friend and comrade showed the very secondary place of Scotland in the Leader's geography: 'Raven Thomson had a great heart and a fine head. He led a dedicated life. It is one of the tragedies of our time that he did not live until his outstanding abilities could serve one of the great positions of England and of Europe which are occupied by lesser men.' In the words of Thomson's biographer, Peter Pugh, 'if Mosley was the Don Quixote of British politics, tilting at windmills in the belief they were giants, then

Raven Thomson was his Sancho Panza'.[30] Thomson did not return to his native land. A memorial service was held on 8 November at St Columba's Church, Shoreditch. Following cremation his ashes were scattered at a tree in a London park. The tree would be blown down in the great gale of 1988.

Despite the efforts of the indefatigable Thomson and others, the UM seemed to lack a certain vitality. On 18 July 1955, Desmond Stewart wrote to Mosley from his holiday home in Elie, Fife: 'I think the *European* has exceeded all our dreams in its presentation, its content, its interest, its reliability, its ability to show over a number of passing months a *Weltanschauung* which had no expression before we started. So much so good. What is disappointing is the small circulation.' There was, continued Stewart, 'an atmosphere of running down, decay, dust, inefficiency at the office . . . I just cannot believe that our magazine would not interest three times more people than take it at the moment. It needs someone Scottish perhaps! Who won't allow a profession of sympathy to pass, without getting a cheque there and here'.[31]

The European may have lacked the dynamism of a canny Scot, but the Scottish national question was often addressed in its pages, either to be denigrated or integrated into the new Mosleyite European line. In September 1955, a review of John MacCormick's *The Flag in the Wind* concluded:

> When Europe is crying out for a surrender of the old national sovereignties, in the cause of European Union, is Scottish nationalism doomed? Larger units of government appear to be indicated, not smaller; less patriotism, not more. But under the syndicates so often discussed in *The European* the control of Scottish industry would pass from nationalised boards or absentee shareholders in London into the hands of local Scottish workers; the myth of 'poor Scotland', for which thousands must emigrate, would be killed. If, at the same time, every encouragement were given to the revival of the Gaelic language and other manifestations of Scottish culture, Mr MacCormick's objections would be attained – although not in quite the form his book advocates.[32]

In January 1956, Desmond Stewart reviewed James Kinsley's *Scottish Poetry. A Critical Survey.* His comments were typically acerbic:

As convincing an argument against Scottish nationalism as any that has appeared recently. Why? Because every Scot, who is conscious of being a Scot, has somewhere in the lumber of his brain, a complex of attitudes to the English. That is his nationalism: not as enthusiasm for his own peninsula, for his own people, (who are so divided anyway), or his own history (which like Kurdish history is brave and exciting, but leads nowhere); but an attitude to the richer, more populous southern half of the island, which in moments of frustration, or periods of bad weather, he accuses of exploiting Scotland.[33]

How 'provincial and unimportant in the world of poetry' Scotland was, compared with the southern half of Britain. 'It shows the Scottish poet, if no one else, what he has to gain from unity in English, and not in Gaelic, a defeated, or in Lallans, a defeating tongue.'[34] After declaring that 'Sir Walter Scott's wisest decision was to write in prose', Stewart concluded:

Today, when England has lost faith in itself, it is natural for young Scotsmen to search in themselves for their own roots: and seeing the built-up horror of the south, to ask whether their own beautiful land, or their own tortured land, whichever way they see it, cannot inspire them, as Ireland inspired Yeats. But it is probably a false way of looking at the question. Both Scotland and England are decadent; and it is more profitable for the intelligent of both nations to track down, as zealously as King Oedipus, the crime, whether conscious or unconscious, which has turned the two kingdoms into their dreary twentieth-century selves – worse than any plague the dreariness of the TV masts – and to try and atone for that crime. The two things that to one Scot seem to blame, far more than English exploitation of Scotland or Scottish infiltration of England: the rule of money, and the isolation of Europe. Re-establish human values, and rejoin Europe. Then, and perhaps only then, will the Poet's tongue be freed, whatever his dialect.[35]

Nevertheless, some signs of vitality had been discerned at the Edinburgh Festival. In November 1957, Edward Bourke-Haliburton hailed the emergence of 'The Theatre of the Resistance':

Of thirteen plays seen, seven were political in character and six dealt with nationalist themes. *The Rising of the Moon*, *The Flowers of*

Edinburgh and *The Queen and the Welshman* typified the reactions of the three submerged Celtic nations to the Saxon overlords; three others commented upon revolutionary situations in Portugal, Hungary and France.[36]

This was, wrote Bourke-Haliburton, 'a most significant development. For twenty years now the policy of management has tended largely to try and keep people off thinking realistically when they go to the theatre'.[37] Such resistance was echoed in the rest of that issue: three poems by Nietzsche, articles on Henry Williamson and the 'risks of Russian science gaining decisive advantage', and a call for an amnesty for Ezra Pound, enemy of 'usurocracy'. Yet the 'resistance' did not seem to make much headway farther north. In June 1958, *The European* analysed the voting strength of the Union Movement at the recent local elections: 11% in East London, with a high of 33% in Shoreditch; 2.4% in Manchester; but nothing north of the Cheviots.

In spite of the patent failure of the Mosleyite message, Bourke-Haliburton preferred to contemplate 'the death mask of constitutionalist nationalism' in Scotland in an article published in September 1958.

> The Scottish political outlook is heavily overcast. Behind those clouds of phlegm and unco-operative thought, the rumblings and groanings of a people can be heard building up to what may be a big explosion. There is less open activity now amongst nationalists than in any period within living memory. Every tactic of pacific constitutionalism and extra-constitutionalism seems to have been tried.[38]

The SNP had scored a record low poll at local elections, with 33 candidates put forward in Glasgow and Edinburgh aggregating only 8% of the total poll; in the country, the party gained only two seats. 'A National movement', declared Bourke-Hamilton, 'has never flourished in a period of political decline':

> The Conservative and Labour Parties retain their monolithic control of electoral business because (and not otherwise) they are primarily British parties. They get the votes because people are aware that no matter how indifferently they may function and how eminently

unsatisfactory their leadership and standards of statesmanship, they operate at the source of power, which is London and not Edinburgh.[39]

Nationalist meetings were 'usually better attended than those of the other parties', and their questions 'more lively and intelligent'; but 'those who come to listen and concur, seldom vote'.[40] This pessimistic view of the prospects of Scottish nationalism was apparently confirmed by the unsuccessful protests of nationalists against the construction of a rocket range on South Uist. *The Tinkers of the World*, a 'powerful and serious play' by Ian Hamilton, had predicted how, in Hamish Henderson's would-be 'folk-lore reservation', 'the support of the islanders would melt under the "carrot" and "stick" technique of the Ministry'. For Bourke-Haliburton, the play was 'entirely prophetic, it was regarded as an utterly pessimistic assessment of the Scottish character, and many people objected to it and stayed away when it was produced by the Gateway Theatre in Edinburgh last year ... "The Scots," wrote Mr Hamilton, "are not dying people; they are dead". For one significant section of political nationalism, South Uist was the funeral service'.[41]

Nevertheless, if the SNP did indeed find itself in the doldrums at the beginning of the sixties, a neo-fascist alternative fared far worse. Scotland's contribution to the reorganisation of the fascist movement in Britain was extremely marginal. But one, more 'mainstream', contribution came in the shape of Ray Bamford, founder of the Racial Preservation Society. Bamford was a wealthy writer of tracts on 'the race soul', which appeared in *Combat*, the *Northlander* and even the German Nationalist-Nordic publication *Nordische Zeitung*. Bamford was also chaplain to the BNP's National Youth Movement, and owner of an Edinburgh bookshop and publishing company which specialised in what its catalogue described as 'good conservative literature', including the works of the South African propagandist Ivor Benson. Bamford also formed the Scottish Rhodesia Society in 1966. According to Martin Walker, Bamford's importance 'lay not only in this width of involvement and contacts, but also in his political respectability. He was close to Scottish Conservatives and to that significant sector of the Conservative Party which supported the Rhodesian rebel government, while being revered by the Nationalist groups as a racialist intellectual'.[42]

Another influential figure on the far right was former St Andrews

University convenor of debates, George K. Young. After university, Young had gone on to make a brilliant career in merchant banking and British intelligence, notably masterminding the overthrow of Iran's elected leader, Mohammad Mossadegh, in 1953. Young's radical right-wing sympathies had not waned. In fact, in the course of the sixties, he was instrumental in building up the Monday Club. He wrote the club's pamphlet advocating repatriation of immigrants to Britain, *Who Goes Home?*, published in 1969, and was chairman of its Action Fund. He cultivated links between the club and the MSI, heir to Mussolini's Blackshirts, while defending the Shah of Iran and his SAVAK secret police, and campaigning to lift sanctions against Rhodesia. Thanks to Young's efforts, membership had grown to 1,500 by April 1969, and the club's activities, with protest meetings on defence cuts and 'The grip of the Left on the BBC' attracting national publicity. It reached a peak of 2,000 members in October 1972. In the meantime, it had attracted the support of the burgeoning National Front, notably in 1970 at the club's May Day rally in Trafalgar Square. But Young and his club's focus was very much south of the Cheviots, as illustrated by their backing of a crude anti-immigration film, *England, whose England?*

To Be a Nation Again

Back in Scotland, the most virulent ultra-nationalism was of the Caledonian kind. In 1962, at the Edinburgh Writers' Festival, Hugh MacDiarmid had not hesitated to brand the Scottish situationist Alexander Trocchi as 'cosmopolitan scum'. Despite having rejoined the Communist Party in 1957, MacDiarmid remained attached both to Ezra Pound, whom he would finally have the pleasure of meeting in 1970, and to the extreme separatist cause.

In February 1968, Colin Bell reported for the *Daily Telegraph Magazine* on 'The skeleton in Scotland's cupboard'.[43] This rather tongue-in-cheek article centred on an 'attack' on Stirling Castle, in the royal burgh that the SNP had recently taken in local elections. Activists pulled down the Union Jack and ran up the Saltire. Bell, himself an SNP supporter, delved into the undergrowth of extreme Scottish nationalism, notably the 1320 Club. The list of members was a secret, but it included Oliver Brown, and had as chairman of its 'Armed Forces Committee' one Major F.A.C. Boothby, retired regular soldier. A 'Scottish Liberation Army', successor to Clann Albain and the Scottish Defence Force, was rumoured to exist. In the absence of concrete military action against the English oppressor, publications such as *Sgian Dubh* and *Catalyst for the Scottish View-point* would denounce the Westminster Parliament as 'Bletherin' Ha'' and dub the Secretary of State for Scotland the 'Gauleiter'. These nationalists demanded the immediate convocation of the 'Thrie Estaits' (as the pre-1707 Scots parliament was properly known), then 'strong, firm Government – say six months' government by 221 experts, not politicians but professional men who know about trade, forestry, health and so on'. They did not hide from Bell their attachment to achieving independence by violent means. MacDiarmid declared: 'I don't know any country that's got its freedom without bloodshed. I'm not advocating it – I think it may be imposed on us by the English. I look towards it with equanimity, remembering the physical nature of our country. The military leadership exists already – large numbers of Scots are ex-soldiers.' For Major Boothby, 'there should be at least a skeleton organisation, which could be activated if the Establishment shows signs of using other than political means'. And Wendy Wood, 76-year-old head of the Scottish Patriots, told the journalist: 'We'll only get independence if there's a threat behind it. The SNP is after votes, it can't threaten – that's why there are others. In the background, there's a skeleton force, you see.'

This fringe was joined by another 'usual suspect', Ronald Mac-Donald Douglas, who would be honorary president of the 1320 Club and editor of its review, *Catalyst*. Douglas had returned to Scotland in 1967, this time settling near Hawick, in the hope that at last his nation would not disappoint. In his editorial of spring 1972, he wrote:

> It's time we began openly to show our contempt. Call them quislings, and they merely laugh; call them Anglo-Scots, and they accept the description as a compliment. Call them traitors – which is, of course, what they are – and with utter lack of understanding they turn to call us that, simply because we insist on being Scottish.[44]

Douglas saw traitors in a Scottish TUC – which, ironically, was outspokenly in favour of devolution. 'In my own lifetime I have watched, with aching heart, the almost total destruction of my country by her own people; and mainly by the working classes – once the pride and the strength of the nation.'[45] Douglas had not lost his paranoid tendencies: elsewhere in the same issue, he denounced informers and agents provocateurs, claiming to be 'the recipient of conspiratorial telephone calls and mysterious letters purporting to come from "activists"'.[46]

Douglas resigned of his 'own free will' as editor of *Catalyst* in the summer of 1972 to devote himself to writing a book on *The Hidden Scotland*. But he continued to contribute to the journal, in particular to put the record straight about his activities before and during the war. He recalled his abortive gun-running attempts from Switzerland, his visit to the Braunhaus in Munich, his meeting with Rudolf Hess and other Nazi leaders, and his flight from the British 'Secret Police'. But he tried to downplay the seriousness of such activities: 'I had (and still have) a fantastic sense of the ludicrous ... All successful revolutionaries have been men lacking in a sense of humour and incapable of self-analysis'.[47] Thus he remembered, as 'Chief' of the Scottish Defence Force, saluting from a drystane dyke the column of its Glasgow Brigade. 'Something atavistic had me in thrall,' wrote Douglas, but 'the elation faded as I began to inwardly laugh at myself: an embryo little Hitler!'[48]

Such whimsy about his proto-fascist past notwithstanding, Douglas gave an extremely selective view of his old Breton comrade, Olier Mordrel. In spring 1973, he reviewed for *Catalyst* Mordrel's autobiography, *Breiz Atao*, saluting 'a Breton Hero'. It was 'the most heart-rending thing I have read for years'. He recalled Mordrel's opposition to war against Nazi Germany. 'In 1939, with a few comrades he wrote, signed and issued a manifesto declaring that Brittany should remain neutral during the war. (Very few people know that an attempt at something similar was made in Scotland at the same time. It was sabotaged by the SNP).' At the same time, Douglas strove to prevent Mordrel being tarred with the Nazi collaborationist brush:

> The Breton movement was outlawed by the German occupying forces as well as the Vichy French, and Mordrel was deported to Germany ... In 1944 Mordrel escaped to Italy, was taken prisoner by the English, and handed over to the French. He dislikes the English as much

as I do: we both have cause. Again he was condemned to death, but this time in absentia, for in 1946 he successfully evaded English, Americans, and French, and reached the safety of Argentine.[49]

Thus Douglas and Mordrel passed over past sympathy and, in the case of the Breton Nationalists, active support for the Third Reich. It is true that Mordrel had spent months under house arrest in Nazi Germany. But he had been allowed to return to Rennes in September 1941 and revive the Breton Nationalist paper *Stur*. During the years of occupation, he was in frequent contact with the notoriously anti-Semitic writer Louis-Ferdinand Céline and contributed to the Nazi mouthpiece Radio Paris. In August 1944, Mordrel fled to Germany with the remnants of the French collaborators, including Céline. He was captured and interrogated by the Allies, but the information he offered on the SD, for which he had been an agent throughout the war, allowed him to leave for South America, then Spain. Nonetheless, these facts do not appear in Douglas's review. Instead, both Celtic nationalists were united in martyrdom: 'For twenty-two years, he lived, studied, and practised, suffering the spirit-aching life that only another who has known enforced exile can comprehend'.[50]

The 1320 Club would eventually merge with Siol Nan Gaidheal (SNG), whose virulent 'cultural' nationalism became a headache for an SNP enjoying its first real electoral success. The SNG's propaganda rejected foreign, and especially English, influence. One leaflet exhorted its readers to 'Buy Scots Goods and keep a Scots Worker Working': 'Jean MacGregor's scotch broth, lentils, vegetables and tomato are cheaper than Heinz'. Another kept alive the 'anti-English Fascist' line: 'Are you pro-Scottish or anti-Scottish (like in Quisling)?'. Trips down to Wembley for the annual Scotland–England clash were an opportunity for propaganda and a right good rammie:

SWEET FA WELCOME
They stole everything they could carry away from India, half of Africa, New Zealand, Australia, Jamaica, Barbados, etc,etc,etc.
   Most of what you see in London is a result of theft and reset on a global scale.
   So' take their grass. They owe it to us.
   [...]

A warning: the English NF party and the so-called British Movement have asked their members to 'kick the shit out of the Scotch bastards'. So watch out. Look after one another when you're here. Remember, united we stand . . .

The SNG supported the aims and policies of the SNP, 'believing that the Scottish National Community has never ceased to exist, despite the foreign culture and ideologies forced upon it during centuries of Anglicisation'.

The SNG attracted a small number of young Nationalists frustrated by the failure of the devolution referendum and the Tory victory of 1979. Their violent ethnic Nationalism was illustrated by their behaviour at annual Bannockburn and William Wallace rallies in 1980 and 1981. United against the common enemy 'Fascist England', they marched with paramilitary uniforms, banners and broadswords. An effigy of Margaret Thatcher was executed and cut into four parts despatched to 'enemies of Scotland', while the Union Jack was placed at the foot of the Wallace monument and walked over. SNG became more boisterous and aggressive as drink took its toll. In the Golden Lion Hotel, Stirling, members sprayed themselves with 'English Bullshit Repellent' and stuck their swords and dirks into tables. Then there was the singing, at a ceilidh, of the Nazi song 'Motherland, oh Motherland'. This could only confirm the suspicions of SNP leader Gordon Wilson, who had shouted at these would-be paramilitaries that they were 'nothing but a bunch of Fascists'. In September 1980, the SNP launched an enquiry, with the ever-vigilant Colin Bell as vice-chairman.

There were some, however, who came to the SNG's defence. On 26 September 1980, William MacRae, four times SNP candidate for Ross-shire, told the *West Highland Free Press*:

SNG are quite frank in admitting they do like to be smart in their turn-out, and they do like to keep in step when they're on a march. But there are far, far too many good people in the organisation to talk of proscription from the SNP. Far from drumming them out of the Party, the SNP should be using those young people as their spearhead.[51]

In the pages of *The Scotsman*, SNG leader Callum Millar defended his organisation. In his living room, reporter Angus MacLeod found a broadsword and a sheathed dirk. 'My mentor is William Wallace,' declared Millar. The SNG was 'neither left nor right'. His 250 to 300 members expressed simply 'a desire to have the SNP develop a greater cultural awareness'. 'You have never seen a Fascist in Highland dress', he concluded, rather disingenuously given the adventures of Ronald MacDonald Douglas.[52] The SNG membership would be expelled from the SNP, but its ethnic nationalism continues to haunt.

The Shock of the Neo

The heirs of pre-war fascism found it particularly difficult to penetrate north of the Border. At the general election of October 1974, the National Front's one Scottish candidate, M.A.B. Brooks, received at Govan the party's lowest national result, a paltry 86 votes (0.5%), miles behind the SNP (41%) and the Labour victor (49.5%). Such a disastrous result contrasted with the NF's national high of 9.4%, in the old stamping grounds of Hackney South and Shoreditch, and a still far from negligible national average of 3.14%. If the NF was extending its electoral influence beyond Greater London to areas of high Asian immigration such as Leicester, West Bromwich, Blackburn and Bradford, its message was not being heard farther north.

Scotland therefore took time to attract the attention of anti-racist monthly *Searchlight*. In 1977, it reported on a proposed NF march opposed by Glasgow Trades Council. Margo MacDonald, SNP senior vice-chairman, declared: 'For the first time in my life I feel racialist and that is towards [NF leader John] Tyndall and his crew. He and his like are just not welcome in Scotland.'[53] In 1978, *Searchlight* noted that Scotland 'has not until now been a very promising recruiting ground for the NF'. However, 'their recent attempts to gain publicity in that direction were quite successful when school pupils in Glasgow and Edinburgh were discovered with NF leaflets and stickers. At Portobello High School, teachers found six NF members led by a 13 year old boy who was openly brandishing his membership card'.[54] In October 1979, the Nazis surfaced again in Scotland:

A sleepy town in South West Scotland is the last place you'd expect to find the NF crawling out of the woodwork. But all of a sudden, Girvan, in South Ayrshire, was swamped with Nazi posters, stickers and leaflets. And what was even more surprising, out of nothing, there appeared about 15 active Fronters, ready and willing to peddle their racist poison. The saddest feature of this is many teenagers are being influenced by only a handful of adults. The Front has been hard at work and two-thirds of the town's housing estates had been leafleted. Their posters didn't stay long as council workers were soon to remove them.

An anti-Fascist meeting attracted 100, but was heckled by 30 'Front-ers'. The local Nazis were 'aided and abetted by a contingent from Glasgow and their Führer Skinner'. A young girl told *Searchlight* that 'the Labour and Tory parties had failed her generation'. The maga-zine concluded: 'there is no great amount of immigration in Ayrshire but what does interest the Front is the vast amount of unemployed and disillusioned youngsters'.[55]

Nevertheless, there was no sign of electoral take-off. At the gen-eral election of 1979 the wife of 'Führer Skinner' had obtained only 104 votes (0.2%) at Glasgow Pollok. In the Glasgow by-election the following year, an Independent NF candidate had done little better, with 148 votes (1.8%). But there was no room for complacency. In September 1981, the Scottish Asian Action Committee claimed that racist attacks were increasing in Scotland. In February 1982, the trial of six Asian men charged after a white mob attacked them on the Beech estate the previous August opened in Dundee. In July 1983, *Searchlight* reported that Fascist slogans had been daubed on walls following a break-in at Edinburgh University. A Fascist newsletter, headed 'Blue Shirt' and claiming to be the voice of Edinburgh Uni-versity Fascists, had been circulated.[56] But the elections of that year were disastrous for the National Front, with an average vote of 0.8% per candidate. If the best result was in Newham North, the worst was, predictably, in Glasgow Shettleston.

The political culture of Scotland in the eighties seemed even more inimical to the Fascists than in the thirties. At the beginning of the decade, Nigel Fielding had interviewed David McCalden, leader of the NF's youth organisation. Fielding wrote:

On an HQ map of Britain NF strength clustered around London, Birmingham and the South Coast. McCalden commented that Scotland and Wales were virtually blank. An observer considered the NF weak because it 'has not yet learnt to play the sectarian game' and has done little to exploit the Protestant 'angle'. McCalden claimed the party was making progress on just this issue. The Scottish NF was gaining support in south-west Scotland, where there is strong support and ties with Ulster Loyalists. The biggest problem here was the SNP. 'We haven't made great inroads in Scotland, we've only run one candidate there, but it's not due to just one single factor, such as the oil. We do feel that the Scottish nationalists have hi-jacked nationalist feeling.' The SNP had drained off voters alienated from the traditional parties.[57]

The Scottish far right emerged intermittently in grotesque incidents. In March 1984, *Searchlight* reproduced a report by the communist *Morning Star* newspaper:

Dundee Trades Council has planned an anti-fascist campaign for 1984, following the abduction of a boy by fascists last year. The 14-year-old boy was taken to a fascist rally in Belgium by members of the National Socialist Action Party, against the wishes of his parents, on a forged passport. Local NSAP organiser Stephen Kerr told the boy's parents that he was taking the lad to an RAF training camp at Loch Lomond. Kerr, who had infiltrated the ROC [Royal Observer Corps], was wearing a full RAF uniform, and all correspondence relating to the non-existent training camp was on official RAF notepaper. The NSAP contingent, including 14 young people, didn't reach the fascist rally at Diksmuide on 3 July. One of the party was found to be carrying a firearm after a disturbance in an Ostend bar, and the entire party was deported. The boy's sister said that he admitted having sworn an oath of allegiance to Hitler at Kerr's home. He said he'd held *Mein Kampf* over his heart and swore the oath promising to get rid of Jews and black people.[58]

In late 1985, a group of Scottish Conservatives, including Nick Fairbairn MP, took part in a meeting at the South African consulate in Glasgow. They announced the formation of the Scottish-South African Union to support the white minority government there. Fairbairn criticised what he called 'that bogus concept of one man one vote'.[59] In March 1986, *Searchlight* protested at the decision by Glasgow University to name a professorship in Scottish Literature after the notorious Lieutenant-Colonel Robert Gayre. Gayre had distinguished himself by his interest in race theories, establishing *Mankind Quarterly*, and appointing as its honorary editor Professor Otto von Vershuer of Munster, former supervisor of none other than Auschwitz's 'angel of death', Dr Josef Mengele.

It was in the arts that Scots were most publicly associated with the toxic legacy of fascism. In October 1979, post-punk band The Skids brought out their second album, *Days in Europa*. The cover alluded clearly to Nazi propaganda, with its gothic lettering and image of a blonde maiden crowning an Aryan Olympian. The song lyrics, by frontman Richard Jobson, may have been obscure, but they conveyed an obsession with war, notably in 'Dulce et Decorum Est'; while 'A Day in Europa' exhibited both nostalgia for order – 'Yes, we had control' – and a defiant rallying call: 'Hail to Apollo, the cleanser of sins/Hail to Europa, she always wins'. This alarmed *Sounds* magazine. Tony Mitchell wrote:

> The . . . thing I find vaguely disquieting about this album, is the thinly disguised Nazi imagery which occurs in places. The sleeve is based on a typically Aryan poster from the infamous pre-war Munich games: the album title derives from a track called 'A Day in Europa' which just happened to be the name for the proposed ideal Aryan state. The whole artwork abounds with Teutonic script and there's a preponderance of distinctly marching music within. Harmless whimsy? Maybe, but these are dangerous times to flaunt such themes.

Bulldog, magazine of the Young National Front, took a radically different view:

> It is not surprising that liberal lefties such as Mitchell should find albums of this sort disturbing. After all, the album promotes White Pride and patriotism, along with an awareness of the power of Wall Street capitalism in tracks like 'Working for the Yankee Dollar'. Mitchell goes on to conclude: 'I only hope fascism isn't going to be the new "inspiration" '. As for Skids themselves, what has lead singer Richard Jobson got to say? 'Modern people in . . . Western Europe . . . should feel within themselves a pride . . . a distinct pride.'

The album was withdrawn from sale, re-mixed and re-released with a different cover. Jobson tried to reassure *Sounds*: 'we checked things out very carefully, even the gothic script we used on the cover which supposedly has Nazi connotations but is actually Jewish.' Yet Jobson and his band persisted by bringing out, with their third album *The Absolute Game*, a complementary disc entitled *Strength through Joy*. Jobson denied this was a reference to the Nazi leisure movement, *Kraft durch Freude*, claiming rather disingenuously that the title was lifted from film star Dirk Bogarde's autobiography. But the song content was again politically provocative: 'An Incident in Algiers', where 'Algeria has gone', and 'Filming in Africa', with its 'virgin plains', seemed to look nostalgically back to white supremacy. Jobson's controversial quotation of the Fascist legacy was not unique: similar accusations had been brought against Manchester's Warsaw/Joy Division/New Order. But the final Skids album, *Joy*, with tracks such as 'Blood and Soil' as well as 'Fields' and 'Iona', showed how the 'fascistic' was being used as part of a quest to create a distinctly 'Scottish' sound. In January 1982, 'Blood and Soil' was number three in *Bulldog*'s 'Rock against Communism' chart, behind The Clash's 'White Riot', but ahead of Skrewdriver's 'Anti-Social'.

Scottish music's appropriation by the far right was not limited to punk and post-punk. At the same time, *Bulldog* proudly reminded its readers that Rod Stewart had declared in 1970 that 'I think Enoch is the man. I'm all for him. This country is overcrowded. The immigrants should be sent home'.[60]

A more international controversy was created by the poet, artist and gardener Ian Hamilton Finlay. An avid reader of Thomas Carlyle's account of the French Revolution, Finlay had found in leaders of the Terror, Louis de Saint-Just and Maximilien de Robespierre, the fusion of word and action, the virtue and the piety which he found lacking in the establishment he rebelled against. These preoccupations, and the overriding theme of a struggle between Nature and Culture, were notably expressed in his neoclassical garden and temple at Little Sparta, near Biggar. His oeuvre incorporated references to the Jacobin Terror, but also to modern weaponry and, fatefully, the Third Reich.

In 1985, the French Ministry of Culture opened discussions with Finlay about a public commission for a monument celebrating the Bicentenary of the Declaration of the Rights of Man. The proposed garden would be on the site where it was proclaimed in August 1789, near the Chateau de Versailles. But this commission fell victim to a campaign against Finlay. The planned garden itself did not provoke controversy. Instead, the pretext for this campaign was one of the works in Finlay's exhibition *Inter Artes et Naturam* at the ARC gallery, Paris, in April–June 1987.

This work, 'Osso', consists of three blocks of rough-hewn marble. The first block is blank. The second is engraved with the lightning-flash insignia of the Waffen SS. On the third block, this insignia is framed by the letter 'o' to form the Italian word for bone. At the ARC, a text taken from the exhibition catalogue was placed near to 'Osso'. In this text, the critic Stephen Bann wrote: 'In the first place we have nature in its primary form – great fragments of marble which are also the "bones" of a future skeleton. Inscribing the fragment with the SS symbol as a streak of lightning used by the German Army, Finlay wished to point out the element of terror and disquiet which is inseparable from nature in its pure state, devoid of any redemption'.

Such a prophylactic interpretation did not stop Catherine Millet commenting in the highly influential *Art Press*: 'At the ARC, in Paris, an English [*sic*] artist, Ian Hamilton Finlay, inscribed the SS sign on some stones . . . God! How modern art is occasionally a farce . . . Just ask [Klaus] Barbie.' The following month, Louis Cane wrote in the same journal: 'On the face of all these sculptures is engraved the Nazi SS insignia . . . and nothing else.' This was an obviously inaccurate description; 'Osso' was in fact the only sculpture exhibited at the ARC which bore the SS insignia, and the description of 'Osso' bears little resemblance to reality. This did not prevent Cane from writing: 'What is at the ARC is fascist quite simply because of what is written on it.'

'Osso' was seized upon by the French press to show that Finlay was an artist of fascist, anti-Semitic leanings, which made him unfit to commemorate the Declaration of the Rights of Man. Other evidence invoked by Millet to 'prove' Finlay's guilt was the presence of sculptured grenades and miniature battleships in Little Sparta, which illustrated a 'strange taste for military things'. Millet also invoked Finlay's correspondence with Albert Speer about his 'secret garden' in Spandau prison. In a statement of symptomatic importance, Millet referred disapprovingly to Finlay's interest in the leaders of the Terror, Robespierre and Saint-Just, rather than 'the men of 1789'.

The campaign was further fuelled by extracts from private correspondence with Finlay, circulated by a disgruntled ex-collaborator, Jonathon Hirschfeld. In this correspondence, Finlay wrote bitterly to Hirschfeld: 'Let it be said, in frankness, that there is an animosity between us which is instinctive and perhaps racial.' He described his ex-collaborator as 'a swashbuckling, bullying Israeli'. In another fragment, he wrote, 'You are rightly regarded as a person fit for deportation.'

At a time when the trial of the 'Butcher of Lyons', Gestapo torturer Klaus Barbie, exhumed yet again France's painful experience of occupation and collaboration, and when the anti-Marxist intellectual consensus equated fascism and communism with the Jacobin Terror, Ian Hamilton Finlay could only be crushed. The Bicentenary commission was cancelled.

The Scot remembered bitterly the hostility of the French. In 1996, he told *Transcript*: 'In 1942, if you wanted to harm someone in Paris, you denounced them as being Jewish. In 1988, you denounced them as being anti-Jewish. But the mechanism of denunciation remained exactly the same.'[61] It is hard to be swayed by such an equation, which is frequently used by neo-fascists. It is even harder to be swayed by Finlay's unpublished remarks to Ralph Rumney, founder of the Situationist International, at Little Sparta in 1989. Comparing his 'persecution' with the public sympathy for the 'schoolboy blasphemy' of Salman Rushdie, Finlay declared: 'I wish they had got him, and a few more of the liberals.'[62]

Nevertheless, back in the world of street politics, the difficult social climate of the late eighties risked being propitious to the 'brown beast'. In September 1986, *Searchlight* raised the alarm about soaring racism: 'Once Bonnie Scotland is becoming anything but "bonnie" for many black, Asian and Jewish people living there. The country's good name as a haven of racial tolerance is now in danger of becoming irreparably damaged.' The racists could prosper in a land 'de-industrialised and bereft of hope': 'In Aberdeen, Dundee, the Lothians, Glasgow and the capital, Edinburgh, there has been a shocking increase in the level of racist attacks and racist behaviour of all types.'[63] There had been frequent attacks on Asian shops in Sighthill, Wester Hailes, Leith and Dundee, where a leaflet had been distributed by the 'Board of Anglo-Saxon Celtic deputies'. In 1984, there had been 7,000 recorded racist attacks; in 1985, the figure had risen to 20,000.

In January 1988, the magazine tracked 'the rise of extremism in Scotland'. Fascist activity had been at its highest in the south side of Glasgow, around Ibrox, 'focal point for racist thuggery'. In fact, the NF and BNP now considered Scotland a priority area, venturing into a sectarian jungle which had been the death of Blackshirts in the past:

> The BNP has put considerable emphasis on working on socially-deprived, unemployment-devastated council housing schemes like Drumchapel and has played on the deep Protestant–Catholic divisions to capture support from young Loyalists. Top Scottish Loyalist and NF nazi David Seawright is based in Glasgow and there is evidence that the city is a staging post for British Nazi thugs en route to Northern Ireland for paramilitary training, along with Swedes and Italians, as guests of Loyalist terrorist organisations.[64]

Sporting events were a focal point for racism and fascism. To religious bigotry was added hostility to black footballers, an almost complete novelty in the Scottish game. Celtic's Paul Elliott and Rangers' Mark Walters were subjected to 'monkey chants' which had nothing to do with the IRA or King Billy. At the same time, the BNP distributed a leaflet at the 1988 Commonwealth Games in Glasgow, supporting South Africa's apartheid regime against 'African Marxists'.

But the BNP and its ilk still came up against the stubborn obstacle of the Scottish national question. In late 1988, its annual St Andrew's Day gathering had to be held two weeks late due to anti-fascist opposition. What's more, when 150 BNP supporters finally gathered to hear their leader John Tyndall, the event turned into a shambles. The BNP was hoping to pick up support from disaffected Scottish nationalists who were worried by the SNP's leftwards drift. And yet, *Searchlight* reported:

> At the rally, a Scottish speaker from outside the BNP was paraded as if to confirm the Führer's prognosis. One Ian, from the hitherto unknown 'League of St Andrew' addressed the meeting but put distance between his supporters and Tyndall by denouncing the Union Jack waving of the NF and BNP.[65]

The BNP continued to hold summer camps in the Western Isles, and their activities were indicated by graffiti concentrated in Pollokshields and Govan, close to Rangers' Ibrox stadium and to Bellahouston Secondary School, which had the highest proportion of black pupils in Strathclyde. But at a rally in Edinburgh in April 1990, they were faced by 1,000 anti-fascists. In November the same year, four Glasgow BNP activists were sentenced to twelve months for a revenge attack on a left-wing meeting. However, the authorities did not find the Nazi daubers who had struck the Jewish cemetery in Dundee that October.

In April 1991, *Searchlight* could announce that 'Scotland shows the way' in the fight against racism and fascism. Proof was given by another catastrophic St Andrew's Day gathering of the BNP, held in Glasgow city centre on 8 December 1990:

> Tyndall's boys, it seems, were due to meet for a prize-giving ceremony in the rather less than auspicious surroundings of the Toby Jug public house, when a mass mobilisation of trade unionists, youth and students and representatives of a string of other organisations persuaded them that, for the sake of their personal safety, they had better abandon their proposed St Andrew's Day bash. Had they not done so, it is a safe bet that the only things getting bashed that afternoon would have been themselves.

Scotland, claimed *Searchlight*, 'has an honourable record of opposition to racism and fascism. In the 1930s Oswald Mosley's BUF was never able to build an organisational base. Attempts by Mosley to do so were met by mass mobilisation of ordinary people, united in their determination to keep the Fascists off the streets'. It was the resolve and determination of that previous generation of anti-fascist fighters that Scotland needed once again: 'Numerically the BNP in Scotland might not have much to shout about, but the street violence of much of its activists had a certain currency among sections of disaffected white working-class youth, particularly on some of the big housing schemes in Glasgow and Edinburgh'. The new heirs to Scotland's proud anti-fascist tradition were the Scotland and Racism Movement, with its charismatic leader, Tommy Sheridan.

The fight was not limited to the West: 'in Dundee, Gareth Norman, the local BNP boy, came badly unstuck when he and some of his boneheads tried to disrupt a rally in the city. The iron bar they were waving about finished up cracking him over the head and he retired injured'. Dundee was a 'hot spot' of racism: recently two BNP activists had been found guilty of threats to the local council leader and the head of the Jewish community.[66]

Racism reared its head in bizarre fashion in Captain Ramsay's former stronghold of Peebles. On 21 June 1991, figures dressed in Ku Klux Klan outfits dragged golliwogs through the streets in chains. The 200 demonstrators said they were protesting at schools' withdrawal of golliwog costumes from the annual Beltane festival. The comedian Craig Charles, in Peebles to record the parade for his series *Them and Us*, declared: 'At one stage I thought they were just being naïve and weren't really trying to be racist. But on the other hand there was a really sinister side to it.' He tried to explain to the local people that their behaviour was racially offensive 'but the black population of Peebles is zero and they were unrepentant'.[67]

Efforts at political organisation continued to be made, although with little success. In August 1991, a BNP march through Edinburgh was banned to protect public order. Their activities had indeed become clandestine. That year, a secret rally in Glasgow was infiltrated by Gary Duncan of *The Scotsman*. Seventy Nazis packed into the Crucible snooker club in Argyle Street for what the journalist described as 'something like a mini Nuremberg on the Clyde'. In a sale to raise funds, a flag of Eugène Terre'Blanche's South African white supremacist AWB party went for £12.

Scottish nationalism did not concern *Searchlight*. On the contrary, in November 1991, it was congratulated on putting the block on fascists: 'Despite the error that led to the SNP adopting a new symbol that strongly resembles the neo-nazi Odal rune, the party took good and strong decisions in support of fighting racism and nazism at its recent annual general meeting.' Nicola Sturgeon, the 21-year-old parliamentary candidate for Shettleston, had called for the SNP to be at the front of the struggle against racism in Scotland, while the party's vice-president, Dr Allan Macartney, stated that the SNP was 'neither anti-English nor anti-immigrant'.[68]

Indeed, *Searchlight*, otherwise vigilant to the point of paranoia, has never sought to illuminate the darker sides of Scottish nationalism. The xenophobic outbursts and proto-fascist paradings of the SNG were never noted. The intimidatory tactics of 'Settler Watch', a group dedicated to driving English immigrants out of Scotland, passed under the radar. Nor was there mention of the *Braveheart* phenomenon. This preposterous bio-pic of William Wallace, violently anti-English and homophobic, received the endorsement of the 'civic nationalists' led by Alex Salmond. The attacks that Mel Gibson's film incited against English 'settlers' in Scotland – a particular form of 'anti-white racism' – never made the pages of *Searchlight*.

'National feeling' in Scotland therefore seemed to belong to the SNP. At the elections of 1992, the BNP's sole candidate in Scotland, D.J. Bruce, came seventh and last in Edinburgh West, with 0.3%. Scotland was a persistent problem area, along with other traditionally weak areas for the extreme right: the North-east and South-west of England, and Northern Ireland. Scotland would be one of the places targeted by the BNP's gradual change of strategy in the mid to late nineties. According to Matthew Goodwin, the BNP sought to tell residents of Glasgow (as well as various places in the North of England) that Labour had 'abandoned ordinary working people' because it was 'more interested in gays, ethnics and their rich money-bags backers'.[69]

In early 1999, *Searchlight* reported that Tyndall had been given 'short shrift' by anti-fascists at yet another unsuccessful St Andrews Day celebration in Glasgow. He was also isolated in his own ranks, for that year saw the triumph within the BNP of a new generation, led by Nick Griffin. The BNP in Scotland would benefit modestly from Griffin's more 'respectable' electoral strategy, which sought to emulate the successes of the far right on the continent. Preying on fears of immigration, globalisation and 'Islamification', especially among the 'disenfranchised' white working class, this strategy bore considerable fruit in local elections, but most spectacularly, thanks to proportional representation, at the European elections, culminating in a million votes and the election of two MEPs in 2009. This success was, however, partially eclipsed by that of the more 'presentable' xenophobes of UKIP.

The path into the mainstream could be a rocky one. At the general election of 2001, Alastair Harper, who had sparred with Raven Thomson on the issue of 'Scotland, Nation and Race' in 1955, stood for UKIP in Dunfermline West, coming sixth and last with 1.5% of the vote. The former leader of the Northern League subsequently joined the BNP, becoming its assistant organiser in Fife, but withdrew as a candidate due to media and family pressures. Harper was not alone: Alistair McConnachie, UKIP's then-organiser in Scotland, was suspended from its National Executive Committee for a year in February 2001 after he questioned the extent of the Holocaust.

Results for the BNP in Scotland were well below those obtained in England and even Wales. But they were not negligible: from 0.4% in the European elections of 1999, the BNP rose to 1.7% in 2004 and 2.5% in 2009, this time well ahead of their sworn enemies on the far left. In October 2009, Jim Murphy, Scottish Secretary and MP for East Renfrewshire, pointed out that BNP support in Scotland had increased ten-fold in the decade, and that Scots were still too complacent about a party which had just won 29,000 votes: 'their support is now sufficiently large that only the largest stadiums in the country could now accommodate all Scottish BNP voters at once'.

The first-past-the-post system was much less favourable: in 2010, Scotland contributed only 13 of the BNP's 338 parliamentary candidates (to be compared with 34 in Greater London and 48 in Yorkshire and Humber). The overall vote for the BNP was a modest 0.4% (+ 0.3%), nevertheless trouncing that for the Scottish Social- ist Party, which had, in the wake of Tommy Sheridan's sordid fall from grace, collapsed by 1.7% to 0.1%. The BNP candidates were concentrated in Aberdeen and Glasgow, with the highest scores in Banff and Buchan (Alex Salmond's former seat) and Glasgow South West, where they both scored an honourable 2.6%. The limits of such popularity in relation to England and Wales are illustrated by the fact that, in Berwick-upon-Tweed, the BNP candidate obtained a healthier 3.2%.

These modest electoral successes corresponded to the distribution of BNP membership, as leaked in 2008. With less than 2%, BNP Scotland made a disproportionately small contribution. Of a mem- bership of less than 200, the largest concentrations were in Glasgow and Aberdeen. The latter seemed to carry on the spirit of the 'Stal- wart of the North', Chambers-Hunter (reinforced by a significant branch of the rival National Front). Edinburgh could muster only 22 members, but Dumfriesshire, with 27, remained solid. Progress was being made in Ross, Skye and Lochaber. However, no part of Scotland could match the membership levels of English constituen- cies such as Pendle, Burnley, Rutland and Epping Forest.

The very Englishness of the BNP can partly explain the relative failure of the party north of the border. The BNP's 2010 election manifesto insisted upon the creation of an English parliament, declaring: 'Englishness especially has been undermined in recent years, as has the entire concept of British identity, which embraces so much of the regional and national characteristics within these islands.'

That said, the BNP did attempt to articulate a vision for Scotland in its 2011 manifesto, 'The voice of ordinary people'. The manifesto denounced the 'great unmentionables': multicultural society and European Union. It lamented the 'decline of the once proud Scottish nation' and the baleful influence of asylum seekers and economic migrants. The BNP proposed to create a new 'society of stakeholders' and act to reverse Caledonia's Spenglerian decline. St Andrews Day would be promoted as a national holiday, while 'key crafts and traditions' would be nurtured by a 'Living Treasures' programme. The BNP would protect the Gaelic, Doric and Scots languages and preserve 'local indigenous culture', notably through the development of 'living participation spectacles, historic re-enactments and pageants'. In a dark warning to funding bodies, the manifesto declared: 'Scotland is part of the western European family of nations and public sponsorship of the Arts in general must reflect that family association.'[70]

But hopes of benefiting from the electoral system were dashed: the BNP obtained 0.78%, down 0.42% on the 2006 elections. The tide of nationalist feeling was overwhelmingly in favour of Alex Salmond's SNP. The BNP's one consolation was that, again, they had out-polled the far left, receiving more votes than Solidarity and Respect put together. Yet this failure, added to the feuding endemic on the far right, pushed the bulk of the BNP membership in Scotland, led by its organiser Gary Raikes, to defect to the anti-Griffinite Britain First! party.

Fascist Scotland therefore, and not for the first time, was in a sorry state. Caledonia has only a very marginal and passing reference in *2083. A European Declaration of Independence*, the sprawling manifesto and user's manual by Norwegian mass murderer Anders Breivik, alias 'Andrew Berwick'. Breivik praised those who had prevented Saracens reaching the Highlands, and contrasted the Scottish Enlightenment approvingly with the French one, which had undermined Europe's 'Judeo-Christian' roots. The BNP Scotland was listed as one of those organisations stoutly resisting multiculturalism, Islam and immigration. As a cover for the 'Justiciar Knight's' accumulation of fertiliser explosive, Breivik suggested the cultivation of porridge oats, among other crops. But a Justiciar Knight might have problems in the Highlands: 'most crofters have second jobs as a living generally cannot be made today.'[71]

Nae Nazis?

For days there had hung the threat of a 'battle royal' in the streets of Dundee. Tayside Police reassured the *Courier* that they did not anticipate trouble and were confident in the effectiveness of their 'community-based' style. But on Saturday, 1 September 2012, it was not the Flower and Food Festival at Camperdown Park, nor an organ recital in the Caird Hall, which taxed their resources. Instead, a three-deep police cordon outside the Nethergate shopping centre would separate the Scottish Defence League from Unite Against Fascism.

It was reported that two SDL busloads, from Edinburgh and Glasgow, would arrive to protest 'against Islamic extremism'. Would they match the 170-strong demonstration in Glasgow that previous February? In the meantime, anti-fascists gathered in Albert Square, where stalls promoted the wares of Unison, Unite, the Socialist Party of Scotland, the Socialist Workers Party and the Marxist-Leninist Komunist Party. 'No Passaran' [*sic*] appeared on placards, alongside 'Dundee says: Nae Nazis!'

The proud memory of Dundee volunteers for the Spanish Civil War was at the forefront of the protestors' minds. A brief march ended at the memorial to those International Brigaders who fell on 'Suicide Hill' at the Battle of Jarama in February 1937. A speaker promised he would never clean his boots as they carried the dirt of that sacred battlefield, before reminding them of the 'sixty years [*sic*] of Franco dictatorship' that had followed the defeat of the Republic. Back at the Square, ex-Communist Stuart Fairweather declared that his was the city of 'the peh, the pizza and the pakora'. 'This is Dundee. You are *visitors*', he sneered in the direction of those SDL interlopers who had been 'scraped into a corner'. For the anti-fascists, Dundonian diversity was not limited to fast food. According to a speaker from the Public and Commercial Services Union, a black member had been asked to give an account of growing up with racism in Dundee, but he couldn't, 'because he had no experience of it'. The woman at the

'United Against Fascism' stall told me: 'I love Dundee. We all love each other here.' Personal memories flooded back of two burglaries in Stobswell, the intervention of the Tayside 'anti-social squad', and young Asian women being insulted in Dura Street. She added: 'Or at least I do . . .'

There was little love lost down at the Nethergate. An ageing skinhead, already the worse for wear, had turned up early at the SDL pen with some cans and a bull terrier in a studded collar. 'You're insulting me,' he told the policewoman after being warned about foul language. 'That's my fucking native tongue!' 'No it's not', she replied, enigmatically. Meanwhile the bull terrier was more interested in my peh.

At last the Scottish Defence League arrived and the excitement ratcheted up. Escorted into the pen, about thirty people, mainly young and often female, denounced the 'Islamic threat'. A pretty blonde from the Edinburgh Division taunted her opponents with 'Islam's contribution to Scotland':

Terrorism
Child Grooming
Forced Marriage
Honour Violence.

Two Dundonian girls held a banner saying no to a '£1 million megamosque' in their city. They were joined by the Ayrshire and Dumfries Divisions and Borders and West Coast 'Infidels'.

Drowned by the cacophony, a young man in a hoody, raybans and combat trousers ranted inaudibly into his megaphone. He was followed by another blonde, this time from Blackburn. At that moment, the young Muslim men (there were no women) who monopolised the 'anti-fascist' megaphone increased their abuse: 'Show us your minge!' The SDL visitors, and especially the women, did not give in. 'Alcoholics!' shouted the Islamists, 'You're all on methadone!' – at which point a gaunt and grey-faced passer-by lunged towards them. 'Master race? You're havin' a laugh!' chanted the descendants of the heroes of Jarama, 'Go back tae England! . . . You're shitebags and you know you are! . . . Get some education, you wankers!' As the verbal violence reached its climax, both sides were shouting: 'Go back home!'

It was not your usual Saturday afternoon. A young woman, heavily-laden with shopping bags, told her friend: 'This the best thing that's ever happened to Dundee!' A group of teenage girls emerged from the Nethergate, attracted by the spectacle: 'Are these . . . the *racists*?!' Then, giggling, they took out their mobile phones to snap each other with the SDL. Everyone, 'fascist', 'anti-fascist' and shopper alike, left with a smile on their face: no one was 'sent home tae think again'. Another tattooed skinhead tottered away, his tee-shirt emblazoned with the saltire and 'Scottish and Proud'. An Asian policeman said: 'At least I'm on double-time. I can't wait to spend it.'

Dundee, it seemed, had yet again repelled the Far Right and done the memory of the Brigaders proud. But the anti-fascists had given an implausible, if laudable, image of the city of 'the peh, the pizza and the pakora'. There are indeed social problems, in Dundee and elsewhere, which can attract fascistic solutions. The fear of an 'Islamic threat' is shared by more people than they might wish to admit. While the Anglophobic, or simply boneheadedly offensive, rhetoric of the counter-demonstrators indicated a well of intolerance that may be mobilised for demagogic purposes, be it in an independent Scotland or a continuing UK. It remains wilfully naïve to think that there can be 'nae Nazis' this side of the Cheviots.

Notes

Prologue

1 All quotations from this letter to 'Buz' in NA: FO 1093/1.
2 NA: FO 1093/1.
3 NA: AIR 16/1266.
4 NA: FO 1093/1.
5 David Stafford (ed.), *Flight from Reality. Rudolf Hess and his Mission to Scotland 1941* (London: Pimlico, 2002), p. 80.
6 Quoted in Stephen McGinty, *Camp Z. The Secret Life of Rudolf Hess* (London: Quercus, 2011), p. 29.
7 NA: FO 1093/2.
8 NA: INF 1/912.
9 Fred Taylor, *The Goebbels Diaries 1939-1941* (London: Hamish Hamilton, 1982), p. 363.
10 NA: FO 1093/1.
11 Quoted in McGinty, p. 48.
12 NA: FO 1093/1.
13 Roy Conyers Nesbit and Georges van Acker, *The Flight of Rudolf Hess. Myths and Reality* (Stroud: The History Press, 2011).
14 *The Times*, 6 October 1939.
15 Richard Griffiths, *Fellow Travellers of the Right. British Enthusiasts for Nazi Germany 1933-39* (Oxford: Oxford University Press, 1983), p. 140.
16 *Anglo-German Review*, March 1939, p. 120.
17 *Anglo-German Review*, May 1939, p. 194.

Chapter One: Mosley's Lost Legion

1 See Panikos Panayi (ed.), *Racial Violence in Britain in the Nineteenth and Twentieth Centuries* (London: Leicester University Press, 1996).
2 Griffiths, *Fellow Travellers of the Right*, p. 13.

3   *The Times*, 16 December 1963.
4   *British Fascist Bulletin*, 13 June 1925.
5   *British Fascist Bulletin*, 20 June 1925.
6   *British Fascist Bulletin*, 11 July 1925.
7   *British Fascist Bulletin*, 25 July 1925.
8   *British Fascist Bulletin*, 29 August 1925.
9   *British Fascist Bulletin*, 27 March 1926.
10 *British Lion*, August 1927.
11 *British Lion*, February 1928.
12 *British Lion*, June 1929.
13 *Morning Post*, 31 December 1929.
14 NA: PRO 30/69/1310.
15 NAS: HH5/332(including quotations from press).
16 *Politisches Archiv des Auswärtigen Amtes*, R 64052.
17 University of St Andrews Special Collections: Minutes of the Union Debating Society.
18 *Blackshirt*, 12 January 1934.
19 *Blackshirt*, 16 March 1934.
20 *Blackshirt*, 30 March 1934.
21 *Blackshirt*, 13 April 1934.
22 *The Scotsman*, 7 April 1934.
23 NA: HO 144/20141.
24 *Blackshirt*, 27 April 1934
25 NA: HO 114/20142.
26 *Blackshirt*, 18 May 1934.
27 *Blackshirt*, 5 June 1934.
28 *The Scotsman*, 2 June 1934.
29 *Blackshirt*, 22 June 1934.
30 *Blackshirt*, 13 July 1934.
31 *Blackshirt*, 27 July 1934.
32 *Blackshirt*, 3 August 1934.
33 *Blackshirt*, 24 August 1934.
34 *Blackshirt*, 14 September 1934.
35 *Blackshirt*, 21 September 1934.
36 *Blackshirt*, 28 September 1934.
37 *Blackshirt*, 5 October 1934.
38 *Blackshirt*, 2 November 1934.
39 *Blackshirt*, 9 November 1934.
40 Colin Kidd, 'Teutonist Ethnology and Scottish Nationalist Inhibition, 1780–1880', *The Scottish Historical Review*, Vol. 74, 1: No. 197 (April 1995), p. 48.
41 *Ibid.*, p. 49.

42 Robert Knox, *The Races of Men: A Fragment* (London: 1850), p. 6.

43 Stewart J. Brown, 'The Social Vision of Scottish Presbyterianism and the Union of 1929', *Records of the Scottish Church History Society*, 24 (1990), p. 93.

44 New College Library, Edinburgh: John White, 'Notes for speech [1928]', John White Papers, Box 9, 'Irish Immigration' folder.

45 Tony Milligan, 'The British Union of Fascists' Policy in Relation to Scotland', *Scottish Economic and Social History*, Vol. 19, Part 1 (1999), p. 5.

46 *The Vanguard*, 27 December 1933.

47 *Blackshirt*, 16 June 1933.

48 *The Vanguard*, 27 December 1933.

49 *The Vanguard*, 15 November 1933.

50 *The Vanguard*, 25 April 1934.

51 *The Vanguard*, 6 February 1934.

52 *The Vanguard*, 1 May 1935.

53 *The Vanguard*, 8 January 1936.

54 *The Vanguard*, 22 January 1936.

55 *The Vanguard*, 29 January 1936.

56 *The Vanguard*, January 1939.

57 *The Vanguard*, 11 May 1934.

58 Stephen M. Cullen, 'The Fasces and the Saltire: The Failure of the British Union of Fascists in Scotland, 1932-1940'. *The Scottish Historical Review*, Vol. 87, 2: No. 224 (October 2008), p. 326.

59 Tom Gallagher, *Glasgow. The Uneasy Peace. Religious Tension in Modern Scotland* (Manchester: Manchester University Press, 1987), p. 163.

60 Cullen, p. 325.

61 Ibid., p. 310.

62 Ibid., p. 324.

63 Oswald Mosley, *My Life* (London: Nelson, 1968), p. 331.

64 Raven Thomson, *Civilization as Divine Superman. A Superorganic Philosophy of History* (London: Williams and Norgate, 1932), p. 24.

65 Ibid., p. 40.

66 Thomson, *The Coming Corporate State* (London: BUF, 1937), p. 24.

67 Ibid., p. 32.

68 *Blackshirt*, 12 October 1934.

69 NA: HO144/20144.

70 NA: HO 144/674, 216/270.

71 NA: HO 144/20147, 674, 216/424.

72 *Blackshirt*, 22 February 1935.

73 *Blackshirt*, 12 April 1935.

74 *Blackshirt*, 26 April 1935.

75 *Blackshirt*, 7 June 1935.

76 *Blackshirt*, 12 July 1935.

77 *Blackshirt*, 6 September 1935.

78 *Blackshirt*, 4 October 1935.

79 *Blackshirt*, 11 October 1935.

80 *Blackshirt*, 27 December 1935.

81 *Fascist Quarterly*, Vol. 2, No. 1 (January 1936), pp. 146–7.

82 Ibid., p. 147.

83 *Fascist Quarterly*, Vol. 3, No. 3 (July 1936), p. 427.

84 Ibid., p. 437.

85 Ibid., p. 433.

86 Ibid., p. 435.

87 Graham Seton Hutchison, *The Highland Division Can Save Scotland* (Perth: SNP, 1945), p. 4.

88 Graham Seton Hutchison, *Machine Guns. Their History and Tactical Employment* (Uckfield: Naval and Military Press, 2004), p. 246.

89 Hutchison, *Silesia Revisited 1929* (London: Simplin Marshall, 1929), p. 111.

90 Seton Hutchison, *Footslogger* (London: Hutchinson, 1931), p. 247.

91 Ibid., p. 269.

92 Ibid., p. 322.

93 Ibid., p. 283.

94 Quoted in Seton Hutchison, *Meteor* (London: Hutchinson, 1933), p. 66.

95 Seton Hutchison, *Footslogger*, pp. 380, 383, 384.

96 Ibid., p. 382.

97 Ibid., p. 382.

98 Seton Hutchison, *Warrior* (London: Hutchinson, 1932), p. 316.

99 Seton Hutchison, *Arya* (London: Hutchinson, 1932), p. 164.

100 Ibid., p. 165.

101 *Meteor*, p. 67.

102 Ibid., p. 56.

103 Ibid., pp. 274–5.

104 Ibid., p. 280.

105 Ibid., p. 281.

106 Ibid.

107 Seton, *Blood Money* (London: Hutchinson, 1934), p. 118.

108 Ibid., p. 233.

109 Ibid., p. 235.

110 Correspondence between Graham Seton Hutchison and Ezra Pound: British Library MS 74270 (892E).

111 Ibid., p. 16.

112 Seton Hutchison, *The Highland Division*, p. 10.

113 *The Times*, 16 February 1940.
114 *Jewish Chronicle*, 13 March 1936.
115 NA: HO 45/24967.
116 Mosley Papers: OMN/C/2/3.
117 *Blackshirt*, 23 May 1936.
118 *The Scotsman*, 16 May 1936.
119 *The Scotsman*, 4 July 1936.
120 *The Scotsman*, 16 May 1936.
121 *The Scotsman*, 13 July 1936.
122 See Henry Maitles, 'Blackshirts across the Border: The British Union of Fascists in Scotland', *Scottish Historical Review*, 82 (213).
123 Ibid., p. 94.
124 *Jewish Chronicle*, 28 July 1899.
125 *The Scotsman*, 16 January 1903.
126 *Jewish Chronicle*, 8 June 1934.
127 Martin Stannard: *Muriel Spark: The Biography* (London: Weidenfeld & Nicolson, 2009), p. 34.
128 David Daiches, *Two Worlds: an Edinburgh Jewish Childhood* (London: Harcourt, Brace & Co., 1954), p. 93.
129 Ibid., p. 193.
130 *Hawick News* and *Hawick Express*, 2 July 1936.
131 *Blackshirt*, 19 September 1936.
132 *Blackshirt*, 26 September 1936.
133 *Blackshirt*, 2 January 1937.
134 *Blackshirt*, 23 January 1937.
135 *Blackshirt*, 22 May 1937.
136 *Blackshirt*, 19 June 1937.
137 *Blackshirt*, 3 July 1937.
138 *Blackshirt*, 10 July 1937.
139 *Blackshirt*, 24 July 1937.
140 *Blackshirt*, 7 August 1937.
141 *Blackshirt*, 21 August 1937.
142 *Blackshirt*, 9 October 1937.
143 NAS: HH 55/704.
144 *The Scotsman*, 20 September 1937.
145 *Blackshirt*, 16 October 1937.
146 NA: HO 21064.
147 *Blackshirt*, 16 October 1937.
148 *Blackshirt*, March 1938.
149 *Blackshirt*, July 1938.
150 NAS: HH 55/705.
151 Ibid.

152 Ibid.
153 Ibid.
154 Ibid.
155 NAS: HH 55/705.
156 NAS: AD 59/38.
157 Cullen, 'The Fasces and the Saltire', pp. 328–9.
158 Ibid., p. XXX.
159 *Northern Blackshirt*, September 1938.
160 Milligan, p. 17.
161 Cullen, 'The Fasces and the Saltire', p. 330.
162 John Blythe, Cornelius Finucane.

Chapter Two: Fasci di Scozia

1 'The Recollections of Joseph Pia', BBC Radio Scotland broadcast, 15 August 1994.
2 Wendy Ugolini, *Experiencing War as the 'Enemy Other'. Italian-Scottish Experience in World War II* (Manchester: Manchester University Press, 2011), p. 81.
3 NA: KV 3/219.
4 Quoted in Ugolini, p. 69.
5 *L'Italia Nostra*, 3 May 1935.
6 *L'Italia Nostra*, 17 May 1935.
7 *L'Italia Nostra*, 9 August 1935.
8 *L'Italia Nostra*, 6 September 1935.
9 *L'Italia Nostra*, 61 November 1935.
10 *British–Italian Bulletin*, 18 April 1936.
11 *British–Italian Bulletin*, 16 May 1936.
12 Ugolini, *Experiencing War*, p. 38.
13 Ibid., p. 39.
14 Ibid., p. 69.
15 NA: KV 3/219.
16 NA: FO 371/19942.
17 NA: KV3/220.
18 NA: FO 371/20739.
19 Ibid.
20 Ibid.
21 NA: FO 371/23035.
22 *L'Italia Nostra*, 5 January 1940.
23 *L'Italia Nostra*, 19 January 1940.
24 *L'Italia Nostra*, 19 April 1940.
25 *L'Italia Nostra*, 26 April 1940.

26 *L'Italia Nostra*, 3 May 1940.

27 NA: KV 3/220.

28 Lucio Sponza, 'The Anti-Italian Riots, June 1940', in Panayi (ed.), *Racial Violence*, p. 133.

29 Ugolini, *Experiencing War*, p. 95.

30 *The Scotsman*, 11 June 1940.

31 Quoted in Ugolini, *Experiencing War*, p. 123.

32 Ugolini, *Experiencing War*, p. 123.

33 Ibid., p. 128.

34 *The Scotsman*, 12 June 1940.

35 *The Scotsman*, 19 June 1940.

36 Sponza, 'Anti-Italian riots', p. 142.

37 Ugolini, *Experiencing War*, p. 31.

38 Sponza, 'Anti-Italian Riots', p. 138.

39 Ugolini, *Experiencing War*, p. 135.

40 Terri Colpi, *The Italian Factor* (Edinburgh: Mainstream, 1991), p. 195.

41 Ugolini, *Experiencing War*, p. 105.

42 Ibid., p. 166.

Chapter Three: Scotland for Franco

1 Daniel Gray, *Homage to Caledonia* (Edinburgh: Luath Press, 2008).

2 See Cullen, 'The Fasces and the Saltire', pp. 306–331.

3 G.K. Chesterton, *My Autobiography* (London, Hutchinson, 1936), p. 88.

4 Sam Johnson, 'Playing the Pharisee? Charles Saroléa, Czechoslovakia and the Road to Munich. 1915–1939', *The Slavonic and East European Review*, Vol. 82, No. 2 (April 2004), p. 296.

5 Saroléa Collection, Special Collections, Edinburgh University Library (SAR), file 88.

6 SAR 60.

7 Ibid.

8 Ibid.

9 Archives of the Institut de France, Paris: Fonds Morand.

10 Blair Castle Archives: Duchess of Atholl papers (DoA), file 44/7.

11 Quoted in Stuart Ball, 'The Politics of Appeasement: the Fall of the Duchess of Atholl and the Kinross and West Perth By-election, December 1938', *The Scottish Historical Review*, Vol. 69, 1: No. 187 (April 1990), p. 56.

12 SAR 60.

13 Ibid.

14 Ball, 'Politics of Appeasement', p. 56.

15 DoA 44/3.

16 DoA 44/9.
17 Ibid.
18 Ibid.
19 Ibid.
20 Archivo de la Administración, Alcala de Henares: 54/7198.
21 DoA 44/5.
22 Ibid.
23 Ibid.
24 SAR 84.
25 SAR 85.
26 Ibid.
27 *The Scotsman*, 22 October 1937.
28 *The Border Telegraph*, 10 August 1937.
29 *The Border Telegraph*, 17 August 1937.
30 SAR 64.
31 *Anglo-German Review*, January 1938, p. 51.
32 *Anglo-German Review*, May 1938, p. 180.
33 SAR 85.
34 For Saroléa–Chandler correspondence: SAR 85.
35 SAR 60.
36 Archives of the Archdiocese of Glasgow: CU 12.
37 Ibid.
38 DoA: 22/18.
39 *The Scotsman*, 18 June 1938.
40 Archivo de la Administración: 54/7206.
41 Ibid: 54/7193.
42 Ibid: 54/7210.
43 SAR 60.
44 Ibid.
45 SAR 86.
46 Ibid.
47 Ibid.
48 DoA 22/18.
49 See Gallagher, *Uneasy Peace*, pp. 206-207.
50 Archives of the Archdiocese of Glasgow: CU 12.
51 Ibid.
52 Ball, 'Politics of Appeasement', p. 58.
53 *The Scotsman*, 29 April 1938.
54 DoA 22/18.
55 DoA 22/22.
56 SAR 64.
57 *The Scotsman*, 25 November 1938.

58 DoA 22/31.
59 *The Scotsman*, 8 December 1938.
60 Ibid.
61 SAR 64.
62 Saroléa, *Daylight on Spain* (London: Hutchinsons Sixpenny Series, 1938), p. 6.
63 Ibid., p. 10.
64 Ibid., p. 15.
65 Ibid., p. 126.
66 SAR 64.
67 Ibid.
68 Johnson, 'a true European and a sincere racist', p. 316.
69 SAR 61.
70 Ibid.
71 *The Scotsman*, 17 December 1938.
72 S.J. Hetherington, *Katharine Atholl 1874–1960. Against the Tide* (Aberdeen: Aberdeen University Press, 1989), p. 215.
73 Ball, 'Politics of Appeasement', p. 73.
74 Hetherington, *Katharine Atholl*, p. xvi.
75 *The Scotsman*, 23 December 1938.
76 Ball, 'Politics of Appeasement', p. 83.
77 Quoted in Ball, 'Politics of Appeasement', p. 83.
78 SAR 86.
79 *The Glasgow Observer*, 23 December 1938.
80 SAR 64.
81 Ibid.
82 DoA 22/31
83 Ibid.
84 SAR 86.
85 SAR 84.
86 SAR 64.
87 Archivo de la Administración: 54/7216.
88 *The Glasgow Herald*, 3 February 1939.
89 *Glasgow Observer*, 10 February 1939.
90 *The Vanguard*, June 1937.
91 *The Vanguard*, August 1937.
92 *The Vanguard*, October 1937.
93 *The Vanguard*, January 1938.
94 *The Vanguard*, April 1938.
95 *The Vanguard*, May 1938.
96 *The Vanguard*, November 1938.
97 *The Vanguard*, March 1939, p. 1.

98   SAR 86.

99   Ibid.

100 *Anglo–German Review*, April 1939, p. 159.

101 SAR 64.

102 *Anglo–German Review*, June 1939, p. 181.

103 *Anglo–German Review*, July 1939, p. 211.

104 SAR 85.

105 National Library of Scotland: MS Dep 217/Box 7.

106 SAR 230.

107 Ibid.

108 Ibid.

109 SAR 64.

110 Ibid.

111 Quoted in Martin Pugh, *Hurrah for the Blackshirts* (London: Pimlico, 2006), p. 295.

112 Quoted in Richard Griffiths, *Patriotism Perverted. Captain Ramsay, the Right Club and British Anti-Semitism 1939–40* (London: Constable, 1998), p. 203.

113 Ibid., p. 207.

114 SAR 65.

115 Ibid.

116 SAR 64.

117 SAR 65.

118 SAR 139.

119 SAR 64.

120 SAR 157.

121 SAR 86.

122 Ibid.

123 Ibid.

124 Archivo de la Administración: 66/3981.

125 *The Times*, 12 March 1953.

126 SAR 139.

127 SAR 183.

128 Johnson, 'A good European', p. 347.

129 *The Scotsman*, 15 January 1931.

Chapter Four: The Nazis and the Nats

1   NLS: Acc. 6914/4.

2   'At the Sign of the Thistle. Programme for a Scottish Fascism', *The Scottish Nation*, 5 (5 June 1923), p. 10.

3   Alan Bold, *MacDiarmid – Christopher Murray Grieve. A Critical Biography* (London: Paladin, 1990), pp. 169–170.

4 Ibid., pp. 486–487.
5 Peter Crisp, 'Pound and MacDiarmid: Fascism, Communism and Modernity', *CUHK Journal of Humanities*, The Chinese University of Hong Kong Press, 1997, p. 161.
6 *Scots Independent*, May 1929, p. 90
7 Bold, *MacDiarmid*, pp. 274 and 278.
8 *Scots Independent*, June 1929.
9 Duncan Glen (ed.), *Selected Essays of Hugh MacDiarmid* (London: Jonathan Cape, 1969), p. 70.
10 Ibid., p. 71.
11 Ibid., p. 71.
12 Ibid., p. 72.
13 Gert Antonius, '"Home Rule" für Schottland?', *Volk und Reich*, November 1934, pp. 837–844 [translation by Daniela Bruns].
14 Wendy Wood, *Yours Sincerely for Scotland. The Autobiography of a Patriot* (London: Arthur Baker, 1970), p. 19.
15 NA: HO 45/25472 for quotations on the DSSO and SDF.
16 *Scots Independent*, December 1926.
17 *Scots Independent*, November 1927.
18 Lewis Spence, *Freedom for Scotland. The Case for Scottish Self-Government*, p. 7.
19 Ibid., p. 131.
20 *Scots Independent*, November 1928.
21 *Scots Independent*, March 1933.
22 *Scots Independent*, November 1933.
23 Quoted in *Jewish Chronicle*, 20 November 1936.
24 Ibid.
25 *Scots Independent*, December 1936.
26 *The Scotsman*, 19 May 1937.
27 *Scots Independent*, April 1938.
28 *Scots Independent*, July 1938.
29 *Scots Independent*, November 1938.
30 *Scots Independent*, December 1939.
31 *Scots Independent*, January 1939.
32 *Scots Independent*, April 1939.
33 NLS: Acc. 9188, 6.
34 Georges Cadiou, *L'hermine et la croix gammée. Le mouvement breton et la collaboration* (Paris: Editions Apogée, 2006), p. 74.
35 Ibid., p. 75.
36 Ibid., p. 73.
37 Daniel Leach, 'The Unwelcome Brothers. Scottish Nationalists in Irish Exile during the Emergency', *Irish Studies Review*, Vol. 15, No. 4 (2007), p. 430.

38 *Scots Independent*, October 1939.
39 *Scots Independent*, April 1940.
40 *Scots Independent*, May 1940.
41 See Trevor Royle: *A Time of Tyrants. Scotland and the Second World War* (Edinburgh: Birlinn, 2011).
42 *Scots Independent*, June 1940.
43 *Scots Independent*, July 1940.
44 *Scots Independent*, September 1940.
45 *Scots Independent*, October 1940.
46 Lewis Spence, *The Occult Causes of the Present War* (London: Rider and Co., 1943), p. 18.
47 *Scots Independent*, November 1940.
48 Cadiou, *L'hermine et la croix gammée*, p. 75.
49 Ronald Macdonald Douglas, *The Irish Book* (The Talbot Press: Dublin 1936), pp. xv–xviii.
50 Ibid., p. xxvi.
51 Ronald MacDonald Douglas, 'War or Peace', *Catalyst*, Vol. 6, No. 1 (Winter 1973), p. 16.
52 Douglas, 'The Mad Nationalist', *Catalyst*, Vol. 6, No. 3 (Summer 1973), p. 5.
53 Ibid., p. 6.
54 *Catalyst*, Vol. 6, No. 4 (Autumn 1973), p. 19.
55 Leach, 'Unwelcome Brothers', p. 426.
56 Ibid., p. 434.
57 Ibid., p. 435.
58 NLS: Acc. 6914/4.
59 Ibid.
60 Quoted in Royle, p. 116.
61 Kevin Morgan, *Against Fascism and War. Ruptures and Continuities in British Communist Politics, 1935–1941* (Manchester: Manchester University Press, 1989), p. 122.
62 Ibid., pp. 123–124.
63 Royle, p. 233.
64 NLS Acc. 3721 Muirhead papers, Box 89/27.
65 John Manson, Dorin Grieve and Alan Riach (eds.), *The Revolutionary Art of the Future: Re-discovered Poems* (Manchester: Carcanet, 2003), p. 42.
66 Ibid., p. 45.
67 Ibid. p. 50.
68 George Campbell Hay, *Collected Poems and Songs*, vol. 1 (Edinburgh: Edinburgh University Press, 2000), p. 52.
69 John Manson (ed.), *Dear Grieve. Letters to Hugh MacDiarmid (C.M. Grieve)* (Glasgow: Kennedy and Boyd, 2011), p. 296.

70 Oliver Smith, *Hitlerism in the Highlands* (Glasgow: self-published, 1941), p. 2

71 Ibid., p. 12.

72 Ibid., p. 12.

73 All quotations from Hamilton file: NA: HO45/23680.

74 NAS: HH55/557.

75 NAS: HH55/558.

76 Manson (ed.), *Dear Grieve*, p. 307.

77 NAS: HH 55/557.

78 NA: HO 45/23801.

79 *Scots Independent*, May 1941.

80 *Scots Independent*, June 1941.

81 NAS: HH55/557.

82 *Scots Independent*, June 1942.

83 *Scots Independent*, August 1942.

84 *Scots Independent*, September 1942.

85 NAS: HH55/557.

86 *Scots Independent*, September 1943.

87 Ibid.

88 *Scots Independent*, October 1944.

89 Graham Seton Hutchison, *The Red Colonel* (London: Hutchinson, 1946), pp. 139–140.

90 Ibid., p. 177.

91 Ibid., p. 181.

92 Ibid., p. 182.

93 Ibid., p. 192.

94 Ibid., p. 65.

95 Ibid., p. 149.

96 Seton Hutchison, *The Highland Division*, p. 3.

97 Ibid., p. 5.

98 Ibid., p. 11.

99 Ibid., p. 12.

100 Ibid., p. 17.

101 Ibid., p. 19.

102 Ibid., p. 19.

103 Ibid., p. 22.

104 Ibid., p. 22.

105 Ibid., p. 23.

Chapter Five: Tartan Treachery

1 *The Scotsman*, 17 May 1938.

2 *Sunday Mail*, June 1938.

3 *Sunday Mail*, 12 June 1938.

4 NAS: HH/6/212.

5 *Sunday Mail*, 19 June 1938.

6 NA: KV2/193.

7 Ibid.

8 NA: KV2/194.

9 *Daily Record*, 21 May 1937.

10 Ibid.

11 NAS: HH16/212.

12 *Bulletin*, 14 November 1938.

13 *Sunday Mail*, 19 June 1938.

14 Ibid. NAS: HH 16/212

15 *Daily Mail*, 1 August 1938.

16 NAS HH 16/212

17 Ibid.

18 NA: HO45/25755 for quotations from the Barlinnie internees' file.

19 NA: KV2/187.

20 *Daily Express*, 6 September 1937.

21 NA: KV2/245.

22 *Sunday Chronicle*, 31 July 1940.

23 *Sunday Pictorial*, 31 July 1942.

24 NA: KV2/185.

25 NA: KV2/186.

26 *News Chronicle*, 21 May 1945.

27 NA: KV2/185.

28 NA: KV2/186.

29 Interview with Farquhar Ewen, Alness, March 2010.

30 NA: KV2/425.

31 NA: KV2/424.

32 NA: KV2/425.

33 NA: KV2/424.

34 NA: KV2/425.

35 NA: KV2/424.

36 Horst J.P. Bergmeier and Rainer E. Lotz, *Hitler's Airwaves. The Inside Story of Nazi Radio Broadcasting and Propaganda Swing* (New Haven: Yale University Press, 1997), p. 203.

37 NA: KV2/425.

38 *Hitler's Airwaves*, p. 209.

39 NA: KV2/424.

40 NA: KV2/425.

41 NA: KV2/424.

42 Ibid.

43 Ibid.
44 Ibid.
45 Ibid.
46 Ibid.
47 NA: KV2/425.
48 NA: HO 283/70.
49 Ibid.
50 Ibid.
51 Peter Richard Pugh, 'A Political Biography of Alexander Raven Thomson', unpublished DPhil thesis, University of Sheffield, (1998), p. 180.
52 NA: HO45/25701.
53 Ibid.
54 Ibid.
55 Ibid.
56 Ibid.
57 NA: HO45/23737 for all quotations from Alexander Proctor's file.
58 Archibald Maule Ramsay, *The Nameless War* (London: The Britons' Publishing Society, 1952), p. 66.
59 Quoted in Griffiths, *Fellow Travellers of the Right*, p. 335.
60 *Peeblesshire Advertiser*, 13 January 1939.
61 *Peeblesshire Advertiser*, 20 January 1939.
62 Griffiths, *Patriotism Perverted*, p. 116.
63 Ibid., p. 117.
64 *Peeblesshire Advertiser*, 10 February 1939.
65 *Peeblesshire Advertiser*, 17 March 1939.
66 *Peeblesshire Advertiser*, 24 March 1939.
67 See Griffiths, *Patriotism Perverted*.
68 NA: KV2/677.
69 NA: KV2/677.
70 Ibid.
71 *Peeblesshire Advertiser*, 23 May 1940.
72 NA: KV2/677.
73 Ibid.
74 Ibid.
75 Admiral Sir Barry Domvile, *From Admiral to Cabin Boy* (London: Boswell, 1947), p. 123.
76 *Daily Herald*, 1 August 1941.
77 NA: KV2/678.
78 Ibid.
79 Ibid.
80 Ibid.
81 *Peeblesshire Advertiser*, 29 September 1939.

82 NA: KV2/679.
83 Ibid.
84 *The Vanguard*, 30 September 1939.
85 *The Vanguard*, 14 October 1939.
86 *The Vanguard*, 25 November 1939.
87 *The Vanguard*, 2 March 1940.
88 *The Vanguard*, May 1940.
89 *The Vanguard*, July 1940.
90 *The Vanguard*, August 1940.
91 *The Vanguard*, September 1940.
92 *The Vanguard*, October 1940.
93 *The Vanguard*, December 1940.
94 Alexander Ratcliffe, *Are You Fighting for Democracy?* (Glasgow, 1941), p. 12.
95 Ibid., p. 7.
96 Ibid., p. 12.
97 Ibid., p. 24.
98 Ratcliffe, *The Truth about the Jews!* (Glasgow, 1943), p. 6.
99 Ibid., p. 7.
100 Ibid., p. 9.
101 Ibid., p. 11.
102 Ibid., p. 14.
103 Ibid., p. 16.
104 NA: HO 45/25398 for all quotations from Alexander Ratcliffe's file.
105 *Jewish Chronicle*, 9 April 1943
106 *Daily Worker*, 12 April 1943.
107 *The Vanguard*, February 1945.
108 *The Vanguard*, May 1945.
109 *The Vanguard*, August 1945.
110 *The Vanguard*, October 1945.
111 *The Vanguard*, February 1945.
112 *The Vanguard*, June–July 1946.
113 *The Vanguard*, January 1947.
114 NA: KV 2/2474 for quotations from Angus MacNab's file.

Chapter Six: The Third Reich No More?

1 Timothy W. Ryback, *Hitler's Private Library. The Books that Shaped his Life* (London: The Bodley Head, 2009), p. 207.
2 Richard Thurlow, *Fascism in Britain. From Oswald Mosley's Blackshirts to the National Front* (London: I.B. Tauris, 2009), p. 277.
3 Tony Kushner, 'Anti-Semitism and austerity: the August 1947 riots in Britain', in Panayi (ed.), *Racial Violence*, p. 8.

4 Ramsay, p. 19.

5 Ibid., p. 37.

6 Ibid., p. 41.

7 Ibid., p. 46.

8 Ibid., p. 90.

9 *Peeblesshire Advertiser*, 18 March 1955.

10 Mosley Papers: OMD 10/2/1–4.

11 Oswald Mosley, *The Alternative* (London: Mosley Publications, 1947), p. 38.

12 Ibid., p. 89–90.

13 Mosley Papers: XOMD/4/3.

14 See Douglas MacLeod, *Morningside Mata Haris* (Edinburgh: Birlinn, 2005).

15 Martin Walker, *The National Front* (London: Fontana, 1978), p. 27.

16 *Union*, 28 March 1953.

17 *Union*, 8 January 1955.

18 *The European*, 14 (April, 1954), p. 44.

19 Ibid., p. 51.

20 *The European*, 24 (February 1955), p. 18.

21 *The European*, 27 (May 1955), p. 13.

22 Ibid., p. 13.

23 Ibid., p. 23.

24 Ibid., p. 24.

25 Ibid., p. 24.

26 Ibid., p. 25.

27 *The European*, 28 (June 1955), pp. 61–62.

28 Mosley Papers: OMN/B/2/4.

29 *The European*, 33 (October 1955), p. 27.

30 Pugh, 'Political Biography of Alexander Raven Thomson', p. 260.

31 Mosley Papers: OMN/B/2/4.

32 *The European*, 32 (September 1955), p. 47.

33 *The European*, 35 (January 1956), p. 49.

34 Ibid., p. 49.

35 Ibid., p. 50.

36 *The European*, 57 (November 1957), p. 175.

37 Ibid., p. 176.

38 *The European*, 67 (September 1958), p. 33.

39 Ibid., p. 34.

40 Ibid., p. 34.

41 Ibid., p. 36.

42 Walker, *National Front*, p. 60.

43 *Daily Telegraph Magazine* (9 February 1968).

44 *Catalyst*, Vol. 5, No. 2 (Spring 1972), p. 7.

45 Ibid., p. 18.

46 Ibid., p. 27.

47 *Catalyst*, Vol. 6, No. 1 (Winter 1973), p. 17.

48 Ibid., p. 17.

49 *Catalyst*, Vol. 6, No. 2 (Spring 1973), p. 17.

50 Ibid., p. 17.

51 *West Highland Free Press*, 26 September 1980.

52 *The Scotsman*, 9 October 1980.

53 *Searchlight*, 27 (1977), p. 16.

54 *Searchlight*, 36 (1978), p. 19.

55 *Searchlight*, 52 (1979), p. 18.

56 *Searchlight*, 85 (1983), p. 13.

57 Nigel Fielding, *The National Front* (London: Routledge, 1981), p. 41.

58 *Searchlight*, 105 (1984), p. 18.

59 *Glasgow Herald*, 25 September 1985.

60 Quoted in *Bulldog*, 16 (late 1979), p. 3.

61 See Gavin Bowd, 'La Cruauté de l'Histoire: Ian Hamilton Finlay et la Révolution française', in David Kinloch and Richard Price (eds), *La Nouvelle Alliance* (Grenoble: Ellug, 2000), pp. 91–114.

62 I thank the late Alan Woods for providing me with the tape of this conversation.

63 *Searchlight*, 135, September 1986, p. 3.

64 *Searchlight*, 151, January 1988, p. 5.

65 *Searchlight*, 163, January 1989, p. 8.

66 *Searchlight*, 190, April 1991, p. 13.

67 *Searchlight*, 195, September 1991, p. 11.

68 *Searchlight*, 197, November 1991, p. 3.

69 Matthew J. Goodwin, *New British Fascism. Rise of the British National Party* (London: Routledge, 2011), p. 51.

70 *The Voice of Ordinary People* (Turriff: BNP, 2011), p. 18.

71 Anders Breivik, *2083. A European Declaration of Independence*, p. 1504.

Select Bibliography

Primary Sources

Archives of the Archdiocese of Glasgow
CU 12 (Papers of John Campbell)

Archivo de la Administración, Alcala de Henares
54/7193, 7195, 7206, 7210, 7215, 7216, 7237 (Glasgow Consulate of the Spanish Republic)
54/7198, 7247, 66/3981 (Nationalist diplomatic correspondence)

Blair Castle Archives
22/18-30, 44/3-9 (Papers of the Duchess of Atholl)

British Library
MS 74270/829E (Graham Seton Hutchison–Ezra Pound correspondence)

Mosley Papers, University of Birmingham
OMD10/2/1–4 (documents on Union movement)
OMN/B/2/4 (correspondence with Desmond Stewart and Raven Thomson)
OMN/C/2/3 (Mosley and mediums)
XOMD/4/3 (correspondence with Douglas Spens)

National Archives, Kew (NA)
FO 371/19942, 20739, 23035 (Foreign Office reports on Nazi Party and Italian Fascist Party in Great Britain)
HO45/23680 (Matthew Hamilton)
HO45/23737 (Alexander Proctor)
HO 45/23801 (The case of Arthur Donaldson)
HO 45/24967 (Imperial Fascist League)

HO 45/25395 (Fascism in Great Britain)
HO 45/25398 (Alexander Ratcliffe)
HO 45/25472 (Wendy Wood and Ronald MacDonald Douglas)
HO 45/25701 (Raven Thomson)
HO 45/25755 (Dundee internees)
HO 144/674, 2014–4 (Special Branch reports on BUF)
HO 216/270 and 424 (SB on BUF)
HO 283/70 (Raven Thomson)
KV2/184–7 (Norman Baillie Stewart)
KV2/193–4 (Jessie Wallace Jordan)
KV3/219–220 (Italian Fascist Party in Great Britain)
KV2/245 (William Joyce)
KV2/424–5 (Donald Grant and Radio Caledonia)
KV2/677–9 (Archibald Maule Ramsay)
KV2/2474–5 (Angus 'Juan' MacNab)
PRO 30/69/1310 (Robert Forgan to Ramsay Macdonald)

National Archives of Scotland (NAS)
AD59/38 (BUF in Aberdeen)
HH5/332 (New Party in Glasgow)
HH6/212 (Jessie Wallace Jordan)
HH55/557–8 (Police actions against Scottish Nationalists in 1941, etc.)
HH55/704–5 (BUF in Aberdeen)

National Library of Scotland
Acc. 3721, Box 89/27 (Papers of Roland Muirhead)
Acc. 6419/4 (Papers of Douglas Young)
Dep. 217/Box 7; Acc. 9188 (Papers of Andrew Dewar Gibb)

New College Library, Edinburgh
John White papers, Box 9

Politisches Archiv des Auswärtigen Amtes, Berlin
R 64052 (DAAD tutor report to German Embassy, London)

University of Edinburgh Special Collections
Papers of Professor Charles Saroléa

University of St Andrews Special Collections
Minutes of the Union Debating Society

Newspapers and Journals

Action
Anglo-German Review
Blackshirt
Border Telegraph
British Fascist Bulletin
British–Italian Bulletin
British Lion
Bulldog
The Bulletin
Catalyst for the Scottish Viewpoint
Daily Express
Daily Herald
Daily Mail
Daily Record
Daily Telegraph
Daily Worker
The European
Fascist Quarterly
Glasgow Herald
Glasgow Observer
Hawick Express
Hawick News
L'Italia Nostra
Jewish Chronicle
News Chronicle
Northern Blackshirt
Peeblesshire Advertiser
Scots Independent
The Scotsman
The Scottish Nation
Searchlight
Sunday Mail
Sunday Chronicle
Sunday Pictorial
The Times
Union
The Vanguard
Volk und Reich
West Highland Free Press

294   FASCIST SCOTLAND

Books

Bergmeier, Horst J.P. and Lott, Rainer E., *Hitler's Airwaves. The Inside Story of Nazi Radio Broadcasting and Propaganda Swing* (New Haven: Yale University Press, 1997)

Bold, Alan, *MacDiarmid–Christopher Murray Grieve. A Critical Biography* (London: Paladin, 1996)

Brown, Oliver, *Hitlerism in the Highlands* (Glasgow, 1941)

Cadiou, Georges, *L'hermine et la croix gammée. Le mouvement breton et la collaboration* (Paris: Editions Apogee, 2006)

Chesterton, G.K., *My Autobiography* (London: Hutchinson, 1936)

Colpi, Terri, *The Italian Factor* (Edinburgh: Mainstream, 1991)

Daiches, David, *Two Worlds: an Edinburgh Jewish Childhood* (London: Harcourt, Brace & Co., 1954)

Domvile, Admiral Sir Barry, *From Admiral to Cabin Boy* (London: Boswell, 1947)

Douglas, Ronald Macdonald, *The Irish Book* (Dublin: The Talbot Press, 1936)

Fielding, Nigel, *The National Front* (London: Routledge, 1981)

Finlay, Richard J., *Independent and Free. Scottish Politics and the Origins of the SNP 1918–1945* (Edinburgh: John Donald, 1994)

Gallagher, Tom, *Glasgow: The Uneasy Peace. Religious Tensions in Modern Scotland* (Manchester: MUP, 1987)

Glen, Duncan (ed.), *Selected Essays of Hugh MacDiarmid* (London: Jonathan Cape, 1969)

Goodwin, Matthew J., *New British Fascism. The Rise of the BNP* (London: Routledge, 2011)

Gray, Daniel, *Homage to Caledonia* (Edinburgh: Luath Press, 2008)

Griffiths, Richard, *Fellow Travellers of the Right. British Enthusiasts for Nazi Germany 1933–39* (Oxford: OUP, 1983)

Griffiths, Richard, *Patriotism Perverted. Captain Ramsay, the Right Club and British Anti-Semitism, 1939–40* (London: Constable, 1998)

Hay, George Campbell, *Collected Poems and Songs* (Edinburgh: Edinburgh University Press, 2000)

Hetherington, S.J., *Katharine Atholl 1874–1960. Against the Tide* (Aberdeen: Aberdeen University Press, 1989)

Hutchison, Graham Seton, *Silesia Revisited 1929* (London: Simplin Marshall, 1929)

Hutchison, Graham Seton, *Footslogger* (London: Hutchinson, 1931)

Hutchison, Graham Seton, *Warrior* (London: Hutchinson, 1932)

Hutchison, Graham Seton, *Meteor* (London: Hutchinson, 1933)

Hutchison, Graham Seton, *Arya. The Call of the Future* (London: Hutchinson, 1933)

Hutchison, Graham Seton, *Blood Money* (London: Hutchinson, 1934)

Hutchison, Graham Seton, *The Highland Division Can Save Scotland* (Perth: SNP, 1945)

Hutchison, Graham Seton, *The Red Colonel* (London: Hutchinson, 1946)

Johnson, Sam, '"A good European and a sincere racist": the life and work of Professor Charles Saroléa, 1870–1933', unpublished PhD thesis, University of Keele, 2001

Knox, Robert, *The Races of Men: A Fragment* (London: H. Renshaw, 1850)

McGinty Stephen, *Camp Z. The Secret Life of Rudolf Hess* (London: Quercus, 2011)

MacLeod, Douglas, *Morningside Mata Haris* (Edinburgh: Birlinn, 2005)

Manson, John; Grieve, Dorin and Riach, Alan (eds.), *The Revolutionary Art of the Future: re-discovered poems* (Manchester: Carcanet, 2003)

Manson, John (ed.), *Dear Grieve. Letters to Hugh MacDiarmid* (Glasgow: Kennedy and Boyd, 2011)

Morgan Kevin, *Against Fascism and War. Ruptures and continuities in British Communist Politics, 1935–1945* (Manchester: Manchester University Press, 1989)

Mosley, Oswald, *The Alternative* (London: Mosley Publications, 1947)

Mosley, Oswald, *My Life* (London: Nelson, 1968)

Nesbit, Roy Conyers and van Acker, Georges, *The Flight of Rudolf Hess. Myths and Realities* (Stroud: The History Press, 2011)

Panayi, Panikos (ed.) *Racial Violence in Britain in the Nineteenth and Twentieth Centuries* (London: Leicester University Press, 1996)

Pugh, Martin, *Hurrah for the Blackshirts!* (London: Pimlico, 2006)

Pugh, Peter Richard, 'A Political Biography of Alexander Raven Thomson', unpublished DPhil thesis, University of Sheffield, 2002

Ramsay, Archibald Maule, *The Nameless War* (London: The Britons' Publishing Society, 1952)

Ratcliffe, Alexander, *Are you fighting for democracy?* (Glasgow, 1941)

Ratcliffe, Alexander, *The Truth about the Jews!* (Glasgow, 1943)

Royle, Trevor, *A Time of Tyrants: Scotland and the Second World War* (Edinburgh: Birlinn, 2011)

Ryback, Timothy W., *Hitler's Private Library. The Books that Shaped his Life* (London: The Bodley Head, 2009)

Saroléa, Charles, *Daylight on Spain* (London: Hutchinson, 1938)

Spence, Lewis, *Freedom for Scotland. The Case for Scottish Self-Government* (Glasgow: Scottish National Movement, 1926)

Spence, Lewis, *The Occult Causes of the Present War* (London: Rider and Co, 1943)

Stafford, David (ed.), *Flight from Reality. Rudolf Hess and his Mission to Scotland* (London: Pimlico, 2002)

Stannard, Martin, *Muriel Spark: the Biography* (London: Weidenfeld and Nicholson, 2009)

Taylor, Fred, *The Goebbels Diaries 1939–1941* (London: Hamish Hamilton, 1982)

Thomson, Raven, *Civilization as Divine Superman. A Superorganic Philosophy of History* (London: Greater Britain Publishing, 1932)

Thomson, Raven, *The Coming Corporate State* (London: BUF, 1937)

Thurlow, Richard, *Fascism in Britain. From Oswald Mosley's Blackhirts to the National Front* (London: I.B. Taurus, 2009)

Ugolini, Wendy, *Experiencing War as the 'Enemy Other'. Italian Scottish Experiences in World War II* (Manchester: Manchester University Press, 2011)

Walker, Martin, *The National Front* (London: Fontana, 1978)

Waugh, Evelyn, *Officers and Gentlemen* (Harmondsworth: Penguin, 2001)

Wood, Wendy, *Yours Sincerely for Scotland. The Autobiography of a Patriot* (London: Arthur Baker, 1970)

Worley, Matthew, *Oswald Mosley and the New Party* (London: Palgrave Macmillan, 2010)

Articles

Antonius, Gert, 'Home Rule für Schottland?', *Volk und Reich*, November 1934, pp. 837–844

Ball, Stuart, 'The Politics of Appeasement: the Fall of the Duchess of Atholl and the Kinross and West Perthshire By-election, December 1938', *The Scottish Historical Review*, Vol. 69, 1: No. 187 (April 1990), pp. 49–83

Brown, Stewart J., 'The Social Vision of Scottish Presbyterianism and the Union of 1929', *Records of the Scottish Church History Society*, 24 (1990), pp. 596–617

Crisp, Peter, 'Pound and MacDiarmid: Fascism, Communism and Modernity', *CUHK Journal of Humanities*, pp. 160–174

Cullen, Stephen M., 'The Fasces and the Saltire: the Failure of the British Union of Fascists in Scotland, 1932–1940', *The Scottish Historical Review*, Vol. 87, 2: No. 224 (2008) pp. 306–331

Johnson, Sam, 'Playing the Pharisee? Charles Saroléa, Czechoslovakia and the Road to Munich, 1915–1939', *The Slavonic and East European Review*, Vol. 82, No. 2 (April 2004), pp. 292–314

Kidd, Colin, 'Teutonist Ethnology and Scottish Nationalist Inhibition, 1780–1880', *The Scottish Historical Review*, Vol. 74, 1: No. 197 (April 1995), pp. 45–68

Leach, Daniel, 'The Unwelcome Brothers: Scottish Nationalists in Irish Exile during the Emergency', *Irish Studies Review*, Vol. 15, No. 4 (2007), pp. 425–449

Maitles, Henry, 'Blackshirts across the Border: the British Union of Fascists in Scotland', *The Scottish Historical Review*, Vol. 82, No. 213 (2003), pp. 92–100

Milligan, Tony, 'The British Union of Fascists' Policy in Relation to Scotland', *Scottish Economic and Social History*, Vol. 19, Part 1 (1999), pp. 1–17

Index